STUDIES IN EDUCATIONAL ETHNOGRAPHY

Volume 2 • 1999

EXPLORATIONS IN METHODOLOGY

90 0485345 3

STUDIES IN EDUCATIONAL ETHNOGRAPHY

EXPLORATIONS IN METHODOLOGY

Editors: ALEXANDER MASSEY
GEOFFREY WALFORD
Department of Educational Studies
University of Oxford

VOLUME 2 • 1999

JAI PRESS INC.
Stamford, Connecticut

CONTENTS

PREFACE

Ethnography has become one of the major methods of researching educational settings. Its key strength is its emphasis on understanding the perceptions and cultures of the people and organizations studied. Through prolonged involvement with those who are being studied, the ethnographic researcher is able gradually to enter their world and gain an understanding of their lives.

Each volume of *Studies in Educational Ethnography* focuses on a particular theme relating to the ethnographic investigation of education. The volumes are closely linked to an annual two-day residential conference which explores various elements of ethnography and its application to education and schooling. The series of Ethnography and Education conferences began in the late 1970s, and was originally held at St. Hilda's College, Oxford University. The series later moved to Warwick University and back to the Department of Educational Studies, University of Oxford in 1996. Each year a broad theme for the conference is chosen and participants are invited to contribute papers. The conference meeting itself is a period of shared work: papers are pre-circulated to participants and critically yet supportively discussed. In their revisions for possible publication, participants are thus able to take account of the detailed critique offered by their colleagues.

The contributions presented in each volume of *Studies in Educational Ethnography* are of two types. Most are revised versions of papers presented at the annual Ethnography and Education conference, but each volume also includes some further specially commissioned pieces. They are selected on the basis of their high quality, their coherence as a group and their contribution to both ethnographic methodology and substantive knowledge.

The series recognizes that the nature of ethnography is contested, and this is taken to be a sign of its strength and vitality. While the idea that the term can be taken to be almost synonymous with qualitative research is rejected, chapters are included that draw upon a broad range of methodologies that are embedded within a long and detailed engagement with those people and organizations studied.

Further details of the Education and Ethnography conference or the *Studies in Educational Ethnography* series of volumes are available from the Series Editor.

Dr. Geoffrey Walford (Series Editor)
Reader in Education Policy
Department of Educational Studies
University of Oxford
15 Norham Gardens
Oxford OX2 6PY, England

INTRODUCTION

Geoffrey Walford and Alexander Massey

The Series Preface makes clear that *Studies in Educational Ethnography* recognizes that the nature of ethnography is contested, and takes this to be a sign of its strength and vitality. It is therefore fitting that the second volume in the series should focus on debates and developments in methodology and the many ways in which ethnographic work interacts with education. The contributions to this volume are diverse and challenging. They indicate that ethnography is a rich field that has much to offer the study of education.

The first two chapters focus on access to undertake research. In the first, Geoffrey Walford argues that ethnographers may have much to learn about gaining access from a study of some of the techniques used by salespeople. Access to research sites is increasingly being seen and experienced as problematic, which means that researchers now have to pay more attention to the ways in which they present themselves and their projects to those who can open doors. Walford draws an analogy between selling a product or service to a new customer and the process that researchers might follow when trying to obtain access. He gives illustrations of where the techniques described in many popular selling and marketing books can be usefully applied to gaining research access. The account is structured around one particular popular formulation where salespeople are exhorted to examine their Approach, then how they develop Interest, and a Desire to purchase on the part of the customer, and finally how they move from this position to completing a Sale. While the techniques described should not be treated as a recipe, they offer a variety of ideas worthy of consideration.

In contrast to this rather optimistic first chapter, the following discussion by Maria Birbili examines some of the difficulties of accepting some particularly well-known advice about gaining access. Her focus is on the common suggestion that personal links between people known to the researchers and others should be exploited in order to gain access to research subjects. In her study of the work experiences of Greek academics she used existing contacts between her friends, relations and colleagues and the academics she wished to research. While this strategy did enable her to interview those academics she wished to focus on, Birbili shows that there are several negative aspects of this method of gaining access as well as those positive features that have been commonly discussed. She urges that other researchers exercise caution before automatically following such strategies themselves.

The following two chapters have in common their questioning of the stance to be taken by the ethnographer. Phil Carspecken argues that, in terms of methodology, there is no agreement about what should be called "critical ethnography." In his chapter he outlines the origins and development of critical ethnography from the work of the Center for Contemporary Cultural Studies in the 1970s onward, and shows that this genre of research has been primarily distinguished by the values of the researchers who identify with it rather than any distinctive epistemology or unique set of analytic methods. However, Carspecken argues in favour of the development of a definite critical methodology and proposes one particular version based upon specific methodological principles rather than on value orientation. Initially drawing on Habermas's theory of validity, and using the concept of pragmatic horizons, he sets out a five stage methodology for conducting critical ethnography where each stage has its own set of validating procedures.

Sam Hillyard tackles the proposition that all ethnographic writing is a social construction, rather than an explication, of reality. The paper considers postmodern and contemporary methodological and epistemological arguments of social constructivism, as advocated by postmodern historian Keith Jenkins and, within ethnography, Atkinson and Hammersley. Working along the theme of uniting theory and practice, she asks questions about the implications for ethnographic writing and representation if arguments of social constructivism are accepted. She investigates the basis on which future ethnographic findings (or claims) can be made. The chapter makes the argument that postmodernist critiques can be faced through the manipulation of unconventional forms of sociological writing and representation. The paper uses the unique sociology of Erving Goffman (1922-1982) to detail and explore different techniques of writing and representation. It argues that elements of Goffman's conception and approach to the task of sociology offer a direction for future ethnography to develop and advocates that the ethnographer's "imagination" has a key role to play.

Marlene Morrison's chapter begins to move the discussion on to a consideration of the problems of undertaking research about a diversity of people. She focuses on a British Library funded project entitled "Public Libraries, Ethnic Diversity and Citizenship," which was based jointly at the Centre for Educational Development Appraisal and Research (CEDAR) and the Centre for Research in Ethnic Relations (CRER) at the University of Warwick and conducted during 1996-1997. The study investigated the role and purposes of public library services among ethnically diverse populations. The desk and field research were conducted jointly by the author, a white female researcher—based at CEDAR—and the project manager, a black male researcher—based at CRER. From the standpoint of the former, the chapter explores the methodological and epistemological challenges in researching ethnic diversity in policy-related and ethnically focused qualitative research, where the author became a gendered and ethnically "minority" figure. Specific attention is drawn to: multi-site case study and issues of typicality and atypicality; research partnership and teamwork; and importantly, to major issues of ethnic symmetry and asymmetry when researching and/or "problematizing" the "other"—in this project, ethnic minority populations. Aspects of the research are considered alongside a critical discourse of citizenship and empowerment, and in relation to the early phases of dissemination. Concluding comments reflect on the aspects of a reflexive research account that remains "unfinished" in terms of its outcomes and aspirations for change.

Mari Boyle's chapter is concerned with the problems and dilemmas of being an adult researcher of the worlds of childhood. In a research project investigating child-meaningful learning in a bilingual school, Boyle wished to investigate the experiences of the bilingual child starting school. This chapter examines her methodological approach during the two year research and focuses particularly on data collection involving the children. She considers the role and status of children as research subjects and partners in the research process. In much ethnographic research the perspectives of the participants has been central to validation of findings, and is often gathered using "adult" techniques through interview. Boyle argues that such techniques may not be suitable when gathering information from young children and outlines alternative strategies for talking with young respondents. The chapter finally considers the impact of the white researcher investigating ethnic-minority pupils.

The following chapter by Angela Xavier de Brito and Ana Vasquez focuses on the use of video in ethnographic research. However, rather than discussing the technicalities and mechanics of video use, the bulk of the chapter is devoted to developing a theoretical understanding of the place of video in ethnography. In doing this, they build on Marcel Mauss's idea of "the gift relationship." They argue that the progressive establishment of trust between the researcher and the subjects of the research is constructed within a framework of exchange, and that video can provide an important part of the resulting gift relationships. They describe some of their own extensive experience of using video and show how relationships were formed and tested through negotiations about the use and showing of video during the research period. Video, they argue, is a gift that binds the researchers and subjects into relationships with mutual responsibilities and privileges.

The next two chapters both stretch the concept and activity of ethnography beyond those commonly accepted. In different ways both argue that ethnography and education are interwoven because ethnography is, in itself, educational. John Schostak uses an ethnographic study of a Canadian newspaper editorial office as the concrete starting point for his discussion of the nature of ethnography and of education. He argues that the texts that journalists produce in their newspaper act as a witness for the people of the city, and might be seen as a "curriculum" of the city that has at least the potential for being educational. Newspapers can challenge the views of their readership, and can confront versions of the "truth" proclaimed by governments, the rich and the powerful. Drawing on the work of Lucan, Schostak discusses the textual production of the witness within newspaper journalism. He argues that, if witnesses are to offer persuasive alternatives for change in the context of the global-local context of contemporary life, the gaze must create those projects in the spaces overlooked by modernist and postmodern visions alike. Alternative forms of personal and social being can be seen only through the cr/eye of the ethnographic witness.

Jim Mienczakowski's chapter offers a different focus on problems of representation in ethnographic research, and reports his own use of ethnography and ethnographically based dramatic performance as a vehicle for student learning in schools and higher education. The chapter uses two extended examples. First, it discusses a relatively small-scale project with senior school students which used ethnography to enable them to develop a new understanding of their community. Second, it describes a funded health research project in which student nurses and professional health workers constructed an ethnographic health narrative for year 11 and 12 students. It describes the use of ethno-drama in educational settings, demonstrates the methodologies, and argues the theoretical cogency of this activity. The chapter then discusses the nature of the analytical dissonance between the aims and values sought by the funding health authority and the nature of the data collected through the ethnographic research process, and continues with an elaboration of the potential of ethnographic performance research to explain, critique and influence understanding of health informants' lives.

The following chapter by Bob Jeffrey illustrates a way of achieving a balance between the need for involvement and the need for distance in undertaking ethnographic research. He argues that both are vital aspects of the research process and shows how he uses memos to develop an appropriate balance. The paper draws upon two of Jeffrey's research projects (conducted with Peter Woods) on the effects of the National Curriculum and of Ofsted inspections in primary schools and classrooms. First, he reproduces some of his research memos to show how he identified with teachers emotionally, experientially, appreciatively and humanely. Next, he illustrates the need for and utility of "playful writing" within memos and vignettes, showing their light narrative or evocative natures and the use of stories and metaphoric analogies. Finally, Jeffrey shows how his own personal interests can impinge on the analysis and help to achieve greater distance. His interests in music, opera and ballet, for example, provide appropriate analogies and metaphors within the written memos and the final published accounts.

In the final chapter Alexander Massey argues that, when applied to methodology, the concept of triangulation is highly problematic. He shows that the metaphor of triangulation exerts a strong hold over many researchers in social science and education, but he argues that the trust they give it is misplaced. The chapter shows that some researchers have mistakenly assumed that the ontological and epistemological bases of certain research activities are the same as those underpinning the triangulation method in surveying. The result of this philosophical and methodological confusion is that many misleading and invalid claims are made in the name of triangulation which play into the hands of those already keen to discredit qualitative and mixed-method approaches to research. He describes and analyses seven different error types that can be found in methodological triangulation, and argues for fresh thinking on how to establish the authority of empirical claims.

Altogether, we believe the sheer variety of chapters presented here and their multiple, contested and sometimes contradictory understandings of ethnography are evidence of the life and vitality of ethnography and its utility within the study of education. Ethnographic research methodology is an area of intense debate. This collection does not seek to provide definitive answers, but it is hoped that these chapters will add further fuel to the debates.

SELLING YOUR WAY IN:
GAINING ACCESS TO RESEARCH SITES

Geoffrey Walford

I've got to the airport just a little early. I'm going on holiday. I've packed the novels, but there is just a slight feeling of guilt that I haven't packed any "work" books. I browse through the airport bookshop and I'm faced with a mountain of books on business, finance and management. Can a good ethnographer learn anything useful from the business shelves?

In this chapter I will argue that ethnographers can, indeed, learn a great deal from some business books, particularly many of the popular books on marketing and selling. I argue that access to a research site has many similarities with the process of selling, and an examination of the suggested ways of encouraging sales might therefore give new insights into the process of gaining access to research sites and to individuals within those research sites.

ACCESS AS A PROBLEM

Gaining access to research sites has long been one of the "classic" topics within methodology books about ethnographic research. Hammersley and Atkinson (1995), for example, devote a whole chapter to "Access," Burgess (1984b) has

Studies in Educational Ethnography, Volume 2, pages 1-15.
Copyright © 1999 by JAI Press Inc.
All rights of reproduction in any form reserved.
ISBN: 0-7623-0563-0

"Starting research and gaining access" for the title of his second chapter, while the even older book by Johnson (1975) has a chapter that discusses "Gaining and managing entree in field research." Access is also a popular topic for ethnographers to consider in their reflexive accounts. The several collections of such accounts edited by Robert Burgess (1984a, 1985a, 1985b) and my own similar edited volumes (Walford 1987a, 1991a, 1994, 1998a) have numerous examples of the genre. These accounts usually offer descriptions of successful and unsuccessful attempts to enter research sites such as schools and classrooms, and offer an array of tactics that have met with success in the past. It is always emphasized that access is fraught with difficulties and that, within ethnography, it is a continuous process. Even after those with power within a school have eventually been persuaded to give access, the researcher continually has to negotiate further access to observe classrooms and interview teachers and students. At a deeper level, access can be seen as a process of building relationships with people within the organization. The aim is that teachers and students learn to trust the researcher to the point where they are prepared to be open and honest about their perceptions and beliefs. Access is thus never total, but might be seen as an incremental continuum, where the researcher is gradually able to move from the initial permission to enter the buildings to a series of developed and trusting relationships with some teachers and students. Access is also always provisional, as permission and trust can be withdrawn at any time by headteacher, teachers, parents or students.

Geoff Troman (1996) has recently suggested that access to schools has now become even more difficult than before. He argues that the macro-changes in the organization, management and content of schooling that have resulted from government legislation over the last decade have led to schools becoming more reluctant to agree to become a site for a research study. Among the changes that he notes as important are: the intensification of teachers' work, the negative views that teachers hold about the usefulness of research, the increased fear of surveillance by external "experts" that has resulted from Ofsted and Key Stage testing, and the increasing numbers of other researchers already in the schools as a result of the growth of Masters and Doctoral students and students undertaking research as part of their more school-based initial teacher training. If Troman is correct that access is becoming more difficult and that these difficulties stem from macro-changes, it is increasingly important that the micro-level interactions that lead to access are effective. Researchers can do nothing directly to reduce the effects of these macro-level changes on schools, so the process of obtaining access needs to take these new constraints into consideration. Just as salespeople conduct research on the commercial environment within which they are selling, and take this into account in the way they promote their products, so educational ethnographic researchers must take macro-changes in the educational environment into account in their approach to gaining access. They must learn to "sell" themselves and their research more effectively.

SELLING YOURSELF AND YOUR RESEARCH

I wish to argue that the popular sales and marketing books to be found at airport bookshops (and, of course, elsewhere) offer numerous insights about how to gain and maintain access. I am not suggesting that any of these books should be followed slavishly, or that their "tried and tested" "secrets of success" or "vital ingredients" that lead to "the perfect sale" should be taken too seriously. But what these books do is to encourage salespeople to think about the access process and how they are presenting themselves and their products to potential clients and purchasers. These books deal in hyperbole, but in advocating selling as "the world's greatest profession" (Denny 1997) and by claiming that "Living life successfully *is* selling!" (Carmichael 1994) these authors remind us that researchers need to take the process of gaining access seriously. We have to be clear how our research can be sold to those who can grant us access and clarify what the potential benefits are to them. In selling, it may have become a platitude to say that "people don't buy products, they buy benefits," but it is nonetheless true. We need to be clear what benefits researchers, the process of research, and the research findings themselves can offer.

The type of book I am suggesting might be useful is hardly likely to find a place on academic booklists. They largely lack any sophisticated theoretical or research base and tend to present anecdote and opinion as fact. Even business schools would be hesitant to recommend them, and most educational research methodologists would probably not see them as having any relevance. These books have titles such as: *The Perfect Sale: All You Need to Get It Right First Time* (Thornely and Lees 1994), *Selling 101* (McGaulley 1995) which promotes itself as "Expert advice for small business," *Selling to Win* (Denny 1997) which is advertised as the "UK number one best seller," *Four Square Selling* (Carmichael 1994) or, perhaps the most "respectable looking," *The American Marketing Association Handbook for Successful Selling* (Kimball 1994). Even books with such titles as: *Persuasive Business Presentations* (Robinson 1993) or *Powerful Presentations* (Ehrenborg and Mattock 1993) have many points of interest. I am suggesting that we swallow our pride and see how highly successful salespeople can help us gain and retain access.

APPROACH

Rather than follow an exact formula from one of these many books, it is more useful to organize an account in terms of a very general structure. One very simple way of thinking about the selling process is through the acronym AIDS, where the four-fold formulation is: Approach, Interest, Desire, and Sale. In most of the following I will use entry to a school as the main example, but the discussion and suggestions are equally applicable to the many other institutions and organizations where learning occurs. Equally, although much of the discussion is framed around the initial entry to a school that might be granted by a headteacher, it can also be applied to individual teachers and students within the school.

According to the "selling" books, in trying to make a sale, the first step is to seek prospects who are likely to want to buy your product or service. A great deal of work is done before any direct contact is made, for it is necessary to approach the correct prospects, and not waste time and energy on those who are unlikely customers. Similarly, in making an approach to a school or any other organization to conduct research, the ethnographer needs to make sure that contact is made with the person most likely to be receptive to the research. "Prospecting" is the term used for looking for someone who might be sympathetic to whatever it is that you are selling. This requires research before making any approach. So, to obtain entry to a school to conduct an ethnography, it is worthwhile doing some preliminary research on people within a number of potentially suitable schools. The aim is to build a file of information on the key people in each school. One obvious possibility is to look for any university connections. Someone who has spent time doing their own research might be expected to be more likely to agree to outside research than someone who has not. It is relatively easy to find the academic qualifications of those in the senior management team of a school and the title of a dissertation for a Masters or Doctoral degree can often be found from the university or on the internet. If someone has a doctorate, it is worth seeing if they have published anything—again, this is now easily done on the internet. If a headteacher has researched and published on management structures or special educational needs, for example, this is certainly worth knowing before making any approach. The approach can then be framed to include elements that might be likely to appeal.

It is usually important that the person approached is "qualified." In this case the term means "qualified to deal with the issue"—in other words, able to grant access. In schools this is usually straightforward as the headteacher will be the obvious qualified person. But this is not so in all schools—in some the Chair of Governors has a major say, while in others the Senior Management Team may expect to be consulted. So it is wise to investigate these people as well as the Headteacher and to try to discover where the power lies. Troman (1996) gives an example where the Headteacher appeared to be enthusiastic about his proposed research, but where the Senior Management Team (whom he did not talk with) rejected it. It is possible to see this as erroneously making his sales presentation to an individual when he should have insisted on making the presentation to the group.

Several of the books on selling emphasize that they are only systematizing what they regard as "common sense." But this act of systematizing and naming is useful, for it encourages us to think through various possibilities. A "referred lead" is a possible new client who has been suggested by an existing client. In attempting to gain access to a research site this might be seen as the use of a mutual friend or colleague. If there is someone else in the school who the researcher already knows, this person might be able to act as a "link" and as a recommendation. Obviously, it is important here to contact the mutual friend or colleague first to ask for help and to try to ascertain the relationship between this person and the "qualified" person. A further development of this idea is that it might be possible to exploit a shared experience or interest. Headteachers are more likely to give access if they can perceive the researcher as being "one of us." A researcher who is able to show some shared experience has a real advantage.

In my own early ethnographic work on boys' independent boarding schools (Walford 1986, 1987b), I approached access in a rather haphazard way. I wrote letters to headmasters and had five refusals before one gave me an interview. I will discuss that interview in more detail later, but one of the important aspects was that the headmaster spent time checking the question "Are you one of us?" As I had briefly taught in three of these schools, he was able to answer that question in the affirmative, but only after he had extracted the name of someone whom we both knew from one of the schools who could act as a "referee" for me. In this case, I had not contacted this person beforehand and I was not even sure that he would remember me with any clarity. But evidently the reference he gave (alongside that from the academic referee that was also demanded) was convincing, for an invitation to conduct the research soon followed. I had been lucky, for I had not thought through these possibilities beforehand and had done very little prospecting. It is also worth noting that, once into the system, it was very easy to be given permission to conduct research in other boys' independent boarding schools. The first Headteacher gave me permission to use his name as a "referred lead" and the Headmaster of the second school simply telephoned him for a reference. I was let loose in this second school for a whole term with hardly a question being asked about what I was going to be doing.

Another important term in selling is "gatekeeper." In ethnography, the term is often used for the person who is able to grant access to the research site but, in selling, the gatekeeper is the person who is able to give you access to the prospect. I have found that secretaries are well worth being good to. They are able to help or halt the research approach according to how they are dealt with. My route into the first City Technology College at Solihull was particularly tortuous. I made dozens of telephone calls to the college before I was eventually able to meet the principal, but the various secretaries were most helpful, and I gradually built up a great deal of information on the activities of the college and the principal before even setting foot in the buildings (Walford and Miller 1991; Walford 1991b).

One of the reasons I probably had so much difficulty in gaining access to the boys' independent boarding schools was that I misunderstood the purpose of my letter to the schools. Had I read any of the "selling" books beforehand, I might have been clearer that the purpose of any letter is to gain an initial interview, and not to gain access. Instead of a short letter that raised interest in the proposal without giving too many details, I wrote fairly long letters that included far too much information. Every additional piece of information gives a chance for an objection or problem to be raised in the mind of the reader. Detailed letters make it far too easy to find a "good reason" to object. Thus, if a letter is to be used, it should be brief. If it is possible to include a referred lead or some aspects of common experience, then this is useful. If a letter is to be used, it should indicate that a telephone call will follow to try to fix an appointment. Having sent such a letter, it may be possible to use this as a way past any secretary who screens calls.

Denny (1997) puts the purpose of letters and telephone calls succinctly: "Remember that the purpose of writing a letter is to sell your telephone call which should, in turn, sell the appointment. Another great principle of salesmanship: *you can only sell one thing at a time*" (Denny 1997, p. 72, emphasis and sexism in the original). In a similar way, Kimball (1994, p. 87) uses large lettering to stress "The purpose of the telephone call is to get the appointment." They both then go into great detail about how a telephone call might be conducted, giving ways of getting past secretaries and, most importantly, not getting into the position where a face-to-face appointment is unnecessary. They indicate ways of avoiding saying too much on the telephone, and making it seem imperative that a meeting occurs. If researchers are just after a single interview it might be possible to explain the need during a telephone conversation and obtain a positive reply. But nobody is going to give permission for an ethnographic enquiry explained through a telephone call—the focus must be gaining a meeting.

Now much of this (once we have read it) does indeed seem to be "common sense," but the "selling" books take far more care with approaches than most researchers. The use of the telephone is one area where "selling" books have a great deal to offer ethnographic researchers trying to gain access. Whereas most research guides have little to say on the issue, these "selling" books are brimming with ideas. Consider (and maybe reject) the "handy hints" about using a telephone. It is obvious that one should plan the call, and be enthusiastic, but is it obvious that one should know what reaction is desired, that we might sound more decisive if we stand up when using the telephone, or that it might be a good idea to smile while on the telephone to project a better manner? (Denny 1997, p. 79). And why not tape record any telephone calls to see how we sound and to learn how to improve performance? (McGaulley 1995, pp. 42-43). And what is the best way of dealing with voice mail? What time should be suggested for a meeting? These selling books have more ideas on these matters than any educational or social research methods books I have read.

INTEREST

The objective of any telephone call is to get a face-to-face interview. In spite of the increasing success of telephone sales, it is widely accepted that the best way to sell is on a face-to-face level. Only fools make large purchases from telephone sales, and ethnographers are not usually dealing with fools. Headteachers and others who can grant access to schools and classrooms are not going to do so without actually seeing the researcher face-to-face. The purpose of the telephone call is to create some initial interest and to fix a date for an interview. The prospect has to become convinced that a meeting is both worthwhile and necessary. On no account should the prospect be given the chance to say "no" on the telephone.

Once an appointment has been obtained, the preparation for and conduct of that interview must also be taken very seriously. One of the central tenets behind any of these "selling" books is that the good salesperson is not born, but made. These books promise that any moderately competent human being can learn skills and improve their techniques such that they can become successful salespeople. I would suggest that the need for such skills might be greater for academics and researchers than for most "moderately competent human beings." In my experience, educational researchers tend to be apologetic about their research; they balk at the idea of selling themselves or their research to others. Yet this is what they must do if they are to gain access.

My early attempts to gain access to the boys' independent boarding schools are indicative:

> My interview with the Headmaster of the first school to express interest lasted for only twenty minutes, but I experienced it as being far longer and more nerve-racking than any of the interviews I had for academic appointments. He was extremely sharp and shrewd and demanded precise answers to a range of questions about my purposes and methodology. I had envisaged presenting myself as an open ethnographer and had thus prepared only a fairly flimsy outline of the sort of areas in which I was interested—I intended, in true ethnographic style, to develop my research strategy once actually in the school. The Headmaster, however, had a rather different view of how research should be conducted, where questions are tightly framed, questionnaires or interview schedules developed, and representative samples drawn from populations. It quickly became obvious that the role of "open ethnographic researcher" was one which he would not entertain (Walford 1991b, p. 50).

I had done insufficient groundwork and I had allowed the prospect to control the situation. In this case I was able to retrieve the situation by showing considerable flexibility in my proposed research methodology, but I was very lucky. More thought about how to interest the Headmaster in the research would have greatly improved my chances.

Although there is now much greater concern about preparation for interviews, in particular where those interviews are with powerful people (for example, McHugh 1994; Fitz and Halpin 1994), I believe that many researchers would benefit from appraising some of the presentation skills suggested in "selling" books. Most educational researchers are now aware of the obvious aspects of self-presentation at interviews. We think about how smart to look, what clothes to wear, and what degree of formality to try to adopt. Of course, we do not always get it right:

In my most recent research on sponsored grant-maintained schools, for example, I went to interview the Headteacher of a Transcendental Meditation Primary school that wished to obtain state funding, but whose application was eventually rejected. I dressed reasonably smartly, but not in a suit. With a tie in my pocket, I checked whether I should wear it with the local taxi driver who was driving me to the school. "No, they're all very laid back. It's all very informal," he informed me. In fact, the staff were all very smartly dressed—all the male teachers had ties, and all the children were in stylish uniforms! I looked and felt out of place with my open collar.

But such aspects are trivial compared with the care that good salespeople take with their interviews. The various "selling" books have pages of ideas about how to make sure your position in the room is a good one, how to control and interpret body language, how to deal with presentation aids and how to sell yourself as much as the product or service. But two points of emphasis in many of these books are the use of questions and the need to listen to the customer. In Denny's (1997, p. 85) words: "If you were to ask me what I consider to be the single most important skill in mastering the art of professional selling, I would say it is the ability to ask questions." Kimball agrees and states:

[W]hen a professional salesperson makes a presentation, he or she will listen more than speak. In a presentation, you should listen—with the prospect talking—at least 55 percent of the time. If you are doing more than 45 percent of the talking, it's time to pull back on the reins, talk less, and listen more. You aren't going to persuade the prospect with your brilliant oratory. On the contrary, you persuade the prospect by getting him or her to talk (Kimball 1994, p. 106).

While we should not take too seriously the exact percentages (they are hardly likely to be the results of systematic research), it is worth stopping and thinking about the general statement. My feeling is that it is unlikely that most educational researchers would try to interest anyone in their research in this way. For most of us, preparation for an initial interview means working out what we want to say; we hardly ever think of what our prospects might want to say. Yet, according to these "selling" books, questions can enable us to tune into the prospect and their thinking, and to identify their needs and motives. Questions can help to establish a greater rapport and, at the same time, give greater control to the person asking questions. They can help us to shape our presentation more carefully such that it is more likely to be accepted.

In my experience headteachers definitely like to talk. When an appointment is arranged by telephone, they are often careful to explain how busy they are and how little time they can spare but, once in the office, they seem to have far more time than expected. In my recent work on sponsored grant-maintained schools (Walford 1997, 1998b), for example, when I interviewed headteachers and sponsors I usually asked for 45 minutes. None of the interviews was that short, and some went on for over two hours. A great deal of that time was spent in them talking about issues that were not directly relevant to my own concerns but, by listening to their agenda, I was able to obtain very full answers to my own specific questions.

In a similar way, when trying to gain ethnographic access, listening to the head-teacher's needs and desires can mean that the research proposal can be framed more closely to be more attuned to those requirements. Listening gives the salesperson "buying signals" and indicates potential hesitations and objections. For the researcher, listening can give similar information about potential concerns which, as discussed in the next section, can then be dealt with before they are even voiced.

The "selling" books use a great deal of space on presentational aids. In this case, questions of how to ensure that over-head projectors and computer graphics actually work are important. How are high quality visuals created? Should the salesperson have leaflets and other promotional materials and, if so, what type, and at what point should they be handed out? They also remind us that the salesperson him/herself is the prime presentational aid. Kimball (1994, p. 110) celebrates this as:

> Remember: It's show time! Your presentation is a performance, designed to interest, entertain, and persuade. To be successful, it needs to be completely and perfectly rehearsed. Note that I said rehearsed, not canned.

Now, it is unlikely that educational ethnographers would wish to see themselves as actors on stage or to use sophisticated aids in any presentation, but it is worth thinking about the impression that we wish to make. Visual inputs can be particularly effective, so some simple aids might be worth considering. In particular, it is worth trying to build and present an image of success, so taking along an example of the results of previous research would be helpful. A book based on previous research also has the advantage of slightly deflecting the discussion away from the details of the particular research that is being planned in this situation. An important book written by someone else might also have a similar effect. However, the aim would not be to deceive, simply to indicate the type of academic "end-product" that the research might lead to.

DESIRE

There are two main aspects to raising the desire to purchase an item or service: overcoming objections and stressing benefits.

Within an interview numerous doubts may arise in the prospect's mind. It is usually thought better to deal with the most obvious possible doubts before they have been voiced. This shows that the salesperson is considerate and recognizes that the prospect may have some misgivings. In research, the doubts that will probably most often come to mind are those that concern the smooth running of the organization and the investment of time that staff and pupils might be asked to make. After all, schools have purposes other than to act as research sites. An ethnographer is in a very good position to quell some of these doubts, as the objective is always to disrupt the everyday life of the organization as little as possible. Any interviews are conducted at times convenient to those interviewed, and any observations are designed, as far as possible, to have no effect on those observed.

In an increasingly market-driven system, headteachers are often concerned about any potential bad effects on the school's reputation. This is easily dealt with by discussing confidentiality and anonymity before these problems are raised. Troman's (1996) list of macro-changes in the school environment are also indicators of potential objections. It is useful making a judicial consideration of how each of these may be relevant to the particular target school, and showing how the particular research will take account of these problems.

If it is correct that "people don't buy goods and services, but buy benefits," it is essential that desire is developed by stressing the benefits of the research. If convincing benefits cannot be found, then the research should be abandoned. It is very unlikely that access to conduct an ethnography will be granted without a clear understanding and explanation of the potential benefits.

Academic researchers often think of potential benefits only in terms of the benefits that might eventually flow from the results of the study. Although this is of prime importance to the ethnographer, such benefits alone are unlikely to convince most headteachers. They offer no immediate benefits to the school and, if there are any long-term benefits, then all schools will benefit whether or not they agree to take part in the research.

An alternative is to offer more direct benefits. Thus many ethnographers have been prepared to become supply teachers when necessary or to take a class or two on a regular basis (e.g., Burgess 1983; Lacey 1970). This trade-off has obvious benefits for the school as it saves money, and it can have benefits for the researcher as well, in that it can help in getting to know the school's culture and in providing a ready group of students. But the role conflicts can be great and the time involved in lesson preparation and marking can overwhelm the research. If this sort of benefit is to be offered, it is probably better to suggest help with sports or other extra-curricular activities.

What researchers often forget is the direct benefits to the school, its teachers and students that the process of research can bring. Just as headteachers can benefit from talking in confidence to someone else about the school, so teachers can benefit from discussions about their work and careers. Students, too, can benefit from the process of being asked to think about their learning activities, their examination preparation or their plans for the future.

A good salesperson will ask past customers about what they liked and disliked about their purchases. If, at the end of any research, ethnographers were systematically to ask headteachers, teachers and students about what benefits they thought they had gained from the research process, future access procedures could be enhanced.

Of course, there is a need to be careful about the agendas of those with power. It is far from unknown for headteachers to suggest that researchers observe certain teachers that they want information about. The teacher may not be able to refuse a request, but the researcher should be very clear that observations and interviews with teachers are confidential and will not be fed back to the headteacher. It is wise to resist any suggestion that the ethnographer's topic be shifted to one that focused on a particular problem for the school. It might be highly tempting, but the problem of feeding back information to the headteacher and others with power will not only compromise the research, but will also lead to severe ethical problems. As researchers, we often have to decide "whose side we are on" (Becker 1968) and it is worth remembering that students may form one of the "sides." However, appropriate feedback to the school is an obvious benefit that most researchers can offer. If the focus is on bullying, for example, the researcher may eventually be in a good position to offer an inservice training session. The researcher's breadth of reading about the issue will be usually far greater than teachers have time for, so much of any feedback session can deal with general findings as well as the findings from the school itself.

The researcher's greater knowledge of the academic literature about the broad area of research should not be underestimated, for it is possible for some ethnographers accurately to present themselves as consultants on particular issues. Where the study focuses on more than one school, the researcher might offer the benefit of knowledge about other (obviously anonymized) schools and about general structural features. Such information can be of great benefit.

SALE

The final stage is the "sale." The prospect agrees to pay for 10,000 widgets or, in our case, the headteacher agrees to grant access in return for the benefits that he or she believes will follow. The "selling" books have many tactics that might be used to bring a discussion to a successful conclusion. Many of these suggestions may involve far more "pressure" than ethnographers would be willing to use, and are unlikely to be appropriate within the education system. But the "selling" books' viewpoint of seeing "objections as your friends" and the reminder that "your objective is to close the sale, not to complete the presentation" (Kimball 1994, p. 175) are well worth the ethnographer's consideration.

There comes a time in all sales presentations when it is best to start closing the sale. This time might be before the salesperson has completed all that could be said, and before some features of the product have been covered. Thus, in an access interview, it may be better to move to a decision at an unexpected time. When there are strong "buying signals," it may be best to ask for a decision at that point. In the research context, such signals can vary considerably. They might include questions on the details of procedures to be followed, indications of who it might be thought desirable for the researcher to meet, or even comments on a more collegial basis. Such signals need to be interpreted with care, and equal care needs to be taken with the method chosen for closing the agreement.

If the researcher has really generated a desire to take part in the research, it may be possible to use the "scarcity" tactic. As Kimball (1994, p. 176) states, "People are motivated to buy when they feel the opportunity to buy may be lost." Only a very limited number of schools will be involved in any ethnographic study, and the researcher selects particular schools to offer the opportunity to take part. The chance to be part of the research is limited, for the researcher does not have unlimited time or other resources. Is it too far fetched that researchers could generate a feeling that schools would be privileged to take part?

Another possibility, which may have only limited applicability, is the idea of the "assumed close." When the prospect has offered no objections, it may be possible simply to ask, "When shall I start? Would next Tuesday be okay, or next Wednesday?" Even said lightheartedly, it might well work in some cases. Another possibility, when there are signs of uncertainty, is to "pass down the hierarchy." If entry to a particular school is very important, and the headteacher is showing indecisiveness, pressure to make a decision may just go the wrong way. In many ways it is easier to say "no" than "yes," and our objective should be to avoid giving the chance of a "no." A suggestion that it might be a good idea to talk with the Deputy Head or other appropriate members of the Senior Management Team, might be one way of avoiding the "no." The advantage is that, once the research has been discussed with that person, it may be possible to again "pass down the hierarchy" such that several members of staff become involved with the research before any decision is made. The school may drift into a positive decision without knowing it.

There is also the possibility of some negotiation on the "price" to be paid by the school in return for the benefits expected. The decision to grant access is not a simple yes or no. Just as salespeople are prepared to reduce their price and offer "special discounts" to particular customers, so the ethnographer can negotiate the extent of access desired. In my rather chaotic negotiations for access to the boys' independent boarding school, I originally asked for six weeks (which I actually thought was too short) unstructured access. I was granted four weeks, under more tightly specified conditions. Perhaps if I had asked for eight I might have been granted six. If the cost to the school of granting access can be reduced, yet the same potential benefits are perceived to be forthcoming, then a deal might be easier to strike.

BUT IS IT ETHICAL?

I have suggested that a selective and critical reading of some of the "selling" guides might be of benefit to ethnographers wishing to gain access to research sites. The enthusiasm and care with which good salespeople approach selling should be a challenge for our own often rather poorly thought through tactics. If we don't take their suggestions too slavishly, these books can offer many insights. Not only can they give ideas about how to gain initial access to the buildings of an organization, they can help ethnographers with the continual process of gaining and maintaining access to the various people who work there. In ethnography, there is a continual need to find "ways-in and to stay-in" (Beynon 1983), and a study of selling might help ethnographers to develop their own procedures.

But is such selling ethical? Denny (1997, p. 10) asks the reader to consider the old saying "A good salesperson can sell anything," and then goes on to say, "It is rubbish. A good salesperson can only sell anything if he or she believes in it. Product belief is essential." Being positive about the research that you wish to conduct, and being able to show the benefits that could be obtained from being involved in the research, does not involve lying or even being "economical with the truth." I believe that if we can't find convincing benefits, then we should not be doing the research.

Selling has a bad name, but good selling is not just concerned with selling to one-off customers, but also to the "repeat buyer." It is widely recognized that repeat buyers need to be cultivated, and the easiest way of doing this is for the product to be of a high quality. People do not purchase twice a product that has not given them the benefits that were claimed for it, or which has actually cost them more than they originally expected. They do not recommend to friends services that have failed to deliver.

But, of course, there are some occasions when the major benefits of doing research do not accrue to the school, teachers or students who are the subjects of the research. There are times when potential benefits are gained by the wider society or wider social group, rather than those directly involved in the research. In many cases researchers can still obtain access by selling the benefits of feeling altruistic and of acting in such a way as to develop teaching as a research-based profession. However, it is still probably easier to gain access to study teachers' working conditions and the possible intensification of work practices than it is to study classroom management techniques.

My research on the City Technology College, Kingshurst, is an example where the direct benefits to the school were very low and the potential threat that research presented was great. As I have described elsewhere (Walford 1991b), Kingshurst was the first of the highly contentious CTCs established by Kenneth Baker while he was Secretary of State for Education. The college was at the center of a political controversy where there was little unbiased evidence, and where the taxpayer was paying far more towards the costs of the college than anyone had anticipated. I recognized that the research might actually cause some harm to the college, and that there would have to be some intrusion into the private lives of those closely involved, but I believed that there was a public "right to know" about how this important policy initiative was working in practice (Barnes 1979;

Pring 1984). My attempts to gain access spread over many months culminating in an unexpected (for her) meeting that I engineered with the principal away from the college. My selling was hard, if not crude. She did not want a book written about the college during its early years but, if one was to be written at all, she felt that she should write it. I intended to write a book about the college whether or not I obtained access to the college itself. The bargain we eventually struck was that I would give her the immediate benefit of space for a 15,000-word unedited chapter written by her in the book that I intended to publish. Importantly, in order for me really to understand the college and be able to write about it, she also insisted that I attend for about two days a week for a term and that I go to some of the special college events. This was exactly what I wanted to do. My actions reduced the potential costs of granting access, and introduced some direct benefits.

CONCLUSION

While the "problem of access" has long been a classic topic within methodology books about ethnographic research, I have not found any that examine the insights that might be gained from the business of selling. Commercial salespeople live on their ability to sell, and they have developed a range of techniques that they can draw upon to help them. These techniques may well not be based upon systematic research and may be idiosyncratic but, at least in some circumstances, they work. I have argued that ethnographers might benefit from knowing about some of these techniques and I hope that, next time readers are in an airport bookshop with its array of business books in front of them, they will invest a little time and money in reading one of these books on selling. Most of them only take an hour or two to read from cover to cover.

ACKNOWLEDGMENTS

I am grateful to Professor David Knights of UMIST for the original idea for this chapter and to Alexander Massey for his copious and helpful comments on an earlier draft.

REFERENCES

Barnes, J.A. 1979. *Who Should Know What?* Harmondsworth: Penguin.
Becker, H.S. 1968. "Whose Side Are We On?" *Social Problems* 14: 239-247.
Beynon, J. 1983. "Ways-in and Staying-in: Fieldwork as Problem Solving." In *The Ethnography of Schooling,* edited by M. Hammersley. Driffield: Nafferton.
Burgess, R.G. 1983. *Experiencing Comprehensive Education: A Study of Bishop McGregor School.* London: Methuen.
Burgess, R.G. (Ed.). 1984a. *The Research Process in Educational Settings: Ten Case Studies.* London and Washington, DC: Falmer Press.

Burgess, R.G. 1984b. *In the Field*. London: George Allen and Unwin.

Burgess, R.G. (Ed.). 1985a. *Field Methods in the Study of Education*. London and Washington, DC: Falmer Press.

Burgess, R.G. (Ed.). 1985b. *Strategies of Educational Research: Qualitative Methods*. London and Washington, DC: Falmer Press.

Carmichael, A. 1994. *Four Square Selling*. London: Concept.

Denny, R. 1997. *Selling to Win* (2nd ed.). London: Kogan Page. First edition 1988.

Ehrenborg, J., and J. Mattock. 1993. *Powerful Presentations*. London: Kogan Page.

Fitz, J., and D. Halpin. 1994. "Ministers and Mandarins: Educational Research in Elite Settings." In *Researching the Powerful in Education*, edited by G. Walford. London: UCL Press.

Hammersley, M., and P. Atkinson. 1995. *Ethnography: Principles in Practice* (2nd ed.). London and New York: Routledge.

Johnson, J.J. 1975. *Doing Field Research*. New York: Free Press.

Kimball, B. 1994. *AMA Handbook for Successful Selling*. Lincolnwood, IL: NTC Business Books.

Lacey, C. 1970. *Hightown Grammar*. Manchester: Manchester University Press.

McGaulley, M.T. 1995. *Selling 101*. Holbrook, MA: Adams Media Corporation.

McHugh, J.D. 1994. "The Lords' Will be Done." In *Researching the Powerful in Education*, edited by G. Walford. London: UCL Press.

Pring, R. 1984. "Confidentiality and the Right to Know." In *The Politics and Ethics of Evaluation*, edited by C. Adelman. London: Croom Helm.

Robinson, N. 1993. *Persuasive Business Presentations*. Singapore: Heinemann Asia.

Thornely, N., and D. Lees. 1994. *The Perfect Sale*. London: Arrow Books.

Troman, G. 1996. "No Entry Signs: Educational Change and Some Problems Encountered in Negotiating Entry to Educational Settings." *British Educational Research Journal* 22(1): 71-78.

Walford, G. 1986. *Life in Public Schools*. London: Methuen.

Walford, G. (Ed.). 1987a. *Doing Sociology of Education*. Lewes: Falmer Press.

Walford, G. 1987b. "Research Role Conflicts and Compromises in Public Schools." In *Doing Sociology of Education*, edited by G. Walford. London and Washington, DC: Falmer Press.

Walford, G. (Ed.). 1991a. *Doing Educational Research*. London and New York: Routledge.

Walford, G. 1991b. "Researching the City Technology College, Kingshurst." In *Doing Educational Research*, edited by G. Walford. London and New York: Routledge.

Walford, G. (Ed.). 1994. *Researching the Powerful in Education*. London: UCL Press.

Walford, G. 1997. "Sponsored Grant-Maintained Schools: Extending the Franchise?" *Oxford Review of Education* 23(1): 31-44.

_____ . 1998a. *Doing Research About Education*. London and Washington, DC: Falmer Press.

_____ . 1998b. "Reading and Writing the Small Print: The Fate of Sponsored Grant-Maintained Schools." *Educational Studies* 24(2): 241-257.

Walford, G., and H. Miller. 1991. *City Technology College*. Buckingham and Philadelphia: Open University Press.

USING CONNECTIONS
TO GAIN ACCESS:
SOME POINTS
OF CAUTION

Maria Birbili

In their book *Analyzing Social Settings*, Lofland and Lofland point out that "it seems quite typical for outside researchers to gain access to settings or persons through contacts they have established. They cast among their friends, acquaintances, colleagues and the like either for someone who is already favorably regarded by the person or the persons with access control or for someone who can link them to such a person." In urging this point, the authors conclude that "wherever possible you should try to use and/or build upon pre-existing relations of trust to remove barriers to entrance" (Lofland and Lofland 1995, p. 38).

Similarly, in their article "Getting in, Getting on, Getting out and Getting back," Buchanan and colleagues advise using "friends and relatives wherever possible" and report that "we have been most successful [in negotiating access] where we have had a friend, relative or student working in the organization. That person can either arrange access themselves depending on their position or they can speak for and introduce you to someone else in the organization who can do this" (Bucha-

Studies in Educational Ethnography, Volume 2, pages 17-28.
Copyright © 1999 by JAI Press Inc.
All rights of reproduction in any form reserved.
ISBN: 0-7623-0563-0

nan et al. 1988, p. 56). In the same vein, in their book *Ethnography*, Hammersley and Atkinson, drawing upon the literature, give several examples of cases where researchers have used personal networks in order to negotiate access or select informants (Cassell 1988; Hoffman 1980; Liebow 1967) and stress the significance of "sponsorship" which can be gained "through the mobilization of existing social networks, based on acquaintanceship, kinship, occupational membership, and so on" (Hammersley and Atkinson 1995, p. 60).

Implicit in much of the research literature is the assumption that using personal connections to get through or around the "wide range of topics, settings and situations that researchers deal with" (Lofland and Lofland 1995, p. 37) is an unproblematic strategy to be preferred "wherever possible" (Blaxter et al. 1996; Buchanan et al. 1988; Moyser 1988). The purpose of this paper is to challenge that notion, and to discuss some of the potential benefits and liabilities of negotiating access through connections as they became apparent while I was conducting a study into Greek academics and the experience of working in Greek higher education. The following review of some of the dilemmas, questions and problems encountered during that study will, I hope, illustrate the range and complexity of issues involved in using connections in order to gain access and provide a stimulus to further, more elaborate discussion.

NOTE ON TERMINOLOGY

In this paper the concern is with using friends, relatives and acquaintances as a strategy to negotiate access to settings and people. For purely presentational convenience, the three words "friends, relatives and acquaintances" will be used interchangeably with the words "personal connections" and "personal sponsors." This does not imply that relationships among friends, relatives or acquaintances are seen as the same, but rather that the argument being made applies to all three kinds of relationships. When it is seen as necessary the nature of the relationship will be defined.

The following discussion is divided into four sections: the first section presents the study and explains the reasons behind the decision to use personal connections in order to gain access to Greek academics. The second section focuses on the advantages of casting among friends, relatives and acquaintances as a strategy for negotiating access to settings and people, whereas the third discusses some of the limitations involved in this. The last section brings together what has been said in the preceding ones and makes some suggestions.

THE STUDY

The starting point for this paper is located in the research I did for my doctoral degree at the University of Oxford. The purpose of the study was to obtain a profile of the workplace experiences of a number of academics from two types of Greek higher education institutions—a university and a non-university type of institution—and to ascertain how the two groups view each other. In the light of a series of governmental proposals to incorporate the non-university type of institution into the university system and a long-standing tension which came to the surface and gave rise to long, bitter debates about the "place" of the non-university type of institution, the study also involved obtaining academics' perspectives on the proposed changes. The study was designed to draw its data from semi-structured, in-depth interviews and was organised around the following broad questions:

- How do the every-day working experiences of academics from the two types of institution differ?
- What do academics perceive to be the main differences between the two types of institution?
- To what extent do the academics from the two types of institution form a single academic community?

Fifty academics selected from four departments—two from each type of institution—were interviewed. Since there is strong support in the professional literature for distinguishing between subject areas when examining academics' perceptions of their workplace (Becher 1989; Thomas 1990), similar departments from each type of institution were chosen. From a list of eight similar departments, four belonging to the so called "hard sciences" (Becher 1989) were chosen on the basis of their accessibility as well as more concrete factors such as their size and their staff composition (for example, departments with only seven or eight people and with only tenured staff were considered a second choice if larger and more varied departments could be found).

NEGOTIATING ACCESS TO GREEK HIGHER EDUCATION

In my attempts to study Greek academics, I soon dismissed the idea of negotiating access to people and institutions directly and decided to make use of friends and relatives to help me gain access to both institutions and individuals. Approaching potential interviewees without any kind of "backup" did not seem a good idea for a number of reasons. The most important one was the issue of my own standing at the time: a young, female research student from Oxford University, former and current member of the staff of the same non-university type of institution I was looking at (but in a different department), and former student of both types of institution with a background in areas as diverse as early childhood education, educational research methodology and higher education. My assumption was that in whatever way I was to present myself—as a colleague, a research student, or both—if I made approaches without any support, there was a greater chance of academics refusing to be interviewed. Keeping other researchers' experiences in mind (Burgess 1991; Easterday et al. 1982; Wax 1986), I believed that ascribed status and roles (e.g. as "one of us" for those at the non-university type of institution and "one of them" for those at the university) as well as attributes associated with a series of stereotypes (young, female, student, student at Oxford University, "colleague") could influence people's responses to my request for interviews negatively. If, however, I were to approach them through an initial introduction from someone they knew and trusted, there was a greater likelihood of achieving their cooperation. This belief was strengthened by my inside knowledge of Greek academia as a rather closed world. Indeed, my experience both as a student and staff member suggested that, as a friend of the family—an academic himself—had put it, the "secret" for getting Greek academics to talk about themselves and their working life was to be defined and introduced as a "friend" by "one of the clique" as they would not accept just "anyone" to study them. Coupled with my experience of Greek society as one in which one can achieve a lot if one knows the right people in the right position, I felt that probably the best way of approaching Greek academics would be through people they knew and trusted.

Operating on the same assumption, another equally important reason for being very reluctant to negotiate access directly was my fear that getting into places where I knew no one involved the risk of managing to talk only to a limited number of academics instead of the larger numbers I was interested in. I believed that having a "peer" or someone they respected to vouch for me could greatly enhance the possibility of accessing more people than I would on my own as my connections' friends could, in order to do a friend a favor, refer me to others, thus setting up a kind of snowball sampling.

In this context, everyone from my personal and family network who had something—anything—to do with the Greek academic milieu, was recruited. As Cassell puts it, "everyone who might possibly know someone or know someone who might know someone" was contacted (Cassell 1988, p. 95). I asked people to introduce me directly to informants and potential interviewees, to vouch for me, or simply to give me names and telephone numbers of people I could interview and who, in turn, could refer me to others. Things worked better than I had imagined or expected. Two very good family friends (friends of my parents), two close relatives and a colleague and personal friend not only did their best to ease my entry to the field by contacting in turn friends, colleagues and acquaintances of theirs working in academia but they also helped me achieve my central aim of interviewing as many academics from each department as possible.

In short, faced with the possibility (and the anxiety) of encountering the same problems, as a result of perceived identity, that many other researchers report having experienced in their efforts to gain access, I tried, as Beynon says, to "simplify the situation through a process which did not involve the complexities of negotiation and discussion" (1988, p. 28). Whether another approach to gaining access—for example, cold calling—would have proved equally successful or not

I cannot tell, as I did not risk testing my assumptions. Various incidents during fieldwork, however (some of them are described later on), and hints I gathered "as everyone does from the atmosphere of one's world" (Landes 1986, p. 127) lead me to the conclusion that, on the whole, my decision was the right one.

ADVANTAGES

The study of the advantages and disadvantages of the different approaches to gaining access has generated and continues to generate a large literature. Compared with other methods and the problems associated with them, as they are presented in a large number of research accounts, I believe that using connections not only greatly facilitated—or "expedited," as Lofland and Lofland (1995, p. 37) say—my access to institutions and academics in many respects but also saved me from some of the anxieties and emotional stresses—all cited several times by field researchers—inherent in the process of negotiating and gaining access (Gans 1982; Hammersley and Atkinson 1995; Lofland and Lofland 1995; Shaffir et al. 1980).

First, it proved to be very convenient in terms of the time taken to locate potential interviewees. A few phone calls were all it took to obtain a list and usually a further phone call was enough to arrange the time and the place of an interview. Second, it proved very convenient in terms of the effort put into encouraging people to participate. Calling or visiting people who already knew something about me and had agreed to talk to me was much easier and considerably less stressful than having to approach the same people from the position of a "rootless stranger" (Rubin and Rubin 1995, p. 117) with the fear of possible rejection. Having already been "introduced" by my personal sponsors (usually, as a "very nice, intelligent girl who is doing her PhD at Oxford," as I found from the interviewees themselves) allowed me to concentrate on how best to explain my research rather than on how to sell myself or convince people to take me seriously (Gans 1982). It was only towards the end of the study, when an academic from the university, whom I approached through the snowball process, politely but firmly asked for proof, "an ID or something that proves that you are who you say you are" (he explained later on that he was worried I might be a journalist), that I realized and appreciated the relaxed state in which I had until then been operating, as a result of being "known."

Having my connections vouching for me was another major advantage. I believe that being vouched for placed me in a non-threatening position and granted me—in the eyes of Greek academics—legitimacy for doing research on such a "serious" topic, namely them. More importantly, however, it probably made most of the interviewees less cautious or reserved than they would have been with a person they knew nothing about and encouraged them (as several of them indicated either directly or indirectly during the interviews) to trust me to make good use of the information they gave me. Their perception of me as someone non-threatening also allowed me, on several occasions, to play the devil's advocate and question or challenge people's views with the ease of someone who knows that she will not be misunderstood. On the whole it has been my experience that my good references and credentials as someone responsible and to be trusted allowed me, as Burgess (1991, p. 51) says, "to access some data that I would not otherwise have obtained," while using such a strategy provided me with "more informative and insightful data" (Hammersley and Atkinson 1995).

The fact that I had someone recommending me also played a decisive part in how people treated me and facilitated the creation of a relaxed atmosphere both before and during the actual interview. For example, in one department where I was introduced by one of the academics as "a good friend" of his I very soon started being greeted as "our girl" and had people doing their best to make me feel welcome and comfortable; I was offered coffee, I was given the opportunity to choose a better place for the interview if I so wished; I was included in their jokes and I was assured, more often than not, that it had been "a pleasure" to talk to me (overcoming my initial discomfort at being called "our girl" by a relatively large group of male academics; I came to see this as an expression that meant nothing more than that I had been appraised as someone to be trusted). At the same time casual conversation with interviewees about our mutual acquaintances or friends provided a welcome opening for the interview process and helped ease the initial discomfort that might exist between two strangers who meet and know that they "have" to talk but they do not know what to expect from one another. On the whole, I felt that I was treated like a welcome guest or the friend of a friend and not that I was "merely tolerated as an inquisitor" (Finch 1984, p. 167).

Another important benefit of using friends and relatives to contact potential interviewees was the fact that suggestions about people I could talk to were often accompanied with useful information on how best to approach them or what to expect. For example, I was once told to be prepared to meet a very talkative interviewee which made me take more tapes than I usually carried with me! Those of my sponsors who themselves were academics also provided me with inside information about relationships, tensions or power arrangement within departments, and anything else I asked for or they thought I needed to know.

Finally, as a female researcher I could not disregard the fact that having people I knew and trusted being the link between me and "strangers" worked as a safety precaution in those few cases where I had to meet an interviewee in his house. Although it did not cross my mind at the time to refuse to interview people in their homes if this was the only option I had, I felt more relaxed in agreeing to this idea than I would have been if I had only my personal judgement about the situation to rely upon.

SOME LIMITATIONS

Nonetheless, for all these advantages, I did experience a number of significant negative effects of casting among friends, relatives or acquaintances in order to gain access to settings and individuals. A combination of factors originating from within me, the people acting as my sponsors and the Greek social context and culture can be said to have contributed to my facing the following four problems.

Relatively early in the study I realized that, as Rubin and Rubin (1995, p. 114) say, calling myself a researcher often did not work, because researcher was not "a meaningful category" in my friends' or relatives' eyes. On several occasions, I felt that it was probably unrealistic to expect people who knew me so well to see me as a researcher and themselves in a role other than that of the friend or the relative (for example, as "informants" or "sponsors"). In this context, I found it difficult to "signal" as Burgess (1991) says "which elements of my work were closed from view, which sets of data were not for public discussion." For example, it was not always easy to convince people who had limited understanding and knowledge about research why I was "refusing" to discuss with them people and situations they very convincingly argued that they knew about (what do you say when your interviewee is a good friend of your connection?) or why I appeared to be so reluctant to answer "simple" questions like "so who else did you see?" "did x tell you about...', "what did you think of what x said?" Reactions varied from "I understand" and "well, if you say so..." to "it sounds a bit funny you know, I introduced him to you and we know each other since we were undergraduates..." and "don't worry, I know all that, you are not revealing any secrets." Moments like this, the fact that in their eyes what I was "refusing" to give them were answers to some "simple" questions, left me with a strong sense that my connections believed I was making a fuss about nothing and was taking my role as a researcher more seriously than I should. Equally strong, at those moments, was my sense of guilt that I was taking and not giving (see Gans 1982).

The dynamics of the interaction with my personal connection were influenced a lot by the nature of the relationship, the age gap and the "degree of intimacy" (Platt 1981) between me and the person who acted as my personal sponsor. For instance, the closer the relationship with my connection the more difficult it was to "play" the researcher or be a close friend while preserving the amount of distance that I believed was necessary in order to value my assurances of confidentiality to those researched. In short, the closer the relationship with my connection the more difficult it was to "segregate," as Platt (1981) indicates, "the formal and the informal interaction." I found this to be the case with my two first cousins and my colleague and personal friend. On the other hand, the bigger the age gap between me and my personal sponsor the more difficult it was for me to "instruct" the person what to do or what to say when he or she was presenting me or the study to potential interviewees. In addition (in their perception), their age granted them legitimacy to act as my advisors and mentors, so that I was faced with the problem of the older of my connections taking "initiatives" (such as for example arranging two interviews for the same day without me knowing it) which, on some occasions, put me into a rather difficult position.

A second problem was my association with my personal connections. As a number of researchers have indicated, the way interviewees perceive the relationship of the researcher with the person who acts as the connection between them can have several implications for the research relationships as well as for the data collected (Burgess 1991; Hammersley and Atkinson 1995). In the same way and for the same reasons that a close relationship between the researcher and her personal sponsor can make interviewees speak openly and be honest, it could, conversely, make them hesitant in talking as they might, quite legitimately, question the researcher's assurances of confidentiality. As Moyser puts it succinctly, "personal sponsorship must be used very carefully, as whilst opening one door it might simultaneously close another" (Moyser 1988, p. 122). In my study I addressed this issue by stating very firmly and explicitly from the beginning of the interview that what was to be said between me and the interviewee was to be kept confidential. I also made sure that interviewees were told about or "reminded of" the fact that my personal sponsor had no connection whatsoever with what I was doing and was only acting as an intermediary (interestingly, while nearly all of them were quick to assure me that they did not have "a problem with that" [my relationship with my personal sponsor] as they did not have "anything to hide," I felt that they were rather pleased by my saying so). In addition, in those cases where interviewees were saying "you probably know about that, x [the name of my personal sponsor] might have told you," I declared ignorance even in cases where my connection had indeed talked to me about that particular issue. On the whole, judging by the quality of the data collected, I believe that my assurances of confidentiality were taken seriously, although of course I have no evidence that people told me "everything" or the kind of things they might have told a complete stranger.

Another price to pay for having contacted interviewees through friends and relatives—that is, through someone else—was that in several cases, until I met them for the actual interview, I did not know whether people had consented to be interviewed out of personal interest or because they were doing a friend, a colleague or an acquaintance a favour. I worried about the latter because I knew that it could affect the quality of the interview process, interviewees' responses, the research relationships and the process of building rapport. Using humor to create a pleasant atmosphere (whenever I sensed that the respondent would appreciate something like that) and calling forth my social skills I tried to make interviewees think of the interview as, at the very least, a pleasant experience. In addition, in those cases where I had not made the initial contact and had not presented the study myself, I was very careful to explain clearly and specifically from the very beginning of the interview what my purposes and the aims of the study were. This was a lesson I learned, fortunately early in the study, when I discovered that what the first four interviewees knew about me and the study ranged from "if I'm not mistaken you're doing something on academics" to "excuse me for asking, but what is it exactly that you're doing?" What these examples suggested was that I had wrongly assumed that my connections would present the study as I had "instructed" them to do or at least in the same detail I had presented it to them. As proved to be the case, what they were actually doing when they were contacting potential interviewees, was to concentrate on talking them into seeing me and leave the "details" to me. While by no means a problem that cannot be solved, meeting interviewees who do not know what the interview is about can be said to have certain disadvantages; some interviewees might feel "embarrassed" or "surprised" (Schatzman and Strauss 1973, p. 24) a fact which could influence the building of rapport and subsequently the quality of one's data.

Finally, while being extremely useful, having friends and relatives vouching for me created the additional anxiety of living up to their and consequently to the interviewee's expectations. The belief that leaving interviewees with only the best impressions of me was the least I could do for those who had helped me so much made me worry about my performance more than I should, and put on me what Agar calls "the strain of maintaining what you think is the correct impression" (Agar 1996, p. 110).

CONCLUSIONS

While the idea of casting among friends, relatives and acquaintances as a means to gain access has increasingly received attention in the research literature, textbooks and articles shed relatively little light on the implications of such a strategy for the researcher, the research process and the data collected.

In this paper I have drawn on my study of Greek academics in order to point out some of the advantages and the liabilities involved in using friends and relatives to negotiate entrée. Although one could rightly argue that the experiences described here are personal and/or culturally specific—and that other researchers might have not faced the same problems, developed the same feelings or defined the situation in the same way—I believe that they might serve as lessons to other researchers who "would do well, when offered the bait of easy access," to borrow Hargreaves' (1987, pp. 28-29) words, through using friends, relatives or acquaintances, to be aware of the tensions that might arise from a situation like this.

As a strategy for gaining access, using one's personal networks has a number of definite advantages. It can be very convenient in terms of time and energy needed to locate and contact potential interviewees and less stressful—or "more comfortable," as Schatzman and Strauss (1973, p. 20) say—than other ways of negotiating entry in terms of the effort needed to convince people to take the researcher and the research seriously and agree to participate. Furthermore, the fact that the researcher has been vouched for can make respondents feel more confident and enable them to talk more easily as well as be more friendly, accommodating and cooperative. However, relying on personal networks in order to gain and maintain access is not without its limitations. A number of problems may arise from the dual responsibility of the researcher to his/her connections and respondents and his/her dual role as a researcher and a friend, relative or acquaintance. Other limitations involve the implications that the association of the researcher with his/her personal sponsor(s) could have for the research relationships and the data collected, the anxiety of the researcher about his/her performance and the risk of "inheriting" one's personal sponsors' decision as "to who is the next suitable interviewee" (May 1993, p. 100). The nature of the problems and the demands made on the researcher depend, among other things, on the setting where research takes place, those researched and the nature of the study itself, the nature of the relationship between the researcher and her connections and the nature of the relationship between the researcher's connections and potential interviewees.

The sheer complexity of human relationships and the fact that, as Gans says, different "topics and settings generate different problems and anxieties," render any attempt for advice extremely difficult (Gans 1982, p. 58). For example, not everybody might feel as anxious about his/her performance as I did or guilty for the reasons I did; according to Roadburg (1980, p. 289), "guilt feelings depend on the researcher's sense of obligation" to those who helped her. Perhaps the best advice is that researchers should consider in advance the extent to which using personal networks to gain access will place any limitations on the study or become a source of "emotional or psychological difficulty" (Lofland and Lofland 1995, p. 47) for them or the people helping them. This would entail looking at the personalities involved and the nature of the relationship between them as well as the setting, the nature of the study and those who are researched (certain combinations of factors—or personalities—are more likely to give rise to difficulties than others). While no one could argue that researchers will be able to predict all potential problems, in trying to do so they are more likely to be, as Letkemann says "mentally and emotionally prepared for situations in which the research role may come into serious conflict with one's responsibilities as a human being" (Letkemann 1980, p. 294). In retrospect, I also believe that it is a good idea to do with your personal connections what some researchers suggest doing with gatekeepers or participants in order to achieve and maintain good research relationships: make as clear as possible at the outset of the research what the research process involves, how much the researcher is willing or able to give and what personal connections should expect—this is particularly useful when one is dealing with people who have no experience of research, as was the case in my study. As Letkemann succinctly puts it, "the clearer the expectations the more likely it is that the research will end in good will" (Letkemann 1980, p. 294).

ACKNOWLEDGMENT

I would like to thank Chris Davies, Alexander Massey, Charis-Olga Papadopoulou and Geoffrey Walford for their valuable comments and suggestions.

REFERENCES

Agar, M.H. 1996. *The Professional Stranger* (2nd ed.). San Diego, CA: Academic Press.

Becher, T. 1989. *Academic Tribes and Territories*. Buckingham: SRHE and Open University Press.

Beynon, H. 1988. "Regulating Research: Politics and Decision Making in Industrial Organizations." In *Doing Research in Organizations*, edited by A. Bryman. London: Routledge.

Blaxter, L., C. Hughes, and M. Tight. 1996. *How to Research*. Buckingham: Open University Press.

Buchanan, D., D. Boddy, and J. McCalman. 1988. "Getting in, Getting on, Getting out, and Getting back." In *Doing Research in Organizations*, edited by A. Bryman. London: Routledge.

Burgess, R.G. 1991. "Access in Educational Settings." In *Experiencing Fieldwork: An Inside View of Qualitative Research*. edited by W. Shaffir and R. Stebbins. Newbury Park, CA: Sage.

Burgess, R.G. 1984. *In the Field*. London: Allen and Unwin.

Cassell, J. 1988. "The Relationship of Observer to Observed when Studying up." *Studies in Qualitative Methodology* 1: 89-108.

Easterday, L., D. Papademas, L. Schorr, and C. Valentine. 1982. "The Making of a Female Researcher: Role Problems in Field Work." In *Field Research: A Sourcebook and Field Manual*, edited by R.G. Burgess. London: Allen and Unwin.

Finch, J. 1984. "It's Great to Have Someone to Talk to: Ethics and Politics of Interviewing Women." In *Social Researching: Politics, Problems, Practice*, edited by C. Bell and H. Roberts. London: Routledge and Kegan Paul.

Gans, H. J. 1982. "The Participant Observer as a Human Being: Observations on the Personal Aspects of Fieldwork." Pp. 53-61 in *Field Research: A Sourcebook and Field Manual*, edited by R.G. Burgess. London: Allen and Unwin.

Golde, P. 1986. *Women in the Field: Anthropological Experiences*. Berkeley: University of California Press.

Hammersley, M., and P. Atkinson. 1995. *Ethnography: Principles in Practice*. London: Routledge.

Hargreaves, A. 1987. "Past, Imperfect, Tense: Reflections on an Ethnographic and Historical Study of Middle Schools." In *Doing Sociology of Education*, edited by G. Walford. Lewes: The Falmer Press.

Hoffman, J.E. 1980. "Problems of Access in the Study of Social Elites and Boards of Directors." In *Social Research Ethics: An Examination of the Merits of Covert Participant Observation*, edited by M. Bulmer. London: Macmillan.

Landes, R. 1986. "A Woman Anthropologist in Brazil." In *Women in the Field: Anthropological Experiences*, edited by P. Golde. Berkeley: University of California Press.

Letkemann, P. 1980. "Crime as Work: Leaving the Field." In *Fieldwork Experience: Qualitative Approaches to Social Research*, edited by W.B. Shaffir, R.A. Stebbins and A. Turowetz. New York: St. Martin's Press.

Liebow, E. 1967. *Tally's Corner*. London: Routledge and Kegan Paul.

Lofland, J., and L.H. Lofland. 1995. *Analyzing Social Settings*. Belmond, CA: Wadsworth Publishing Company.

May, T. 1993. *Social Research Issues, Methods and Process*. Buckingham: Open University Press.

Roadburg, A. 1980. "Breaking Relationships with Research Subjects: Some Problems and Suggestions." In *Fieldwork Experience: Qualitative Approaches to Social Research*, edited by W. B. Shaffir, R. A. Stebbins, and A. Turowetz. New York: St Martin's Press.

Rubin, H., and I. Rubin. 1995. *Qualitative Interviewing: The Art of Hearing Data*. Thousand Oaks, CA: Sage.

Schatzman, L., and A.L. Strauss. 1973. *Field Research: Strategies for a Natural Sociology*. Englewood Cliffs, NJ: Prentice Hall.

Thomas, K. 1990. *Gender and Subject in Higher Education*. Buckingham: Open University Press.

Wax, R. H. 1986. "Gender and Age in Fieldwork and Fieldwork Education: Not Any Good Thing is Done by One Man Alone." In *Self, Sex and Gender in Cross-Cultural Fieldwork*, edited by T. L. Whitehead and M. E. Conaway. Chicago: University of Illinois Press.

THERE IS NO SUCH THING AS "CRITICAL ETHNOGRAPHY":
A HISTORICAL DISCUSSION AND AN OUTLINE OF ONE CRITICAL METHODOLOGICAL THEORY

Phil Francis Carspecken

There is no such thing as "critical ethnography." There are ethnographies that are called "critical" by their authors and there are researchers who call themselves critical ethnographers. But at the time of writing this chapter, no consensus exists on any explicit methodological theory among those who identify themselves as critical ethnographers.

This chapter will introduce readers to one version of critical ethnography that is distinguished by a fairly explicit, though continuously developing, methodological theory. Illustrations will be provided that focus mainly on educational research. Readers must bear in mind the fact that this is a version of critical ethnography, not what critical ethnography is. In fact, some researchers who identify themselves as critical ethnographers will not be readily attracted by the research methods and principles I advocate.

Studies in Educational Ethnography, Volume 2, pages 29-55.
Copyright © 1999 by JAI Press Inc.
All rights of reproduction in any form reserved.
ISBN: 0-7623-0563-0

Through a brief historical discussion of the origins of critical ethnography I will first try to clarify why this genre of research has been primarily distinguished by the value orientation of those who identify with it, rather than by a distinctive epistemology or a unique set of analytic methods. I will then suggest reasons why it makes sense to formulate an explicit methodological theory for critical ethnography. Distinctive epistemological principles for this methodology are then outlined, and this is followed by a summary of analytic principles and methods characteristic of this mode of research. I intend to make the discussion useful to researchers and students wishing to add perspectives and methods to their repertoire, whether they wish to call themselves "critical" or not.

WHAT IS CRITICAL ETHNOGRAPHY?

The term "critical ethnography" seems to have originated during the 1980s. It was first used to refer to qualitative educational research informed by critical theories of education, such as critical pedagogy theory, feminist theories of education, and neo-Marxist theories of education (Anderson 1989; Lather 1986; McLaren 1989, 1993; Thomas 1993). During the late 1980s postmodern modes of thinking also became an important influence on many of those who called their work critical ethnographies (Lather 1990, 1991). The influence of these various theoretical perspectives appeared in the final stages of data analysis rather than in the research methodology.

During the 1990s the small community of researchers who call themselves critical ethnographers has grown to include people working in departments of sociology, anthropology, and cultural studies as well as education (Herzfeld 1989; Hymes 1996; Levinson et al. 1996; Sefa Dei et al. 1997; Street, A. 1992; Street, B. 1995; Thomas 1993; Treuba et al. 1990; Treuba et al. 1993; Treuba and Zou 1994; Zou and Treuba 1998). Handbooks of qualitative methodology and anthologies of qualitative social research now commonly include at least one chapter on critical ethnography (Kincheloe and McLaren 1994; Quantz 1992; Zou 1998). Very recently, introductory college texts on basic research methods for the social sciences have begun to include substantial sections on critical ethnography (Gall et al. 1999).

The number of self-defined critical ethnographers is growing but the critical ethnographies they produce differ in fundamental ways. No consensus exists on what a critical ethnography is, how it should be conducted, how its conclusions may be supported, how it is distinctive from other forms of qualitative social research. Research designs, analytic methods, and the concept of validity vary amongst those who call themselves critical ethnographers.

The principal criteria that have been used by critical ethnographers to distinguish their genre of research have been the value orientation of the researcher and a broadly defined belief that society is structured so as to produce disadvantaged and oppressed groups of people. This shared orientation is not hard to specify. Critical ethnographers generally research social sites, social processes, and cultural commodities like text books, films, and video games in order to reveal social inequalities. All such researchers basically begin their research with the assumption that contemporary societies have systemic inequalities complexly maintained and reproduced by culture. They are opposed to inequality, which they conceptualize as a structural feature of society, and they wish to conduct research that will support efforts to reduce it.

Education has been a particularly attractive site for those conforming to this orientation. This is because education is a key social institution for both promoting and constraining social mobility and for encouraging or discouraging a critical view of society in young people. Not surprisingly, most critical ethnographies of education have supported the argument, in one way or another, that schools and universities do more to sustain a fundamentally unequal society than to produce citizens motivated to, and capable of, producing positive social change.

By the end of this chapter I will have proposed an alternative conception of critical ethnography that emphasizes an epistemological theory and a related set of analytic techniques. The version of critical ethnography I advocate can be conducted by researchers of any initial value orientation. The methodological principles I advocate are consistent with many published studies currently regarded as critical ethnographies but at odds with those critical studies that support relativist epistemologies.

SOME HISTORICAL ROOTS OF CRITICAL ETHNOGRAPHY

There are historical reasons why critical ethnography has not been a methodologically distinctive genre of research. During the 1970s qualitative, ethnographic-like research was conducted by members of the Centre for Contemporary Cultural Studies (CCCS) at the University of Birmingham (CCCS 1978; Hebdidge 1979; Willis 1977). These studies became highly influential and were frequently imitated by Marxist and feminist researchers during the early 1980s. The CCCS ethnographies were conducted at least partially to resolve theoretical problems in neo-Marxism. Heated debates were occurring at this time between Marxist-structuralists (Althusser 1969) and Marxist-culturalists (Thompson 1963, 1978; see Johnson 1979). An issue central to these debates was the question of whether social structure *determined* human choices and social routines (the structuralist argument) or whether, to the contrary, social structure was a *result* of human choices patterned by cultural milieu and social environment (the culturalist argument). Structuralists wished to downplay human agency by regarding the human subject as a social construction. Culturalists wished to emphasize human agency by regarding all acts as the product of volition that is, however, constrained by cultural milieux and social environments. The ethnographic studies produced by CCCS basically supported a culturalist position. Human agents were shown to construct their own life routines but within physical environments, job markets, opportunity structures, and traditional cultural milieux that are largely outside their control.

From the perspective of the neo-Marxist debates, the distinctive feature of these early CCCS ethnographies was their use of ethnographic research to answer questions in social theory. Prior to these studies participants in the debates were either armchair theorists (Althusser 1969) or historians (Thompson 1963).

From the perspective of qualitative and educational research traditions, however, the distinctive feature of these ethnographies was their neo-Marxist interpretation of qualitative findings. The research methods used were not distinctive and little attention was given to the question of how one might validate one's findings and interpretations.

Early work at the Centre for Contemporary Cultural Studies established something like an initiating template for critical qualitative research. The paradigmatic work was *Learning to Labour* by Paul Willis (1977). Other studies produced by the Centre between the mid 1970s and early 1980s were also formative for what was later called critical ethnography (Hebdidge 1979; McRobbie 1978). During the late 1970s and early 1980s various American researchers also produced studies influenced, to various degrees, by CCCS work (Anyon 1980; Everhart 1983).

This basic template was short on epistemology and methodology but strong on value orientation and a neo-Marxist view of society. The class structure of contemporary society and its evils, and later gender and racial inequality, were the orienting framework which produced a triadic structure of social inequality, assumed a priori, the dynamics of which, however, remained mysterious and worthy of investigation. Of empirical interest were the specific roles played by culture and the agency of individuals in reproducing or challenging these given structures of inequality. Qualitative studies used interviews and observations but paid little attention to validation procedures, analytic methods, or research design. Findings were interpreted in light of neo-Marxist and feminist theories of society, usually in order to show the complex ways that the culture and the agency of subordinate groups maintain their subordinate position in a society structured by class, gender, and racial inequalities.

These early ethnographies functioned as exemplars for qualitative educational researchers who were already convinced of the existence of basic social inequalities. Because nothing much was said or written about methodology, a loosely defined community of educational researchers formed, sharing only a very basic and vaguely explicated view of society (that it is structured by unequal relations between classes, genders, and races) and a basic value orientation (that this state of affairs is undesirable). Research was conducted in order to raise critical consciousness of social inequalities. Research was simultaneously social critique.

The Initiating Template

I wrote above that early CCCS ethnographies, especially *Learning to Labour*, established a sort of template for critical qualitative studies. Other researchers used these early CCCS ethnographies as exemplars in constructing their own studies. Results were interpreted in a manner highly similar to that used by members of CCCS though usually with important innovations. An "initiating template" for critical qualitative research resulted; a roughly defined template that was formative for the community of researchers who eventually came to call themselves critical ethnographers. It is worth outlining core features of this template because it is still influential today and because it begs epistemological questions that my specific version of critical ethnographic methodology seeks to address.

I risk being misleading in my choice of the word "template" to describe the role played by CCCS ethnographies in the development of critical ethnography. By template I do not wish to suggest anything too fixed or rigid. Rather, this initiating template helped to generate a genre of research rather like the way in which a prototype functions to generate a category according to recent theories about the structure and nature of categories (Lakoff 1987). According to prototype category theory, a category is based on a prototypical member and other members of the category are included by virtue of their "family resemblance" to the prototype. Category boundaries are usually blurred, by consequence. If we consider the category of "houses," for example, we will probably find ourselves envisioning a house and in possession of a tacit assumption about the qualities all houses must share in order to be houses. Closer scrutiny of the category will pose problems: Is a hut a house? Is a cardboard structure under a bridge a house? We base the concept of house on our own particular image of a house prototype and use resemblance relations to try to determine whether or not other structures belong to this category. Most categories have blurred boundaries and depend upon resemblance relations to a prototype.

It is much the same with critical ethnographies except that instead of an image it is a template that serves as a prototype; a template prescribing the rough form and tone of a research report. The community of critical ethnographers follows no rigidly defined rules, rather, they take inspiration from earlier critical studies and their research reports bear some resemblance to the initiating template. Critical ethnography is a category of research with blurred boundaries that has been partially generated through the prototypical template of early CCCS work.

Four Components

The initiating, prototypical template for critical ethnography has at least four central components. First, the critical researcher investigates a small cultural community whose members usually belong to a subordinate social class, gender, or racial/ethnic group. Most critical ethnographers have chosen groups related to the education system in some way: school boys (Willis 1977), school girls (McRobbie 1978) and teacher education classes (Ginsburg 1988) are examples. The investigation is conducted qualitatively, emphasizing interviews, group discussions, and observations made from a participant-observer role.

Second, core themes from the culture of this community are reconstructed. The themes are articulated, "reconstructed," from the realm of tacit understandings shared by group members into explicit linguistic formulations. These themes are then related to identities routinely constructed by members. They are cultural themes through which group members construct and maintain social identities. School-resistant boys were found to have constructed a culture in which street knowledge is valued over book knowledge, aggressive forms of masculinity are striven for, sexist and racist attitudes are prominent (Willis 1977). School-resistant girls were found to emphasize appearance and sexuality, to value romance, and to look forward to an early marriage rather than to a successful educational career (McRobbie 1978).

Third, these core themes are then explained as the products of human agents who resist dominant cultural definitions and dominant social relations that place them in a subordinate category. Both the boys studied by Willis and the girls studied by McRobbie were of working-class origin. Within the value structure of their schools they had fewer opportunities than their middle-class peers for constructing positive identities. Lack of an emphasis in their homes on education, book knowledge, and educational degrees are part of the reason why their opportunities to succeed in school were restricted. Moreover, success in school might even have stimulated cultural sanctions in their neighbourhoods and friendship groups. Their response was to base their identities and sense of dignity on the values and cultural forms of a friendship group that openly scoffed at the values and assumptions taught by their teachers. Within their friendship groups were values and identity-repertoires that reversed, subverted, and in general rejected the values that teachers wished these students to embrace.

The cultural themes are argued to play an important role in routine modes of resistance to dominant cultural values and norms by supporting acts in opposition to them. Willis's "lads" disrupted classrooms and made fun of both teachers and serious students. The emphasis in this sort of analysis is on human agency and the need of all humans to have a dignified sense of self. Resistance identities and a resistant cultural milieu supportive of them are conceptualized as products of human agency.

In addition, these cultural themes are described as the product of actors who must employ a pre-existing cultural milieu in order to construct their own culture and social identities. This pre-existing milieu is usually also resistant in nature because it is organic to the social class, gender and race of the actors. But pre-existing culture may have features out of date with current living, work, and technological environments. McRobbie's schoolgirls tacitly embraced values appropriate for the traditional role of a working-class housewife during a time when family structures were changing. Willis's lads celebrated physical strength and hard, dirty, manual work during a time when new technologies were making work cleaner and less physically demanding.

Hence the reconstructed culture is explained both in terms of human responses to the school, work, and community environments within which the subordinate group must live, and in terms of cultural tradition and inertia. Culture is always created anew, primarily through the motivation to construct a valued social identity, but cultural production must make use of the cultural materials at hand and these cultural materials are not as quick to change as are work environments, technologies, and family structure. Newly created culture will introduce innovations in the surface forms of cultural traditions but underlying interpretative frameworks remain much the same.

Fourth, the role played by this reconstructed culture in social reproduction is examined. The themes of resistance reconstructed from the culture of the group under study turn out to support actions and attitudes that reproduce the subordinate social position of the group based on class, race, and gender. By developing identities and cultural forms that in many ways oppose the dominant social order, members of the group unwittingly reproduce their place within it. Willis's boys moved from school into working-class jobs when taking school seriously might have enabled some of them to move into middle-class or professional careers. McRobbie's girls married early, had children, and became housewives when taking school more seriously might have enabled some of them to become economically independent and career-oriented. There is, therefore, at least an implicit distinction made, within this initiating template for critical ethnography, between action orientations (the resistance culture produced by the subjects of one's study) and action consequences (the unintended result of social reproduction). The latter, action consequences, have a function to play within the larger social system. Analysis thus implicitly shifts between the hermeneutic reconstruction of cultural themes and a systems analysis of the function played by action consequences.

The functions of culture are often found to do more than just reproduce subordinate social positions. Within the classic template certain features of the reconstructed resistance culture actually function to make life easier within alienating working conditions, patriarchal social relations, and a white-dominated society. Young men already skilled in making the most of the way they are expected to work for teachers or bosses can better adapt to the boredom and meaninglessness of factory work. An early investment of one's identity into the hopes of romance and sexual attraction later on serve isolated housewives in their escapist fantasies (Radway 1991). Therefore, the active production of culture by resistant members of a subordinate population functions not only to reproduce social structure at the level of job choices and gender roles, it also socializes the members into skills and dispositions that serve the social system.

In summary, the initiating template for critical ethnography prescribes qualitative research methods but provides nothing distinctive with respect to them. Research design, validation procedures, and data analysis are not specified by the template. The template does emphasize a critical value orientation towards a society already deemed unequal. It emphasizes agency, culture, and the social system as objects of analysis but does not specify any social theory that could be used to distinguish among these three terms.

Expansions and Permutations

As the 1980s moved on a number of studies employed the template inaugurated by early CCCS ethnographies while often modifying and stretching it in various ways (Carspecken 1991; McLaren 1993; Weiler 1988; Wexler 1992). Richard Johnson's influential paper, "What is Cultural Studies Anyway?" (1983) also appeared during this decade, expanding the interests of CCCS to include critical content analyses of cultural commodities and providing a clearer social theoretical framework ("the circuit of cultural production") from which to produce research designs.

Johnson's work has encouraged studies of cultural commodities like films, music, books, television, and advertising. These sorts of studies usually call themselves "cultural studies" rather than "critical ethnographies," but they are clearly informed by the same orientation as that which informs critical ethnographies. Films, books, and other cultural commodities are reconstructed in much the same way as early critical ethnographers reconstructed the living cultures of small groups. Innovations have developed from the study of cultural commodities, however, through borrowings from literary criticism. All cultural commodities may be considered "texts" to be "read." New ethnographies of small groups have subsequently been able to employ some of the concepts used in literary criticism by treating a living culture as a type of "text" (Brown 1992). Many critical researchers have conducted both sorts of inquiry at different times. A couple of examples, from many possible, of this sort of critical research include bell hooks's *Outlaw Culture* (1994) and Steinberg and Kincheloe's edited volume *Kinderculture* (1997). Such research is clearly relevant to more direct forms of educational research since schools must increasingly compete with the mass media in socializing children and young adults.

The 1980s was also a decade in which postmodern thought made its way into educational research. Those who adopted it often attempted to conjoin it with critical ethnography. Deconstruction was a popular form of text analysis and it became employed in the analysis of living cultures during the late 1980s. Those influenced by postmodernism called their ethnographies of schools and youth cultures critical ethnographies but employed postmodern frameworks in their analysis and critique of cultural forms. Patti Lather's work is a prominent example of this (1990, 1991). Methods and modes of thinking employed by postmodern literary critics were found highly useful for revealing and deconstructing the root metaphors of school ideology, youth culture, and the mass media.

The 1980s was the same decade in which the phrase "critical ethnography" began to appear in various literature on educational theory and educational research (e.g. McLaren 1988). Coining the term "critical ethnography" attracted some educational anthropologists working within the tradition established by Paulo Freire (Freire 1995; Zou and Treuba 1998).

During the 1990s the initiating template has undergone even more permutations as researchers working in departments and traditions other than education (Denzin 1994) have become interested in critical ethnography. Certain comparative educators (Ginsberg 1988) and educational anthropologists (Zou 1998) have also begun to call their qualitative research critical. The basic initiating template has been expanded in some places (Carspecken 1991; McLaren 1993; Weiler 1988), challenged in others (Wexler 1992), supplemented with post-colonial theory (Gandhi 1998; Moore-Gilbert et al. 1998), and even conjoined with educational psychology and theories of human development (Korth 1998).

Thus, by the late 1990s interest in critical ethnography has grown markedly from its origin in early CCCS work on education and youth cultures. Researchers from many of the social sciences and influenced by diverse but convergent academic traditions are now calling themselves critical ethnographers. Yet the term "critical ethnography" refers to little more than a prototypical template specifying analytic results and the tone of a research report. The prototypical template, moreover, has undergone many expansions and permutations since its inception. Critical ethnographies that share the basic orientation differ markedly in terms of how they conceptualize inquiry. From a methodological perspective, there is to date no such thing as "critical ethnography."

A CRITICAL ETHNOGRAPHIC METHODOLOGY

There are several good reasons for constructing a methodological theory suited to critical ethnography. Early critical ethnographies were conducted before postmodern ideas became popular among certain critical theorists, feminists, and those who identify their work as cultural studies. Neo-Marxist frameworks were used to interpret observational and interview data and, since neo-Marxist frameworks have a realist ontology, very basic and traditional notions of validity could inform these studies. *Learning to Labour* and other early ethnographic studies have been rightly criticized as producing generalized conclusions that go further than the data warrant. But no one, to my knowledge, has questioned the validity of the cultural reconstructions presented in these studies, nor the validity of the very idea of comparing these cultural reconstructions with an a priori theory of society as a whole.

As the 1980s progressed, moreover, postmodern ideas started to influence the way that critical ethnographers conceptualized validity itself (Lather 1986, 1990, 1991). A parallel movement occurred within non-critical qualitative traditions when the genre of constructivist methodology formed (Lincoln and Guba 1985; Guba 1990a; Lincoln 1990). Those who were influenced by either constructivism or postmodernism began to argue that all research is always only an interpretation strongly coloured by the value orientation and the social position of the researcher. Multiple incommensurable interpretations were thought always to be possible and "multiple realities" were said to exist. The distinction between reality and knowledge of reality was deemed an illusory one. This relativist view of social inquiry is still influential in many circles at the time of writing.

The idea that all knowledge is simply an interpretation constructed according to the interests of one group or another has been useful to certain critical projects. If some of the dominant views held within society are found to be oppressive to certain groups (e.g. deep-seated and subtle gender and racial stereotypes), then the argument that these are merely one interpretation rather than the way things really are has critical bite. If some research findings have negative implications for women or minorities, then the argument that all research findings are simply biased interpretations will be found appealing. Women, minorities, and members of the lower economic classes can be argued to have their own equally valid views of things, but without many opportunities to formulate these views or have them heard by others.

Relativism of this sort, however, does not long serve critical purposes. The original project of critical qualitative research was based on the belief that a real society exists and is exploitative. The interpretations that one can reconstruct of this same real society from the culture of a subordinate group were argued to distort reality so that members of the group were not fully conscious of their own oppression. A realist ontology is central to this project and, therefore, a non-relativist epistemology is required. For this project to have any potency an argument must be made that critical ethnographies illuminate conditions and processes that really occur, as described and analyzed by the critical ethnographer. An epistemology is required to make this argument.

Thus one reason for constructing a methodological theory for critical ethnography is to counter the relativism inherent in the over-use of postmodern and constructivist theory. There are other reasons as well. A tight methodological theory will provide more rigor to critical ethnographies, improving their quality, and will accordingly win a broader audience for positive appraisals of critical ethnographic work. Many quantitative researchers in education and the other social sciences are highly sceptical of any sort of qualitative study. Because quantitative research generally pays close attention to validation procedures, the frequent absence of such explicit attention in published qualitative studies fails to convince more mainstream researchers.

A third reason for constructing a critical methodological theory is that critical theory provides a sound framework for constructing an epistemology appropriate for all endeavors to understand social life; including quantitative endeavors. "Critical epistemology," as I have chosen to call it (Carspecken 1996), escapes philosophical problems encountered by naïve realism, positivism, and post-positivism. At the same time it avoids a relativistic framework. A genuine critical epistemology should strive for the status of being epistemology proper.

I will outline basic epistemological principles distinctive to critical ethnography as I conceive it in the next section. In subsequent sections I will briefly summarize analytic procedures characteristic of critical ethnography.

Epistemological and Analytic Principles

Critical ethnographies are mainly defined through the value orientation of those who conduct and publish them, but the prototypical template that initiated critical ethnography is nevertheless suggestive for basic epistemological principles. As we have seen, this template suggests a distinction between cultural reconstruction and systems analysis. It also places a great deal of emphasis on human agency as mediated by culture and on the social identity as a motivating force for the production of cultural forms. The initiating template is also inescapably realist because critical ethnographies usually aim to critique "real" social structures and usually distinguish between reality and human knowledge of reality. In terms of educational research, critical ethnographies basically attempt to describe what really takes place in schools and universities, to describe the cultures that one can really find within these sites, to consider the location of schools and universities within a larger social system or set of social systems, and to examine the function played by action consequences for maintaining social systems and/or for supporting a direction of largely unplanned system change.

Validity

Traditional methodologies for the social sciences (Gall et al. 1996) conceive of validity primarily in terms of objective validity claims. Great care is taken to produce valid "measurement" procedures and instruments. Non-objective items of study, such as attitudes and beliefs, are usually operationalized into objective forms. The "internal validity" of operational definitions, however, is usually determined through methods that involve consensus formation among members of an "expert panel" or a sample of individuals from the target population. The structures of consensus formation and their relationship to the concept of validity are not themselves carefully examined.

I have used the consensus theory of truth developed by Jurgen Habermas (1987) to specify the concept of validity used in this critical methodology. I have not done so because I think there is a specific concept of validity appropriate for critical ethnographers that differs from other concepts of validity appropriate for other types of research. Rather, Habermas's critical theory presents a compelling theory of validity applicable to all social inquiry, one that escapes problems encountered by positivism, post-positivism, and relativism (Bernstein 1976, 1983).

Habermas's theory of validity links the concept to the pragmatics of human communication. All meaningful acts implicate validity claims that must be at least tacitly understood if the meaning of the act is to be understood. The validity claims from meaningful acts fall into a number of categories, three of which are most fundamental: objective validity claims, subjective validity claims, and normative-evaluative validity claims.

Put as briefly as possible, objective validity claims are claims about a shared world to which there is multiple access. Usually, access to this world is through the senses. Objective claims are claims about what objects and events exist and take place in the world. Objective claims include the specification of relationships between different objective entities; cause-effect relationships and relationships of correlation are examples. When an ethnographer writes: "The teacher began her science lesson at 12:45," an objective claim has been made. When any educational researcher writes: "Standardized test scores are negatively correlated with student-teacher ratio," then another sort of objective claim has been made.

Subjective validity claims are claims about states within a world to which there is only privileged access. Emotions, other sorts of feelings, and intentions are examples. When an ethnographer writes: "Most students in Ms. Nelson's mathematics class appear to adore her," then a subjective claim is made. One understands, from this assertion, that actions of the students themselves claim states of adoration. Only the students themselves know whether they adore Ms. Nelson or not and only these students know, additionally, whether they pretend to adore her when they really have other feelings. The ethnographer writes the assertion with the emphasis on *appearing* to adore in order to take into account the extra uncertainty that accompanies subjective validity claims. But the inference the ethnographer has made from appearances to subjective states has conformed to the logic of the subjective validity claim. "Appearing to adore" is not at bottom an objective validity claim because an inference to a possible subjective state closed off to the researcher's direct access must be made.

Normative-evaluative validity claims are claims about a shared but non-objective world of norms and values. Included in such worlds are beliefs in what is right, wrong, good, bad, and proper. Norms and values are placed into the same category by myself because the logic that argumentation over norms takes is nearly identical to the logic that argumentation over values takes (Carspecken 1996). While norms emphasize what is right, wrong, and proper the ultimate justification of a norm usually resides in some concept of what is good. Values directly concern what is good. Norms are sort of "applied values" that have won the consensus of a group.

When an ethnographer writes: "All the Asian-American families studied placed a high value on academic success and considered academic failure something shameful for the whole family," then normative-evaluative claims have been *reconstructed*. Usually, most normative-evaluative claims presented in an ethnography will be reconstructions of those typical to a cultural group, rather than those the ethnographer herself holds to. In critical ethnographies, however, it is common for an entire state of affairs to be judged as oppressive. In this case we have a normative-evaluative claim made by the researcher rather than a reconstructed claim. Carefully constructed critical ethnographies will be able to make such judgements according to a standard internal to the culture studied such that the researcher's judgement is in line with actual or implicit judgements made by those studied. A rather complicated theory of cultural power is necessary to understand this internal standard; one that I will not detail here (Carspecken 1996).

On one level, the theory of meaning-constitutive validity claims immediately suggests various methods for qualitative data interpretation. If one is studying a classroom by observing it and one hears a child say: "It's my turn to talk!" in a loud voice indicating a feeling of anger or irritation, then a number of validity claims must be understood for the meaning of the statement to be understood. The relevant validity claims are internal to the meaning of the act. The objective claims in this case would probably include: "So-and-so has already talked for a while." The subjective claims would include: "I am feeling frustrated!" And the normative-evaluative claims would include: "It is rude to talk too long," "People should not talk when it is not their turn to talk," "People should not make it necessary for others to have to declare their right to talk, people should rather stop and wait for the next person's turn when their own talking time is over."

Thus validity claims are part of what one studies in qualitative research. The people studied make their own objective, subjective, and normative-evaluative claims every time they act meaningfully. A culture will be partially characterized by thematic validity claims that members routinely employ when they construct their social routines and take part in routine social interactions. Turn-taking is a prominent norm in some cultures but not in others. The expectation that people will strongly assert their rights rather than wait for others to honor them is a norm in some cultures.

A classroom will always have a hidden curriculum that can be partially described by its thematic validity claims. Textbooks, educational computer software, and other cultural products all carry both tacit and explicit validity claims that will either be learned and accepted or negotiated or rejected by students. Both lived cultures and cultural commodities are infused with many recurring validity claims about what is good, bad, right, wrong, and proper. Both are infused with beliefs about what objects and events exist in a world of shared access and what relationships exist between such objective entities. Everything said refers to the intentions and feelings of the actor as well as objective and normative-evaluative validity claims.

That is one level upon which Habermas's theory of validity may be applied in a critical ethnography. Validity claims are part of what one studies. The three main categories of claim are also important on the epistemological level. The concept of validity as it applies to research methods, research design, and inference procedures must be derived from the origins of validity in the pragmatics of communication if Habermas's critical theory has any merit.

On the epistemological level, Habermas's three categories of validity claim are each necessarily addressed in data interpretation and research reports. When researchers report that the students they observed were routinely bored, or stimulated, or hurt, or frustrated in the classroom, then they are making subjective validity claims. When researchers provide verbatim reports about what a teacher, student, or administrator said and when they report what such people did they are making objective validity claims.

Researchers also seek to reconstruct the norms and values typically upheld in a classroom or school. In this case they are making claims that objectify, through hermeneutic-reconstructive procedures, the lived norms and values of others. Finally, researchers sometimes explicitly judge the school or classroom they study as successful or unsuccessful, liberating or oppressing. Even studies that attempt to adopt a strictly descriptive and neutral tone usually carry tacit evaluations of what was studied as desirable or undesirable, good or bad, right or wrong. In these cases the researcher is making her own normative-evaluative claims. It is best, of course, to make such judgements explicitly and to support them through the use of the internal standard already alluded to. Doing so is a distinctive feature of critical ethnographies.

There are specific procedures for supporting each type of validity claim. These I have outlined elsewhere (Carspecken 1996). The attention given to each type of claim and the validation requirements specific to each is one distinctive feature of critical ethnography. Though each type of claim carries its own unique requirements for providing support, all three claims share one requirement that provides another distinctive characteristic for critical ethnography. This I will describe next.

All validity claims are ultimately supported to the extent that they can win the consent of a universal audience. Habermas's theory of validity is a version of pragmatism. Consent must be given freely, without any coercion or non-rational influence (such as deference to status). Though it is always impossible to present one's validity claims to a universal human audience whose members experience no differences in power or status, this principle serves as a basis that directs one's efforts to support findings and interpretations. The people studied can often be given an opportunity to consider one's findings and conclusions and to present their own perspective. Power relations between the researcher and the researched are to be equalized as much as is practically possible in a critical ethnography.

The consensus theory of truth fundamental to Habermasian critical theory is also what provides the standard by which to spot the workings of cultural power and by which to judge a social situation as oppressive or not. If the routine roles and social identities constructed by members of a cultural group fail to win their consensus when their audience-horizon is expanded, then cultural power is at play and the conditions within which this group lives may be judged oppressive. This is a complex idea and as it could itself easily occupy a chapter-length discussion, I will say no more about it here (see Carspecken 1996, 1999).

Data Analysis

Critical ethnographies may use many of the analytic methods long employed by qualitative researchers. But the theory of communicative action, when supplemented in various ways (Carspecken 1996, 1999) provides a sort of "bottom line" conceptual framework for meaning reconstruction. This analytic bottom line distinguishes critical ethnography from other forms of qualitative research.

A meaningful act is partially constituted by validity claims falling into the three categories mentioned above. Such validity claims can be reconstructed into an array that locates specific claims within the appropriate category and that specifies the degree to which each specific claim is foregrounded or backgrounded by the meaningful act. Yet another dimension of analysis concerns the degree to which the actor is aware of each validity claim constitutive of her meaningful act (Carspecken 1991, 1992). Usually, interviews and extensive observations are required to analyze along this last dimension.

I have introduced the concept of "pragmatic horizon" to help with the reconstruction of meaningful acts (Carspecken 1996, 1999). The actual number of validity claims carried by any particular meaningful act is indefinite. Moreover, there is never a precise way in which to articulate tacit validity claims. Many articulations are always possible, each having slightly different nuances. The meaning delivered by an act, however, is bounded such that actors can spot clearly incorrect articulations of the validity claims. The metaphor of the horizon, long used in phenomenology to describe perceptual experiences, works well to represent the complex and indefinite nexus of claims and assumptions unified in every meaningful act. Speech act horizons are not perceptual in nature, they rather refer to the meaning that a complex social act embodies when everything about the act is taken into account: the words spoken, the gestures made, the tone of voice employed, the facial expression accompanying the act and so on. Thus I have named this the *pragmatic* horizon. It is not constitutive of a perception and it goes well beyond semantics alone. It is constituted by the full pragmatics of the speech act.

The most fundamental structure in a pragmatic horizon is the validity horizon. The basic idea of a validity horizon can be delivered with an example. One of my students, a high school English teacher named Lawrence Kohn, recently had an interesting experience. He went into a restaurant to order a cup of coffee and noticed a lot of young men sitting at various tables who had tattoos, leather jackets, earrings, and other apparel of the sort that gang members often wear. He felt uneasy and noticed that the only seat available was at a service counter next to a seat occupied by one of these young men. He sat next to the man and ordered a cup of coffee. The young man turned to him and said in a gruff voice, "I don't know what's hotter in here, the coffee or the women." My student felt intimidated and ignored the remark. To his relief no further interactions occurred between him and the young man sitting beside him. I will use this incident to illustrate the validity horizon.

To reconstruct the pragmatic horizon of a meaningful act we begin with the reconstruction of a *meaning field*: a bounded range of possible meanings that the act conveys. All meaningful acts will usually have several possible meanings. Both actor and the audience are aware of at least some of these possible meanings and are aware, to varying degrees, of the fact that the act has an uncertain meaning because of its field nature. I ask my ethnography students to practice articulating meaning fields until they can automatically do so mentally. Here is a meaning field for the above act:

> I'm a tough macho male.
> AND
> I'm testing you, are you a "real man"?
> OR
> I'm taunting you, I don't think you are a "real man."
> OR
> I'm funny and I want to make friendly conversation with you.

To reconstruct a validity horizon specifically, just one of the above possible meanings must be chosen. All of the above possibilities, however, share certain elements within their pragmatic horizons. An ethnographer will usually wish to reconstruct terms *typical* to pragmatic horizons routinely exhibited by members of a cultural group or by a key person in one's site of study such as a teacher in her classroom. Thus an ethnographer must be aware of the field nature of meaning but need not be too troubled by it. Often most possible meanings in a field will share precisely those features of routinely constructed pragmatic horizons that qualitative researchers call "cultural themes." All the above meanings would have an *identity claim* that we can articulate as "macho male" in their horizons, plus a related value for a sexual and almost predatory orientation towards women.

Let me take just one of the above meanings, however, and reconstruct its validity horizon specifically so that I might illustrate what a validity horizon is. Remember that a validity horizon is one portion of a full pragmatic horizon. I will take the friendliest one, the interpretation of the act as a joke and as a bid for some friendly chit-chat.

I don't know what's hotter in here, the coffee or the women.

Portion of meaning field to reconstruct: *I'm funny and I want to make friendly conversation with you.*

    Possible Objective Claims
        Highly foregrounded
            There are women in this restaurant at this time.
        More background
            I have frequent sexual experiences with women.
    Possible Subjective Claims
        Foregrounded
            I feel like talking to you.
            I feel friendly toward you. I have benign intentions.
        Less Foregrounded
            I expect you to laugh or chuckle.
        Backgrounded
            (less certain) I am feeling sexually frustrated right now.
    Possible Normative-Evaluative Claims
        Foregrounded
            It is good, manly, to talk about sexual desires for women.
            It is funny to talk about sexy women.
        More Backgrounded
            There are two main types of men: macho (desirable) and not macho (undesirable).
            Women should be thought of as sexual objects.

It would be possible to think of other possible validity claims implied by this speech act as well. So it goes with all validity horizons. They have an indefinite number of components.

Many things other than validity claims can be reconstructed from pragmatic horizons. All meaningful acts carry an *identity claim* that can be reconstructed. The man in the restaurant made an identity claim that could be reconstructed as: "I am a tough, macho male who is sexually potent." Notice that identity claims can be analyzed in terms of validity claims. The above identity claim suggests certain activities regularly conducted by this man (objective claims), certain subjective states commonly experienced by this man (subjective claims such as fearlessness), and certain values (sexual prowess is good). Since identity claims usually reflect important features of culture they are particularly important to reconstruct in ethnographic analysis.

Semantic categories and their relationship to each other are often worth reconstructing from pragmatic horizons. Although the man in the restaurant did not use the term "macho male" an interview with him might have elicited this or some similar term. A cultural category like "macho male" will depend on a contrast set of other categories for its meaning to members of the cultural group. Perhaps this group distinguishes between macho men and "sissies" in certain contexts within which meaningful acts are made. In other contexts the contrast set might be more complex for these same young men: macho men, sissies, nerds, old dudes, and so on. Such semantic categories can be arrayed in complex relationships to each other. In this hypothetical culture, it might be the case that nerds may or may not be sissies but are never macho men. Semantic categories are meaningful only structurally; that is, they take their meaning only through relations of similarity, contrast, binary opposition, hierarchical subordination, and so forth, with other categories. To understand one category one must understand the entire structure of categories within which it has a place.

The culture of a group will be partially distinctive via the specific semantic categories it makes available to its members. Some of these categories will have culturally specific names (e.g. "nerds") and some will not but will be implicated within the semantic structures employed by group members. In my study of Croxteth, Liverpool, for example, I found that local residents called themselves "ordinary" very frequently to distinguish themselves from middle and upper class people (Carspecken 1991). "Ordinary" was a semantic category named by those who used it. The full sense of "ordinary," however, depended on its contrast to an unnamed category that I had to call "non-ordinary" for analytic purposes. "Non-ordinary" was a semantic category organic to Croxteth culture that did not have a name.

Cultures are also distinguished via the type of structural relations that exist between their semantic categories. Relations that depend on analogy, homology, and binary opposition are less rationalized than relations that depend on hierarchical subordination and intersection. It is easier to reflect upon categories that are linked to other categories through hierarchy and intersection (much in the manner of set theory) than it is to reflect upon categories embedded within relationships of analogy (Carspecken 1992).

The reconstruction of semantic categories typical of a cultural group and the complex relationships between categories (relations of binary opposition, hierarchical subordination, horizontal intersection, contrast set, and so on) is a common method of ethnographic analysis (Spradley 1979, 1980). One cannot fully understand what a category means to members of a culture unless one understands the set of categories it implicates and the relationships between categories.

In this critical ethnographic methodology, however, this same practice of identifying culturally specific semantic categories and the relationships between them is related to the concept of a pragmatic horizon. The structures existing between semantic categories, as well as the categories themselves, can always be analyzed in terms of validity claims because the meaning of each category will depend on a simultaneous grasp of specific validity claims. "Macho man" as used by members of this gang culture we are imagining carries objective claims (what such men do and don't do), subjective claims (the typical intentions of macho men, the common state of feeling bold) and normative-evaluative claims (the judgement that it is good to be macho, bad to be a sissy). The various claims constitutive of semantic categories display the same sort of array determined by back-ground-to-foreground relations as do validity horizons proper (Carspecken and Cordeiro 1995).

Qualitative research generally employs many other concepts in its analysis of data. Examples include roles, role sets, interactive power claims and power relationships, settings, setting bids and setting negotiations. All such things can be employed usefully within a critical ethnography and related to the concept of pragmatic horizon. Interactive sequences and rhythms are also analyzed in critical ethnographic studies and grounded in the concept of the pragmatic horizon.

Clearly, no ethnographer would ever be able, much less want, to reconstruct pragmatic horizons of all recorded meaningful acts. The idea is to understand the concept and use it as a ground or baseline from which typical patterns and cultural themes may be articulated. Cultural themes are often best articulated as validity claims that show up in the backgrounds of many pragmatic horizons for a particular group of people. Cultures also carry "implicit theories" that can be reconstructed and examined for each type of validity claim they carry. Parents who believe that one of the purposes of schools should be that of strictly disciplining children, for example, will generally hold to some sort of implicit, unarticulated, theory about human nature and the maturation process (see Carspecken 1991, 1992, for field-based examples of this). Children who are not strictly disciplined are believed to be at risk of turning out "bad." An assumption is held that aggressive and other sorts of destructive drives are core features of human nature that can only be mastered through strict discipline during the formative years.

When cultural themes and implicit cultural theories or assumptions are included in a research report these can always be defended by going back to the field notes and interviews and showing where these themes and assumptions routinely appear within the pragmatic horizons of recorded meaningful acts. Such themes and assumptions can also be broken down by the critical ethnographer into specific validity claims about the objective, normative, and subjective worlds so that the cultural views under study may be considered very precisely. The researcher might find that an implicit theory held by a community of parents about the purposes of education is based on objective facts with which many other communities would concur but interprets these facts alongside very unique values and concepts of what is "right." The opposite sort of thing is also easy to imagine.

Systems Analysis

This version of critical ethnography is additionally distinguished from other forms of qualitative research through its distinction between reconstructive-hermeneutic analysis and systems analysis. Five stages of conducting a critical ethnography are recommended and each stage has its own set of validation procedures (Carspecken 1996; Carspecken and Apple 1992). The first stage is the compilation of a primary record; a set of thick field notes on observed interactions and a set of journalistic notes that do not seek verbatim act-by-act descriptions but rather summarize and gloss what one sees and hears on the field site.

The next two stages prioritize hermeneutic-reconstructive analysis. Using the pragmatic horizon as the analytic ground, many modes of meaning and cultural reconstruction can be conducted. All reconstructions should be traceable back to specific meaningful acts and located within a horizon articulated from them. Observation and interview schedules followed in stage one must have been constructed so that each reconstruction can be determined to be typical or atypical of the cultural group. A coding scheme based on the pragmatic horizon concept is recommended.

Stage two involves preliminary reconstructive analysis of recorded data. Stage three adds interviewing, group discussions, and Interpersonal Process Recall (known as IPR: Carspecken 1996; Kagan 1980, 1984; Kagan and Kagan 1991) to the data collection procedures.

Stages four and five, however, shift from reconstructive-hermeneutic to systems analysis. The above sections have already argued that the prototypical template that helped to initiate critical ethnography contains at least an implicit distinction between hermeneutic-reconstructive and systems analysis. Critical ethnographies generally seek to reconstruct a culture and then explain the functions this culture has in relation to larger social systems. Does the hidden curriculum of a given classroom (a form of culture) socialize students so that they move into jobs as required by the job market (a feature of a system)? Does the lifestyle of a particular working-class youth group (a form of culture) orient its members so as to discourage educational achievements and encourage movement into lower class or underclass positions when they become adults (a feature of a system)? Do popular films watched by young children fill them with gender and racial stereotypes (a form of culture) so that they grow up to act out gender-differentiated roles related to the division of labor (a feature of a system)?

However, early critical ethnography did not articulate a clear theoretical distinction between culture and system even while using such a distinction in the interpretation of data. Are there different ways to study culture and system? Are different validation procedures required in each case? Without a clear distinction between culture and system it is really impossible to say.

I have used Habermas's distinction between lifeworld and system to address this problem. The concept of "lifeworld" is much the same as the concept of a "lived culture." Habermas deduces the concept of lifeworld from his theory of the meaningful act. A lifeworld is a horizon of indefinitely receding cultural milieux upon which agents draw when acting meaningfully. It is from a lifeworld that actors fashion the cluster of validity claims that constitute their meaningful acts. It is from a lifeworld that actors draw semantic categories and roles and construct typical interactive sequences and rhythms with others. Themes, patterns, and implicit theories characterizing a particular group come from a shared lifeworld.

A lifeworld, in other words, is a lived culture. Actors draw upon cultural milieux when they act, often constructing slightly new forms of culture by acting creatively with existing material. Cultural milieu is never exactly reproduced when humans act, it is rather iterated to form permutations and cultural drifts as time moves along. One feature of culture is that it has many diverse structures such as the various relations that can be found to constitute semantic categories. Every meaningful act is partially constituted by a number of diverse structures and every meaningful act reproduces or modifies a number of diverse structures as part of its outcome.

Habermas describes the lifeworld, which I will from here on call "culture," as that which supplies action orientations. Cultural milieu orients actors without determining exactly how they will act, and each act has the potential of creatively changing or adding to the cultural milieu. Stages one to three of this critical methodology are designed to produce reconstructions of action orientations.

The system is distinguished from culture through its dependence on action consequences rather than action orientations. Aggregate action consequences functionally interconnect to produce a system with self-maintaining tendencies. The capitalist economic system, for example, has a self-maintaining logic of its own. Action orientations that support consumerist notions of happiness, that distinguish between work and leisure, and that encourage the belief that schooling should mainly be about job preparation, will result in action consequences supportive of the system. Such action orientations will be reinforced in a variety of ways and through a variety of complex processes. By contrast, action orientations that counter system tendencies will fail to attract resources and encounter various problems traceable to the self-maintaining tendency of the economic system.

If one wishes to ask why a certain social group has its particular culture one must look in two major directions to find answers. In one direction lie cultural traditions which possess some inertia. Certain cultural themes might best be explained simply in terms of their history. They were themes common within the parent's generation and perhaps the grandparent's generation. They were learned in childhood and they are exemplified in routine acts of the community.

The other direction one must look is toward the social group's position within social systems. What action consequences are generated by these cultural themes and what function do these consequences serve for self-maintaining systems?

Culture is accessible to a researcher only through taking an insider's position and reconstructing central themes. This requires meaning-reconstruction, or hermeneutic analysis.

The system, on the other hand, is accessible only by taking a third-person perspective on observed human action in order to examine the functional interconnection of aggregate action consequences. The social system requires culture so that actors will be oriented to act. In other words, without culture there could be no system. But actors are not aware of the function many of their action consequences play in maintaining a social system. To conduct systems analysis the researcher must acquire a view of her findings that is not organic to the culture she is studying. There are specific procedures to be followed to ensure that systems analysis does not simply become the imposition of a priori beliefs held by the researcher (Carspecken 1996).

Social systems are little understood, at this time, in their entirety. The initiating template for critical ethnography emphasized a certain type of system relationship: social reproduction and the role played by schools and friendship groups in bringing it about. The capitalist social system requires a division of labor roughly captured in the formula: working class, middle class, and owners of capital. The system requires a selection process such that some children will move into adulthood by assuming working-class jobs, others by assuming middle-class and professional work. This selection process cannot be too explicitly reproductive without putting the system at risk by social discontent. The selection processes operating to produce the movement from school to work have not been too obviously reproductive in modern western societies; they have been legitimated in terms of individual abilities and preferences. Action orientations that help maintain social reproduction (selection of young people for future adult occupations and the legitimization of this selection) receive subtle forms of functionally generated support. Any action orientations that challenge system maintenance and reproduction will receive subtle forms of functionally generated "discouragement." Generally, there will be difficulties in maintaining and distributing cultural forms that challenge system reproduction.

Hence many critical ethnographies have examined such things as resistant youth cultures, gender cultures, and hidden curricula in order to investigate social and cultural reproduction. Critical research has also examined the economics of textbook production and its relationship to textbook contents which, of course, influence action orientations (Apple 1986). Social policy has also been researched critically. Standardized examinations constrain both curriculum and pedagogy and tend to select those forms generative of the most reproductive types of socialization. Comprehensive schools, an explicit effort to equalize schooling and push job selection more towards ability and preferences than towards favouring those of higher class birth, have been studied to reveal new forms of old class reproduction. De facto segregation of comprehensive schools and the use of ability grouping often work against the rationale of comprehensive schools. Mass media products produced for children are also studied in terms of their cultural content (gender roles, consumerist values, and so forth) to determine how action orientations might be influenced by what is at bottom an economic, system, imperative (Steinberg and Kincheloe 1997).

Systems analysis must avoid the argument that functions determine other sorts of social phenomena. System "imperatives" do not determine what teachers teach, nor how they teach, nor what youth cultures consist of, nor how people read cultural commodities. Rather, system processes work blindly and in a manner analogous to ecological/evolutionary systems in nature. In a sense, action orientations produced and reproduced by actors within their cultural milieu serve as the genetic-generative principle in social systems. Beliefs, values, identities, moral systems, and norms are continuously drawn upon, reproduced and recreated. They are also material from which innovations may be produced and in modern western societies the rate of innovation is high.

The existing social system, however, is the selection mechanism analogous to the environment and pre-existing ecological systems in nature. Some innovations are selected for, and some are selected against. Those that supply a function for the existing system, or for a trend in system change, will often attract resources and gain distribution. Those innovations that threaten either existing system relations or a continuing trend in system change will encounter discouragements. People who invest themselves in cultural innovations that threaten the system will often find themselves marginalized and/or criticized. If they wish to popularize their innovations they will have to overcome many barriers, but the eventual success of structural innovations is not foreclosed by the system, only discouraged.

In educational studies systems analysis will usually focus on the position of schools within the economy and the position of schools within large organizations such as local government and school districts. Both money flows and bureaucratic organizations generate self-maintaining processes and both types of processes affect schools. Critical ethnographers can spot these system processes and determine what sorts of "anchors" they have within specific cultures. The tendency to de-skill teachers and make their work more like that of technicians is one such process. Teachers' work, originally a highly communicative and self-directed sort of work, has become more like wage labor employed within a system of objectives beyond teachers' control. The constraints of standardized examinations, curriculum packages, state inspection of schools have all pushed teachers' work in this direction. Tendencies to blame teachers and educational philosophies for social ills generated by the economy is another system process. Pedagogies that replace normative forms of authority with contractual forms have a function in socializing students for our "contract society." Many educational phenomena have functional significance in the social system as a whole.

Methodologically, systems analysis should be conducted through two recommended stages towards the end of one's ethnography. These stages begin after one has compiled a primary record, held interviews and group discussions, and conducted hermeneutic-reconstructive analysis on one's data.

In stage four the culture of interest is compared to other cultures in some sort of relationship with the focal culture. The culture of a friendship group at school can be compared to the culture of the homes and neighborhoods from which the children come and these cultures can in turn be compared to the cultures of the sites within which the parents work. Since these three basic sites—home, school, and workplace—are connected by the actual movement of people between them, a small system may be discovered. If many similar systems seem to exist throughout a society, then a general system process of macro-level consequence has been found.

Stage four also includes efforts to identify cultural commodities influencing the focal culture. A friendship group may have modes of humor, attitudes, and typical identities strongly influenced by films, videos, video games, and popular music. The relationship between the sites on which these cultural commodities are produced and the focal culture is another kind of system relationship.

In stage four one may look for the influence of educational reports, tax laws, educational law, publications of the religious right, and so on, on educators and their pedagogy. Stage four is an empirical stage of systems analysis.

In stage five one takes one's findings from all previous stages and tries to interpret them in light of an existing, well supported, social theory. Traditionally, critical ethnographies have well exemplified stage five forms of analysis by using neo-Marxist, feminist, and post-colonial theories to explore the ramifications of their findings. In dialectical fashion, critical ethnographies have also offered new concepts and models to these very theories.

The validation procedures used for stages four and five are described in my book on critical ethnography (1996). They are based on Habermasian critical theory as are the validation procedures to be employed in stages one through three.

CONCLUSIONS

In terms of methodology there is currently no broad consensus on what critical ethnography is. Critical ethnography has been a value orientation conjoined to a barely explicated view of modern society. This chapter has suggested reasons for this state of affairs. It has also presented arguments in favor of the development of a critical methodology. The final sections of this chapter have outlined a version of critical ethnography based on methodological principles rather than value orientation. The distinctive features of my proposed critical methodology include use of Habermas's theory of validity in the epistemology, use of the concept of pragmatic horizons as an analytic ground for reconstructive analysis, and use of both hermeneutic-reconstructive analysis and systems analysis in coordination with each other to produce a full ethnography.

REFERENCES

Althusser, L. 1969. *For Marx*. London: Allen Lane.

Anderson, G. 1989. "Critical Ethnography in Education: Origins, Current Status, and New Directions." *Review of Educational Research* 59(3): 249-270.

Anyon, J. 1980. "Social Class and the Hidden Curriculum of Work." *Journal of Education* 162: 67-92.

Apple, M. 1986. *Teachers and Texts: A Political Economy of Class and Gender Relations in Education*. New York and London: Routledge.

Bernstein, R. 1976. *The Restructuring of Social and Political Theory.* Philadelphia: University of Pennsylvania Press.

_____. 1983. *Beyond Objectivism and Relativism: Science, Hermeneutics, and Praxis.* Philadelphia: University of Pennsylvania Press.

Brown, R.H. 1992. *Society as Text: Essays on Rhetoric, Reason, and Reality.* Chicago: University of Chicago Press.

Carspecken, P. 1991. *Community Schooling and the Nature of Power: The Battle for Croxteth Comprehensive.* London and New York: Routledge.

_____. 1992. "Pragmatic Binary Oppositions and Intersubjectivity in an Illegally Occupied School." *International Journal of Qualitative Research in Education* 5 (1) (January-March).

_____. 1996. *Critical Ethnography: A Theoretical and Practical Guide.* New York and London: Routledge.

_____. 1999. *Four Scenes for Posing the Question of Meaning, and Other Explorations in Critical Philosophy and Critical Methodology.* New York: Peter Lang Publishing Inc.

Carspecken, P., and M. Apple. 1992. "Critical Qualitative Research, Theory, Method, and Practice." In *Handbook of Qualitative Research in Education*, edited by M. LeCompte, W. Millroy, and J. Preissle. San Diego: Academic Press.

Carspecken, P., and P. Cordeiro. 1995. "Being, Doing, and Becoming: The Identities of High-Achieving, Secondary, Hispanic Students." *Qualitative Inquiry* 1 (1).

CCCS (Centre for Contemporary Cultural Studies). 1978. *Women Take Issue.* London: Hutchinson.

Denzin, N. 1992. *Symbolic Interactionism and Cultural Studies.* Cambridge: Basil Blackwell.

Denzin, N. 1994. "The Art and Politics of Interpretation." In *Handbook of Qualitative Research*, edited by N. Denzin and Y. Lincoln. Thousand Oaks, CA: Sage.

Denzin, N., and Y. Lincoln. 1994. *Handbook of Qualitative Research.* Thousand Oaks, CA: Sage.

Everhart, R. 1983. *Reading, Writing, and Resistance: Adolescence and Labor in a Junior High School.* London: Routledge and Kegan Paul.

Freire, P. 1995. *Pedagogy of the Oppressed.* Translated by M. Ramos. New York: Continuum Publication Group.

Gall, J., M. Gall, and W. Borg. 1999. *Applying Educational Research: A Practical Guide* (4th ed.). New York and London: Longman Inc.

Gall, M., W. Borg, and J. Gall. 1996. *Educational Research: An Introduction* (6th ed.). Reading, MA: Addison-Wesley Publication Co.

Gandhi, L. 1998. *Postcolonial Theory: A Critical Introduction.* New York: Columbia University Press.

Ginsburg, M. 1988. *Contradictions in Teacher Education and Society: A Critical Analysis.* London and New York: Falmer Press.

Guba, E. 1990a. "The Alternative Paradigm Dialog." In *The Paradigm Dialog*, edited by E. Guba. Newbury Park, CA: Sage.

Guba, E. 1990b. *The Paradigm Dialog.* Newbury Park, CA: Sage.

Habermas, J. 1981. *The Theory of Communicative Action, Volume I: Reason and the Rationalization of Society.* Boston: Beacon Press.

Guba, E., and Y. Lincoln. 1994. "Competing Paradigms in Qualitative Research." In *Handbook of Qualitative Research*, edited by N. Denzin and Y. Lincoln. Newbury Park, CA: Sage.

Habermas, J. 1987. *The Theory of Communicative Action, Volume II: Lifeworld and System, A Critique of Functionalist Reason.* Boston: Beacon Press.

Hebdidge, D. 1979. *Subculture: The Meaning of Style.* London and New York: Methuen.

Herzfeld, M. 1989. *Anthropology Through the Looking Glass: Critical Ethnography in the Margins of Europe.* Cambridge: Cambridge University Press.

hooks, bell. 1994. *Outlaw Culture: Resisting Representations.* New York: Routledge.

Hymes, D. 1996. *Ethnography, Linguistics, Narrative Inequality: Toward an Understanding of Voice.* London: Taylor and Francis.

Johnson, R. 1979. "Three Problematics: Elements of a Theory of Working Class Culture." In *Working Class Culture: Studies in History and Theory*, edited by J. Clarke, C. Critcher and R. Johnson. London: Hutchinson.

Johnson, R. 1983. "What Is Cultural Studies Anyway?" Occasional Paper SP No. 74. Centre for Contemporary Cultural Studies: University of Birmingham.

Kagan, N. 1980. *Interpersonal Process Recall: A Method of Influencing Human Interaction*. Houston: IPR Institute, University of Houston.

Kagan, N. 1984. "Interpersonal Process Recall: Basic Methods and Recent Research." In *Teaching Psychological Skills*, edited by D. Larsen. Monterey: Brooks Cole.

Kagan, N., and H. Kagan. 1991. "Interpersonal Process Recall." In *Practical Guide to Using Video in the Behavioral Sciences*, edited by P. Dowrick. New York: John Wiley and Sons.

Kincheloe, J., and P. McLaren. 1994. "Rethinking Critical Theory and Qualitative Research." In *Handbook of Qualitative Research,* edited by N. Denzin and Y. Lincoln. Newbury Park, CA: Sage.

Korth, B. 1998. "A Reformulation of Care as a Pragmatic Concept: A Qualitative Study of an Adult Friendship Group." Unpublished Doctoral Dissertation: University of Houston. Ann Arbor, MI: UMI Dissertation Services, Bell and Howell.

Lakoff, G. 1987. *Women, Fire, and Dangerous Things: What Categories Reveal about the Mind*. Chicago and London: University of Chicago Press.

Lather, P. 1986. "Research as Praxis." *Harvard Educational Review* 56 (3): 257-277.

_____. 1990. "Reinscribing Otherwise: The Play of Values in the Practices of the Human Sciences." In *The Paradigm Dialog*, edited by E. Guba. Newbury Park, CA: Sage.

_____. 1991. *Getting Smart: Feminist Research and Pedagogy With/in the Postmodern*. New York and London: Routledge.

Levinson, B., D. Foley, D. Holland and L. Weis. 1996. *The Cultural Production of the Educated Person: Critical Ethnographies of Schooling and Local Practice*. New York: SUNY Press.

Lincoln, E. 1990. "The Making of a Constructivist: A Remembrance of Transformations Past." In *The Paradigm Dialog*, edited by E. Guba. Newbury Park, CA: Sage.

Lincoln, E., and E. Guba. 1985. *Naturalistic Inquiry*. Beverly Hills, CA: Sage.

McLaren, P. 1989. *Life in Schools: An Introduction to Critical Pedagogy in the Foundations of Education*. New York and London: Longman.

_____. 1993. *Schooling as a Ritual Performance: Towards a Political Economy of Educational Symbols and Gestures* (2nd ed.). New York and London: Routledge.

McRobbie, A. 1978. "Working Class Girls and the Culture of Femininity." In *Women Take Issue*, edited by the Centre for Contemporary Cultural Studies. London: Hutchinson.

Moore-Gilbert, B., G. Stanton and W. Maley. 1998. *Postcolonial Criticism*. Reading, MA: Addison-Wesley Publication Co.

Quantz, R. 1992. "On Critical Ethnography (with Some Postmodern Considerations)." In *The Handbook of Qualitative Research in Education*, edited by M. Lecompte, W. Millroy and J. Preissle. San Diego: Academic Press.

Radway, J. 1991. *Reading the Romance: Women, Patriarchy, and Popular Literature*. University of North Carolina Press.

Sefa Dei, G.J., J. Mazzuca, E. McIssac, and J. Zine. 1997. *Reconstructing "Dropout": A Critical Ethnography of the Dynamics of Black Students' Disengagement from School*. Toronto: University of Toronto Press.

Spradley, J. 1979. *The Ethnographic Interview*. New York: Holt, Rinehart, and Winston.

_____. 1980. *Participant Observation*. New York: Holt, Rinehart, and Winston.

Steinberg, S., and J. Kincheloe. 1997. *Kinderculture: The Corporate Construction of Childhood*. Westview Press.

Street, A. F. 1992. *Inside Nursing: A Critical Ethnography of Clinical Nursing Practice*. New York: SUNY Press.

Street, B. 1995. *Social Literacies: Critical Approaches to Literacy Development, Ethnography, and Education.* Reading, MA: Addison-Wesley Publication Co.

Thomas, J. 1993. *Doing Critical Ethnography.* Thousand Oaks, CA: Sage.

Thompson, E. P. 1963. *The Making of the English Working Class.* London: Victor Gollancz.

_____. 1978. *The Poverty of Theory and Other Essays.* London: Merlin Press.

Treuba, H., L. Jacobs and E. Kirton. 1990. *Cultural Conflict and Adaptation: The Case of Hmong Children in American Society.* London: Falmer Press.

Treuba, H., C. Rodriguez, Y. Zou and J. Cintron. 1993. *Healing Multicultural America: Mexican Immigrants Rise to Power in Rural California.* London: Falmer Press.

Treuba, H., and Y. Zou. 1994. *Power in Education: The Case of Miao University Students and Its Significance for American Culture.* London: Falmer Press.

Weiler, K. 1988. *Women Teaching for Change: Gender, Class, and Power.* South Hadley, MA: Bergin & Garvey.

Wexler, P. 1992. *Becoming Somebody: Toward a Social Psychology of School.* London and Washington: Falmer Press.

Willis, P. 1977. *Learning to Labour: How Working Class Kids Get Working Class Jobs.* London: Gower.

Zou, Y. 1998. "Dilemmas Faced by Critical Ethnographers in China." In *Ethnic Identity and Power: Cultural Contexts of Political Action in School and Society,* edited by Y. Zou and E. Treuba. New York: SUNY Press.

Zou, Y., and E. Treuba. 1998. *Ethnic Identity and Power: Cultural Contexts of Political Action in School and Society.* New York: SUNY Press.

RESPONDING TO
TEXT CONSTRUCTION:
GOFFMAN'S REFLEXIVE
IMAGINATION

Sam Hillyard

> ...*The notion of reflexivity recognizes that texts do not simply and transparently report an independent reality. Rather, the texts themselves are implicated in the work of reality-construction. This principle applies not only to the spoken and written texts that are produced and interpreted by social actors, but to the texts of social analysts as well. From this point of view, therefore, there is no possibility of a neutral text. The text—the research paper or the monograph, say—is just as much an artefact of convention and contrivance as is any other cultural product (Atkinson 1990, p. 7).*

The above statement by Atkinson represents popular, contemporary (albeit contested) methodological thinking and marks an extension of the argument that, at every stage of the research process, the researcher is less involved in the explication of social reality (what is really "out there") and more in artful interpretation and construction (cf. Atkinson 1990; Coffey and Atkinson 1996; Delamont 1992; Hammersley and Atkinson 1995). Similar conclusions have been reached in post-

Studies in Educational Ethnography, Volume 2, pages 57-71.
Copyright © 1999 by JAI Press Inc.
All rights of reproduction in any form reserved.
ISBN: 0-7623-0563-0

modernist quarters (Scheurich 1997; Stronach and MacLure 1997). The implication is that all disciplines involved with making claims to authentic and authoritative writings on the social works, including anthropology, biography and history, become equally susceptible to such charges of text construction. These disciplines perhaps also offer suggestions on how to defend the value of the ethnographic monograph. The issue of how to respond is the focus of the following discussion. After initially offering a brief account of the reasoning behind Atkinson's (1990) statement and how other disciplines have also moved in similar directions, I want to move to concentrate on the sociology of Erving Goffman. Goffman is used as a case study for discussion, examining how he has constructed his own arguments, accounts and texts. Goffman's sociology, I suggest, imaginatively uses techniques which future ethnography may enjoy (and benefit from) using.

Historiography, the methodological wing of history, has engaged with questions on accuracy and authority in interpreting past social phenomena, reaching conclusions similar to Atkinson's (1990). For example, postmodernist historian Keith Jenkins critiques the Rankean notion of history's task "simply to show how it really was" as naively simplistic, on the grounds that such a traditional skill-based approach to history fetishes method with a naïve belief that "doing it properly" allows the "facts" to emerge.

Jenkins (1991) criticizes two assumptions with traditional skills-based history on grounds which are equally applicable to disciplines, like ethnography, involved with representing reality. First, he challenges the assumption that the "facts" speak for themselves. Jenkins (1991) argues that this implies that the researcher's role is neutral and objective, reducing him or her to a role of impassive translator. Second, that fact (or truth) is out there waiting to be accessed or "discovered," as Glaser and Strauss's (1967) notion of grounded theorizing suggests. Historians (indeed, researchers generally) are not neutral mediums through which the documents are given voice, an argument famously made in historiography by Carr (1987). Carr established that the historian is a product of his or her own time and therefore subject to the socio-economic, political and cultural influences of that period. Such influences, Carr argued, affect the way the historian will interpret sources.

So, by concluding that sources do not speak for themselves but involve interpretation by the historian and manipulation into intellectual arguments which draw on sources as "evidence" to substantiate their accounts, Carr (1987) returns us to concerns of textual construction. More than one reading of the social past or present becomes possible, as the researcher is involved in an act of interpretation and construction, rather than explication, of a given social phenomenon (Carr 1987; Jenkins 1991).

However, on the second point, (the realist assumption that the truth is out there) Jenkins (1991, 1995) moves to make a sustained critique of Carr's position. Jenkins's (1991) and Carr's (1987) rejection of conventional skills-based history lies with the distinction between history and history's object of enquiry (the past).

Jenkins argues that history is one in a series of discourses about the world, its distinctiveness derived from its subject matter, "the past." The key differentiation he makes is the separation of the two: history and the past. Jenkins (1991) argues history belongs in a different category to its subject matter and, therefore, history and the past are quite separate things. The key implication here is that history and the past are not inherently stitched together. Jenkins argues that Carr's position does not move beyond the acknowledgement that more than one historical reading of the past is possible and ask what makes historical readings different; in the case of ethnography we can take historical reading to mean the interpretation of a social situation or phenomenon. Jenkins adds personally:

> All history is theoretical and all theories are positioned and positioning.... You always select a version of the past.... Those who claim to know what history is for them (as for me)...have carried out an act of interpretation (Jenkins 1991, p. 70).

Interpretation becomes placed at the forefront, playing a part, for example, not just in analysis, but also in our perceptions of what constitutes valuable data in the first place; ethnographic research is a way of hearing, but also describes what counts as hearing. So Jenkins's move beyond the acknowledgement that ethnographers actively construct their texts returns us to the opening challenge of how to respond to textual construction. It is Jenkins's (1991) premise that our very definition or conception of a discipline (applicable equally to history and sociology) is vital to the activity that discipline entails, for it defines it. Our ontology ultimately defines the interpretations we offer as researchers. For example, the point over which Jenkins departs from Carr is their respective theoretical stances, namely their differing conceptions of the task of history. Jenkins is a self-admitted postmodernist, whereas Carr (to Jenkins) is an out-of-date, certaintist modernist. This is not to suggest that Jenkins consigns Carr's ideas to a historiographical scrap heap; rather, he argues that 30 years after "What Is History?" first appeared in 1961, thinking has changed.

So what is postmodernism for Jenkins and how does it reject modernism? Jenkins (1991) argues that Lyotard's notion of a loss of "center" is reflected in modern, pluralist society. For Jenkins, postmodernism holds that:

> there are not—and nor have there ever been—any "real" foundations of the kind alleged to underpin the experiment of the modern; that we now just have to understand that we live amidst social formations which have no legitimising ontological or epistemological or ethical grounds for our beliefs or actions beyond the status of an ultimately self-referencing (rhetorical) conversation (Jenkins 1995, p. 7).

Recognition of this when expressed at the level of theory (as opposed to the actualities of living in the postmodern condition—postmodernity) is postmodernism. Postmodernism's rejection of ontology and epistemology as grounds for legitimization is, to use Jenkins's term, "anti-epistemological." When translated to writing authoritative accounts, postmodernism holds that one account cannot automatically be privileged above another as categorical statemnts about social phenomena are not possible; that there is no absolute, objective truth that is out here and accessible. Recognition of this, Jenkins (1991, 1995) argues, renders "the old shibboleths of Carr and Elton" out of date (Jenkins 1995, p. 5).

To reach this conclusion—that not only is all historical work socially constructed but there is no absolute truth to aim towards (an argument easily transferred to ethnography)—on what basis can future historical work be defended if it cannot be realist? Jenkins did not see history as inevitably trapped in a relativistic conundrum, in which contemporary postmodern scholarly historical writing (because it rejects the notion of truth) is brought down to the lowest level, or common denominator, of fictional writing or journalism. Rather, he said, "the only choice is between a history which is aware of what it is doing and a history that is not" (Jenkins 1991, p. 57). The next step is awareness: to lay open the processes of production inherent in historical writing. For Jenkins, this is "positive reflexive scepticism" (Jenkins 1991, p. 57) (and, therefore, it can be argued that perhaps Jenkins is not a "true" example of a postmodernist. He hereby retains notions of rigor within the discipline of history, even within a postmodernist framework which acknowledges social constructivism. This is not to imply postmodernism negates any notion of rigor, but rather counter the idea that postmodernism automatically implies a free-for-all, "anything goes" approach to research).

Jenkins (1995) therefore responds to Atkinson's (1990) opening argument on the socially constructed nature of research and the challenging of textual authority and suggests how future writing and representation can be legitimated. For Jenkins, a way forward from the knowledge that representations of the social world can appear in a variety of, perhaps contradictory, modes is (from a historiographical perspective) adopting "positive reflexive scepticism," which makes accounts

> less mystifying than others inasmuch as they overtly call attention to their own processes of production, clearly flag their own assumptions, and indicate explicitly and repeatedly the constituted rather than the found nature of their referent, "the historicised past" (Jenkins 1995, p. 10).

There is a danger in not adopting a reflexive position. Accounts which write in an objective style, failing to lay bare their assumptions and realize that there is no independent reality or "fact," risk being read as a kind of cover-up or as containing some hidden complicity (Jenkins 1995). Ironically, the scholarly objectivity—neutral and detached—once considered the bastion of all classic virtues is replaced by its one-time ridiculed and suppressed opposite: an open style which lays bare the autobiographical and subjective position of the author (Jenkins 1995). Western culture's irrational passion for dispassionate rationality is ironically reversed.

So Jenkins provides a future direction for history to develop. He argues that it is not the cynical, all-dramatic "end of history," but rather the end of modernist renditions of history. However, his solution is not complete in relation to ethnography. The value in rejecting the Enlightenment/modernist idea of the onward march of progress (Jenkins 1991, 1995) is outweighed by the real problem in the implication that all accounts are ultimately as much constructions as the fictional novel. Jenkins's (1991, 1995) notion of reflexivity, returning to Atkinson's opening proposition, is not a resolution of the problem of writing as a form of social construction, but a strategy for coping. Indeed, Jenkins's (1995) anti-epistemological argument is ultimately self-referencing; his statement involves making a value judgement and relies on that same judgement as a source of authority. The question becomes, how exact are the parallels between Jenkins's picture of the historian and the ethnographer and, secondly, what can we learn from Jenkins's position?

In terms of commitments and resources, historian and ethnographer are remarkably similar (Atkinson 1990). That is, each discipline is committed to attempting to provide a systematic and thorough account of a cultural phenomenon, yet the resources they draw on cannot be reproduced in their entirety. For example, Atkinson (1990) makes a further distinction that "writing down" during fieldwork inevitably does not record all aspects and details of the phenomenon studied and is reduced further in the "writing up" process which funnels detail into examples and illustrations to be included in the research report. As in Carr's (1987) argument, sources (or examples) become meaningful when utilized as evidence in support of a particular interpretation. Atkinson (1990) and Hammersley (1992) likewise recognize that "the 'facts' of the case do not imprint themselves" (Atkinson 1990, p. 9). Therefore, like Carr (1987) and Jenkins (1991), Hammersley and Atkinson recognize that we are part of the social world we live in, and that interpretations therefore cannot escape this existential fact:

> "...We are part of the social world we study, and...there is no escape from reliance on common-sense knowledge and methods of investigation" (Hammersley and Atkinson 1995, p. 21).

If ethnographic research inevitably entails common-sense knowledge, it topples the notion of "fact" from its reified status in traditional, skills-based history. Both the notion of "doing" research (methodological fetishism) and the notion that direct experience of the social world allows the facts to emerge (methodological reification) are problematized. By reducing our reliance on these, comparisons between the scholarly monograph and the fictional novel again arise, as both construct representations of reality. Whilst they are constructed for different purposes and in different ways, why bother with the extra effort and cost of ethnography in relation to armchair reflection? This is problematic in that it leaves the ethnographic monograph in a challenged position regarding its legitimacy and reliability—legitimacy in terms of its claim to authority and reliability in whether it actually studies what it claims to study. Where does ethnography's authority lie?

Hammersley and Atkinson (1995) are adamant that acknowledging that ethnographic monographs employ techniques traditionally seen to be the preserve of fictional novels does not undermine or weaken ethnography's scholarly credibility and status. Rather, like Jenkins, Hammersley and Atkinson (1995) employ the notion of reflexivity as a defense, arguing that identifying research constructs at every stage of the research process (reflexivity) makes research more sophisticated.

The importance of reflexivity is stressed both by Jenkins (1991) and Hammersley and Atkinson (1995), but they differ over their notions of what reflexivity exactly entails, and over where they choose to place themselves in the current debate on constructivism: between the "old certaintist" (realist) position and the new "rhetorical postist" (relativist) (Jenkins 1995, p. 7). Hammersley advocates a "subtle realism" which rejects the goal of macro, law-like social theory, but is nevertheless committed to the belief that there is a "bedrock of direct knowledge" which, while not directly accessible, can be studied (Hammersley 1995, p. 60). The guide behind investigation is "a concern with truth, in which we guard against the illegitimate influence of the other values" (Hammersley 1992, p. 27). Postmodernism rejects the notion of truth, indeed, the possibility of realism or closure (Jenkins 1995; Stronach and MacLure 1997). However, Hammersley and Atkinson (1995) are less persuaded to take that step:

> We do not see reflexivity as undermining researchers' commitment to realism. In our view it only undermines naive forms of realism which assume that knowledge must be based on some absolutely secure foundation (Hammersley and Atkinson 1995, p. 17), sophisticated ethnography, they argue, constructs a sociological account which is conscious of its own limitations. Reflexivity for them involves the recognition that research is constructed at every stage of the process, by theoretical ideas beforehand and throughout. Readings of the monograph itself are also open to interpretation. So having identified the meaning of reflexivity, let us take one of ethnography, its writing, to see what techniques can be used to represent the social world or, rather, how one interpretation seeks to offer an account. Like Atkinson's (1990) clear intention to heighten our awareness of this problem rather than offer a prescriptive textbook, the aim here is to consider some options rather than suggest they are the only way forward.

Atkinson's *The Ethnographic Imagination* (1990), however, is problematic. Like a lot of methodological treatises, it ultimately heaps further points on an already complex research style, leading us into a maze without offering a plan for getting out. This is not to suggest that there is a methodological "map" or solution to every issue arising during the research process; conducting ethnography is inherently messy. It is the possibility of a "game-plan" I want to consider here. Having acknowledged the importance of reflexivity, I want to use it to move beyond the tendency to adopt bi-polar modes of thinking which conceptualize along dualist lines such as: problems to be met by solution; relativism countered with realism; Manning's "aesthetic sensitivity" against "evidential sensitivity" (Manning 1992,

p. 143) and rather acknowledge that ethnography works somewhere in between. Using Atkinson's (1990) theme of the "poetics of sociology," how can the acknowledgement of the incommensurability of reality and research into that reality provide a new direction, value or goal for ethnographic research?

Jenkins's (1991) consideration of the gaps unreflexive history has produced provides hints. For example, the emphasis upon rigor and method underplays (even suppresses) the role of thought and imagination. Method comes to be seen in opposition to imagination. On different lines, Jenkins(1991) identifies that the development of conceptual apparatus by which historians could move to more general statements about the past was likewise repressed. Additionally, the poetic moment in historical writing, not acknowledged to be part of or even present in historical writing, was ignored. Jenkins (1991) argued that historical writing (indeed every form of language use) contains elements of the poetic.

These points all hint that the process of documentary analysis, and ultimately scholarly writing, is more artful. They suggest writing involves much more than staid redescription and quoting of sources as evidence:

> ...The sociology itself may be sustained by various "literary" devices. Arguments are conveyed and coded implicitly in the descriptive writing that ethnographers employ. The authenticity of the account itself is claimed in and on behalf of texts that vividly construct their social worlds (Atkinson 1990, p. 80).

If the neglected elements in writing Jenkins (1991) identifies were recovered and developed, perhaps future possibilities for both historical and ethnographic writing would arise. Then writing would become vivid and mindfully artful; consisting of a subtle blend of sociologically imaginative and reflexive writing. For the ethnographer, writing is simultaneously "grounded" in the richness of qualitative and yet a creative act. Style and sociological imagination become more important. Can an acknowledgement, and even an adoption, of the more literary elements in ethnographic writing open up possibilities for future ethnographic development? What new forms of rhetorical technique can sociologists "play with" to offer an account and explanation of the social world?

GOFFMAN'S REFLEXIVE IMAGINATION

Goffman is discussed here as a case study. He represents a sociologist with a unique style and distinctive flair (even panache) whose sociology has been considered "maverick" in comparison to mainstream sociology. The aim is to analyze his interpretation of the task of sociology and his presentational style. How did Goffman choose to represent his social world? Is Goffman's a reflexive sociology by which to represent social/sociological reality? And does his "style" of sociology open up possibilities for future ethnographic writings to adopt?

Goffman's own reticence to talk on methodological issues (Manning 1992) makes this problematic and suggests it would be unfair to categorize his work or look for evidence in his work that he himself would not have intended to be present or found. But as the above arguments by Carr (1987), Jenkins (1991) and Hammersley and Atkinson (1995) established, personal characteristics and asocial context are important influences on the researcher. Therefore, I want to "get inside" Goffman's view of the task of sociology and, once this is established, evaluate it in the face of criticism of social constructivism. Whether he achieved his own objectives is, at this moment, of secondary importance.

Aside from the one pre-doctoral statistical study, Goffman's focus remained very much upon micro-level face-to-face interaction. This focus on micro sociology, as the preceding arguments established, reflects a researcher's theoretical ideas (Jenkins 1991) and Goffman's interest and adoption of Simmel's sociology stemmed from graduate time at Chicago (Manning 1992). Goffman utilized Simmel's recognition that writing about and describing social phenomena is highly problematic, as social life is in a constant flux. "Flux" is used in the sense that phenomena are constantly affecting each other and what appear as apparently small actions can later prove to be highly consequential, the key implication of this position is that no elements can be known in advance to be trivial. Simmel had used the now familiar functionalist organic analogy to demonstrate this idea which, through equating society to the human body, stresses the importance of social organizations such as the state, religion and the family through comparisons with the major biological organs (heart and lungs). However, it was Simmel's extension of the analogy to the rest of the body which captured Goffman's imagination, particularly Simmel's argument that the multitude of innumerable unknown or unnamed "tissues" are equally essential to the healthy functioning of the body and society as the major organs, but surprisingly receive little attention from the sociologist. Goffman attached considerable importance to this idea:

> Sociologists have traditionally studied face-to-face interaction as part of the area of "collective behavior"; the units of social organization....The other aspect of the problem...uneventful face-to-face interaction...has been neglected until recently (Goffman 1961b, p. 7).

Simmel's idea, to Goffman, "served as a mandate for the detailed study of everyday life" (Manning 1992, p. 19). A basic feature of Goffman's theoretical perspective, writing and representation hence came to actualize this idea and show:

> ...Observers actively project their frames into the world immediately around them, and one fails to see their so doing because events ordinarily conform to these projections, causing the assumptions to disappear into the smooth flow of activity (Goffman 1974, p. 39).

The aim behind Goffman's sociology was to create an account which leads the reader to problematize the taken-for-granted. His methods actualized this aim by focusing on breakdowns in the social encounter; cases which did not work, such as examples when interaction encounters problems such as conflict and the result conflict produces, such as stigma (Goffman 1963). Goffman's suggestion of an inherent fragility in interaction also echoed ethnomethodology's celebration of social order's "awesome" fragility, made and maintained through every encounter. Goffman's challenge of the taken-for-granted is similar to ethnomethodology's notion of tacit knowledge, that successful interaction depends on actors' ability to fill in background assumptions (Garfinkel 1967).

Goffman is therefore not taking order as automatically given; rather it is constructed. Here Goffman is working along lines like those of Jenkins (1991) and Hammersley and Atkinson (1995). So the methodological challenge for Goffman, and the would-be ethnographic writer, is to offer an account which juggles two objectives:

(1) to understand and investigate the social world at a micro level of social actors' behavior (to see how individuals' interaction sustains reality and recreates it with every encounter);
(2) to become detached from common-sense interpretation which is unaware of problems of order (i.e. problematize seemingly everyday encounters).

The first of the above points is reflexive in that it, by simple extension, shows reality and therefore representations of that reality are constructed. This is acknowledged by both Goffman and Simmel, when they argue that accounts are inevitably partial representations of the complexities (flux) of the social world. In this sense, Goffman's sociology is reflexive. However, the second task remains tantalizingly unobtainable; the researcher attempts at the same time to become "an outsider." This second point (in ethnographic terms, "make the familiar strange") is impossible considering that the researcher is inevitably a product of his or her time and social context. Perhaps the contradiction is where Goffman's sociology progresses from a position which acknowledges that sociologists construct their accounts. If so, it is the way Goffman attempts to get behind the everyday which becomes crucial; his ideas in methodological action.

Manning (1992) identifies three main methods in Goffman's work: an extended use of metaphorical description, and systematic naturalistic observation (ethnography). The third of these tactics by Goffman, like conventional ethnography (if enough homogeneity exists to warrant this term), entails drawing from both its own fieldwork and existing scholarly texts to support its arguments and the construction of its accounts (Atkinson 1990). This is therefore nothing radically new—the whole process of undergraduate and postgraduate training could be seen as an extended means of brainwashing the next generation of scholars into adopting the field methods and ideas of existing conventions.

However, Goffman's second strategy of unsystematic naturalistic observation tackles the difficult second objective in Goffman's approach to the social world. Unsystematic naturalistic observation allowed Goffman to move beyond drawing solely from his own fieldwork or existing scholarly literature, to include "eclectic" and "fantastically diverse database" of newspapers, autobiographies, fictional novels and made-up examples (Manning 1992, pp. 17, 21), such as made-up hypothetical, everyday social encounters which are not based on direct field observation. Such ungrounded eclecticism could be criticized for being subjective and haphazard. However, in some ways, recognizing that the social world is constructed (and ethnographic text with them) has a positive outcome as all aspects of the social world become legitimate resources; either as examples to quote or as analytic tools. As Atkinson (1990) argued, all sources are socially derived, whether from the sociologist's imagination or quoting a document or field-based observation. All are equally subject to interpretation and manipulation by the author. However, some are more topical, engaging or fun, than others. This idea echoes Weber's argument that all sociological investigations make use of ideal types. That is, a one-sided accentuation of one or more points of view. As such, they are not descriptions of reality, rather abstractions or composites of many actually existing phenomena.

This returns to the theme and problems involved in writing and representation. It echoes Carr's (1987) argument that sources only really become evidence when used in support of an interpretation. Indeed, perhaps it is worth bearing in mind Nietzsche's observation that disciplines are made up of what we are forbidden to do with them (Nietzsche 1886 trans. 1973). Goffman sometimes broke conventional sources by using diverse examples as a resource to generate concepts and provoke ideas through contrast, aiming to shape the familiar strangely. Goffman's "socio-literary method and procedure" therefore helps problematize the social world in order to study it, and also serves as a basis for conceptual development (Manning 1980, p. 262). In terms of writing, Manning observed that Goffman's ethnographies are more ethnographies of concepts than of places:

> The overall system is a conceptual scheme or frame of reference rather than a theory. Early Goffman provides us with something like a long "shopping list" with which to perform sociological analysis. And, he performs a kind of abstract ethnography organized around his own concepts rather than around those of a particular set of natives (Lofland 1980, p. 34).

Therefore, Goffman's kind of ethnography is distinctive. He remains close to the minutiae of face-to-face interaction, but not wedded to the one case study of his fieldwork. The aim is to problematize social life and see beyond the everyday, while recognizing that researchers can never fully achieve this, being themselves part of what they study. Goffman perhaps was less interested in seeing what was there and more concerned with moving beyond fieldwork both to create new concepts and to make the task problematic *to himself* (Manning 1980). Whereas some ethnographies attach importance, even celebrate inside the social actor's perspective, Goffman remained (deliberately) detached. Hence, his almost chatty style of using the term "we" when describing action within a social situation takes the side of the general reader, looking at social situations through the eyes of the common, everyday actor, rather than a native of one of his field studies' social situations.

Returning to debates on writing and representation, the acknowledgement of social constructivism takes Goffman away from the focus on reporting fieldwork and more into the realm of theorizing. An artful tactic by Goffman could be interpreted as merely a literary flair rather than an intrinsic part of his style and content. Both, fortunately enough, have the effect of drawing the reader into his account of social interaction and Goffman's interpretation of it. His detachment is not motivated by the old certaintist tradition which believed objective, removed research gets us closer to "the truth." Indeed, its general style—in which the eclectic database and chatty style lends a feeling that this could happen to you in any kind of social situation—is more evocative of a pluralist testing of concepts, which the reader can choose to "buy" or not. Ultimately, however, Goffman's writing is persuasive toward his own argument and interpretation. It could be argued that his "chatty" style even dulls our critical faculties, leaving us tempted to challenge the account Goffman is presenting.

The three elements of Goffman, as an ethnographer of concepts rather than place, his general (rather than particular) style plus the overall aim to cast the familiar in a strange light are all present in the third methodological strategy identified by Manning (1992): metaphor. Perhaps this is why this particular method of Goffman, 30 years on, stands out in his work, because it attempts to achieve so much.

Goffman's metaphors cast insights onto problems by "perspective by incongruity," merging categories which are usually mutually exclusive. This fits perfectly with Goffman's aim to problematize banal, everyday experience, as it "focuses and defocuses an aspect of social life" (Manning 1980, p. 252). Common criticisms of metaphor use argue that it eventually falls down when applied in detail. However, Goffman's use of metaphor was not necessarily aimed as a categorical statement about how exactly the world is (i.e., as a realist theoretical framework). Rather, his use of metaphor aimed to hint at a myriad of possibilities, as (following earlier discussions) the only certainty in social research can be the unendingly provisional nature of the ensuing research. Hence Goffman's use of metaphor can be argued to be applying "an idiosyncratic map to the social world," acting more as a guide (or game-plan), than an instruction (Manning 1992, p. 15). This would make metaphor the perfect foil to constructivism while also possessing a thought-provoking quality through incongruity.

Expressed another way, Goffman's metaphor was not used as a metaschema, but rather as a simile; love is like a red, red rose, rather than love is a red, red rose. It emphasized multiple perspectives, sometimes in conflict, rather than a dominant one (Goffman 1961a, 1963). In this sense, metaphor consisted of a preliminary ordering device for writing and representing social situations, a theme rather than a categorical statement. Goffman used metaphor as a reflexive analytical tool, recognizing that metaphor emphasizes some characteristics of the given social phenomena but suppresses aspects which do not fit that analogy. That is, even the most incongruous metaphors still make us think in certain ways whilst blinding us to other possibilities. But his intent through metaphor was to provide an analytic form of *verstehen*, rather than a prescriptive *weltanschauung*. The options were always intended to remain open.

Returning to the issue of constructivism, Goffman's use of metaphor is not over-stretched into a tool to represent and construct an overall, metaschematic interpretation of reality. His application of metaphor is a means to aid understanding, provoke ideas and represent reality, not to develop grand theory (Collins 1980; Manning 1992). Indeed, considering that all sociological knowledge is unavoidably a simplification of the unmanageable complexity of the social world, Goffman's use of metaphor can be seen to be quite the reverse: a way to handle this unmanageable complexity by deliberately simplifying it with a one-sided metaphor. However, we should be sensitive to Simmel's argument that moves to reduce the complexity of the world are merely expedient to the level of the theorist's own analytic limits. As Ricoeur (1981) summarized, metaphor is no more than a concise way of expressing ideas and Goffman used it as such. Metaphor therefore gives a flavor of thinking generally, a way to bridge the gap between theory and method and to balance conceptual elegance and loyalty to empirical detail.

In summary, Goffman makes use of metaphor's descriptive potential (through analogy) in his writing but applies metaphor's real strength as a strategic research tool in its power to create wild contrasts which challenge common sense, and taken-for-granted understandings (and render Simmel's unseen "tissues" of the body visible). It offers insight into the dynamics behind the everyday. Goffman's methodology strikes at social constructivism by ironically recognizing the inescapability of conventions, while trying to step outside them nevertheless. It is that which makes Goffman's use of metaphor so novel.

There are, however, problems. Using such socio-literary writing tactics has a double-edged implication for the text. Manning (1980) warns that, while the incongruous application of metaphor may be dramatic and hold a certain shock tactic, such dramatic flourishes can detract or even overwhelm the analytic point being made. That is, too much of a good thing spoils the effect. Rather, metaphor should be used reflexively and the writer must recognize that once the initial impact has worn off, the metaphor becomes stale and its power to shock is reduced—the novelty of a new metaphor subsides in inverse proportion to metaphor's nervous energy. However, does acknowledgement of this imply Goffman's style of sociology—of which metaphor is a large constituent—therefore has a limited shelf life? For example, Atkinson (1990) cites Goffman as a sociologist whose conceptual apparatus has entered the mainstream fashion so that one expects to see it included. Perhaps Goffman's unconventionality has ironically suffered at the hands of its own tactics and become all too conventional, his once startling images becoming the "dead" metaphors of mainstream sociology.

Looked at through the eyes of Jenkins (1995) or Carr (1987) it is more a case of Goffman's work being part of the social construction of its own time (i.e., like Carr's ideas and modernism) and therefore losing its appeal and power 30 years on.

Goffman's sociology is not anachronistic to modern sociology. He is admittedly not certaintist, grand theory not being an overriding preoccupation. Rather pluralism is celebrated in Goffman's metaphor's inherent ambiguity which leaves his analysis open-ended and ironically forestalls any sense of closure or "fact." Goffman is not postmodern to the same degree as Jenkins because his work contains a moral tone and hence does not reject the notion of center.

An example of this is Goffman's (1961a) critical presentation of the medical profession in *Asylums* (Lofland 1980). This moral tone, and the irony that perspective by incongruity produces, ultimately rely on some form of value consensus to be able to identify the incongruity or see the negativity in social relations (e.g., that total institution). Goffman, therefore, is not anti-epistemological. The humanist tone to Goffman also predisposes his sociology away from postmodernism, particularly his argument that "universal human nature is not a very human thing." This directly evokes themes of reflexivity and social construction as outlined by Atkinson (1990) more than his moral tone suggests. That is, he criticizes unquestioning acceptance of the social world as given, arguing it is constructed. For example, every time actors conform to the hegemony of meaning in a frame of reference's definition of the situation, they lose a bit of humanity by accepting the frame's constraints. Therefore, Goffman's writing deliberately manipulates our cognitive ability to extend metaphors to a multiplicity of settings to see the construction of encounters redescribe society and reflect and challenge this hegemony of meaning. When, in the following paragraph, Goffman is talking about a definition of self, he could be discussing his own methodological tactic of unconventional eclecticism which challenges meaning:

> Our sense of being a person can come from being drawn into a wider social unit: our sense of selfhood can arise through the little ways in which we resist the pull. Our status is backed by the solid buildings of the world, while our sense of personal identify often resides in the cracks (Goffman 1961a, p. 320).

The little cracks Goffman refers to, when placed in this discussion of techniques of writing and representation, could be Goffman's breaks with the conventional ethnographic forms of presentation, such as poetry or film. Goffman's subtlety and intellect, Lofland (1980) argues, lie in his synthesis of traditional and novel techniques.

Hammersley and Atkinson (1995) argue that unsophisticated realist assumptions are, to some degree, countered by reflexivity. Goffman attempts to provide another solution through his refusal to assume the world comes in logically inter-related categories. His writing tends to make assertions, rather than statements to be tested; to focus on explications, rather than propositions. However, all sociological accounts attempt to do more than merely describe, they seek to analyze: that is, explain and understand (Geertz 1973). Postmodernism's claim to an anti-epistemological and anti-ontological position is self-contradictory as, by arguing this position, postmodernism itself is making judgements and setting itself up as a metanarrative. Manning (1980) makes a similar point to Goffman. *Frame Analysis* (Goffman 1974), he argues, is not a frame itself, but is a book about frame analysis and therefore a text on the sociology of knowledge. This makes it just as much an artifact of contrivance as that which attempts to capture (Atkinson 1990).

In this sense, we return full circle to modern ethnography's identification that monographs are not so much an explication as a construction of it (Atkinson 1990; Hammersley and Atkinson 1995; Stronach and MacLure 1997). One way to proceed from this position is to recognize (like Goffman) that texts wed style with content to manipulate an argument. In this case of Goffman, style and content were so closely bound together that perhaps Lofland's (1980) observation that Goffman's style was more important than his content, should be reversed: his style was his content. Whereas there are dangers in reifying anti-conventional methods to solve problems of representation (i.e., Jenkins on traditional history's fetishism of method), anti-conventionality can be defended on the grounds that it challenges hegemony and recognizes the social constructed nature of the social world. In this sense, Goffman's methodology is not only reflexive, but contains a critique of inequality in power relations from its moral tone.

There remains, however, a puzzle in Goffman. Collins (1980) identifies him as "hip to the point of unwillingness to take any strong stance, even the stance of his own hipness" (Collins 1980, p. 206). If Goffman's sociology can be seen to be reflexive—and it has on a number of points—does his unwillingness to take a stance and explicate his own methodology and processes of construction make him unwittingly reflexive? Or is such a term self-contradictory? Is it fair to have evaluated his work in the terms here, or has there been too much read into his sociology? Perhaps his eclecticism has worked against him; he has become all things to all people.

The intention here (similar to Goffman's) has been to explore possibilities rather than reach categorical conclusions. The unreflexive assimilation of "Goffmanisms" into research practice has not been advocated. Yet the resolved questions surrounding Goffman's approach do not undermine his imagination and eminence in the discipline of sociology, nor negate the scholarly application of his ideas to different concerns. A second wave of Goffman into sociological fashion recommends itself as a style to adopt in ethnographic research and Goffman's maverick, eclectic "hipness" has been seen to be one that ethnographers can respond to the challenge of postmodernism and constructivism. Goffman's style blends ontological suppositions on the nature of social reality from a number of intellectual schools into a highly distinctive methodological approach. The sophistication with Goffman is that he achieves this with considerable panache, his intimacy of tone, the deceptively informal structure and accessibility of his books plus the easy familiarity of examples from everyday life. While it could be countered that these only serve to dull our ability to challenge Goffman critically, the strength in Goffman is that he keeps all the postmodernist themes alive while actually getting some empirical inquiry done. While Goffman lacks a contribution toward formal theory generation and development—metaphor being inappropriate toward this end—the style's open-ended eclecticism, in a postmodern world, seems all the more appropriate.

ACKNOWLEDGMENTS

I would like to thank the following for their comments on various drafts of this paper: Martyn Hammersley, Charles Turner, Alexander Massey and Christopher Pole.

REFERENCES

Atkinson, P. 1990. *The Ethnographic Imagination.* London: Routledge.
Carr, E. H. 1987. *What Is History?* (2nd ed.). London: Penguin.
Coffey, A., and P. Atkinson. 1996. *Making Sense of Qualitative Data: Complementary Research Strategies.* London: Sage.
Collins, R. 1980. "Erving Goffman and the Development of Modern Social Theory." In *The View from Goffman,* edited by J. Ditton. London: Macmillan.
Delamont, S. 1992. *Fieldwork in Educational Settings.* London: Falmer.
Garfinkel, H. 1967. *Studies in Ethnomethodology.* New Jersey: Prentice-Hall.
Geertz, C. 1973. *The Interpretation of Cultures.* New York: Basic.
Glaser, B. and A. Strauss. 1967. *The Discovery of Grounded Theory.* Chicago: Aldine.
Goffman, E. 1961a. *Asylums: Essays on the Social Situation of Mental Patients and Other Inmates.* Harmondsworth: Penguin.
_____. 1961b. *Encounters: Two Studies in the Sociology of Interaction.* Indianapolis: Bobbs-Merrill.
_____. 1963. *Stigma: Notes on the Management of Spoiled Identity.* Harmondsworth: Penguin.
_____. 1974. *Frame Analysis: An Essay on the Organisation of Experience.* New York: Harper and Row.
Hammersley, M. 1992. *What's Wrong with Ethnography.* London: Routledge.
_____. 1995. "Theory and Evidence in Qualitative Research." *Quality and Quantity* 29: 55-66.
Hammersley, M., and P. Atkinson. 1995. *Ethnography* (2nd ed.). London: Routledge.
Jenkins, K. 1991. *Rethinking History.* London: Routledge.
_____. 1995. *On "What Is History?" From Carr and Elton to Rorty and White.* London: Routledge.
Lofland, J. 1980. "Early Goffman: Style, Structure, Substance, Soul." In *The View from Goffman,* edited by J. Ditton. London: Macmillan.
Manning, P. 1980. "Goffman's Framing Order: Style as Structure." In *The View from Goffman,* edited by J. Ditton. London: Macmillan.
_____. 1992. *Erving Goffman and Modern Sociology.* Oxford: Polity.
Nietzsche, F. 1973, first published 1886. *Beyond Good and Evil.* Translated by R. J Hollingdale. Harmondsworth: Penguin.
Ricoeur, P. 1981. *Hermeneutics and the Human Sciences.* Cambridge: Cambridge University Press.
Scheurich, J. 1997. *Research Method in the Postmodern.* London: Falmer.
Stronach, I., and M. MacLure. 1997. *Educational Research Undone: The Postmodern Embrace.* Buckingham: Open University Press.

RESEARCHING PUBLIC LIBRARIES AND ETHNIC DIVERSITY:
SOME BLACK AND WHITE ISSUES

Marlene Morrison

INTRODUCTION

The aim of this chapter is to explore the methodological and epistemological challenges of researching ethnic diversity in policy-related research, specifically in public library service settings. The methodological debates concerning ethnicity and research have been long, and often heated (Connolly 1998, p. 1). Reason enough for some trepidation! For this writer, my involvement as field researcher on a project entitled *Public Libraries, Ethnic Diversity, and Citizenship* was the first occasion when, as a white, female "career researcher," the potential for criticism from supporters of a paradigm that sees all ethnically focused policy research conducted by white researchers as "politically maladroit" (Troyna's 1998 reference to Bourne 1980, p. 100), might need to be faced. Moreover, this

Studies in Educational Ethnography, Volume 2, pages 73-89.
ISBN: 0-7623-0563-0

chapter adds to a growing genre of reflexive accounts, which, some might argue, have not necessarily produced "better research" (Patai 1994, p. 69). Yet the intention is to look at the challenges in exploring first, a research arena rarely investigated by those outside the professional world of libraries, and second, policy issues that have ramifications for other public services, but were largely ignored prior to the research study. As importantly, the aim is to reflect upon the research processes and outcomes that emerged from data analysis conducted by two researchers—a white female and a black male—each located in different research centers within the same university, and upon their construction, operation, and early dissemination of the research. Such reflections are "stories" from the white researcher and are, as such, influenced by my multiple identities as white, female (and middle-aged), and partial in the sense of being particularistic "stories"; however, they are informed by the context of discussions and publications that were, and remain joint enterprises (Morrison and Roach 1998; Roach and Morrison 1997, 1998a, 1998b).

THE PROJECT

In 1996 the British Library funded the first major study to examine the relationship between public libraries and communities characterized by ethnic diversity. The study looked at public service responsiveness to the implications of ethnic diversity, and specifically to the way library services are constructed, managed, and reviewed. A number of critical questions were posed, in particular whether (and in which regard) such services were made accountable to, and seen as legitimate by, ethnically diverse communities. Based on the findings from research evidence, the sponsors sought recommendations for developing strategic policy and practice at local and national levels. The 18-month project was jointly developed by Patrick Roach and myself, based respectively at the Centre for Research in Ethnic Relations (CRER) and the Centre for Educational Development Appraisal and Research (CEDAR).[1] My academic background stemmed from extensive case study research in library and educational settings; Roach's role as Research Development Officer at CRER was enhanced by his previous career in public library service management. In addition to British Library funding, additional financial support was received from four local authorities.

THE METHODOLOGY

There were three main aspects to the research. A literature review informed the development of conceptual frameworks for the research (see also below). A focused postal audit sought questionnaire data responses from 12 geographically dispersed English library authorities that included the four case study authorities.

The audit was designed in order to provide useful benchmarks for evaluating the data from the extended case studies, and, as importantly, for the development of national benchmarks for assessing public library service provision. In particular, the audit focused upon policy planning, monitoring, needs analysis, citizen involvement, and marketing and promotion.

Extended case studies took place in four library service areas and examined in detail a range of issues that related to the provision of library services in ethnically diverse settings. The main issues identified related to: the library's place in the local community; performance targets and assessment measures for achieving racial equality; the public library service as an information provider; and strategic changes in public policy as they were linked to service provision for young ethnic minority adults. Each of the case studies was given a pseudonym, and interview responses were anonymized.

QUALITATIVE RESEARCH AND MULTI-SITE CASE STUDIES

In each of the case study authorities, a predominantly qualitative approach to fieldwork was used, combining documentation, interview, and observation analysis. The rationale for the approach was underpinned by a view that, although making links between qualitative research and social policy is "difficult, complex and demanding" (Finch 1985, p. 186), specifically in relation to growing sponsor demands for shorter run research in the field (Burgess et al. 1994), it is "not impossible." The scope of each case study reflected the specific issues identified in each authority, and was part of the overall strategic aim. This meant that while there were common features to all of the case study methodology—namely, desk research and interviews with library service representatives, library users, and members from a range of community service organisations—the emphasis in some approaches was specific to the interests of the case study. By design, and in process and outcomes, the research straddled the challenging policy-focused path between research that met the needs of the powerful and influential, and that which prioritised the interests of a diverse group of clients and user groups, to use the current terminology. Case study design and process, therefore, included a quantitative survey of library users at three service points in one authority, focus group interviews with young people in another, and interviews with local authority personnel beyond the library service in two of the case studies. The research, in its final form, produced five reports: a national report of findings for the British Library and four reports of case study findings for each of the local authorities who had provided supplementary funding. In the final reports, neither the methodology nor the challenges arising in the conduct of the report receive major attention. In the competitive world of research funding this is hardly surprising. As noted in other library-focused studies (Morrison et al. forthcoming), other than in terms of sponsor-researcher crises, such concerns remain largely implicit in the reporting of research outcomes.

The research literature provides limited glances at the challenges as well as the advantages of multi-site research, particularly in the area of ethnic diversity, and specifically for sponsors whose interest in not just in qualitative studies but primarily in informing key issues that have wide-ranging applicability. An important exception is Ward Schofield (1993) who argues that conducting heterogeneous case studies enhances the possibility of qualitative studies to speak beyond the confines of the actual situation to address the multiple interests of, in this instance, five sponsors. The objective was to draw comparisons and common themes between the case studies. In the research literature, cursory attention is still paid to issues of "meaningful comparison" (see Burgess et al. 1994), where passing reference is made to the tensions in selecting research sites, that are often summarized by brief statements that refer to "the kind of compromise which is common in research allowing research and evaluation to be conducted rigorously, yet within the confines of a specified budget" (pp. 131-132).

TYPICAL AND ATYPICAL CASES

For this project, research efforts to negotiate with the individual authorities were considerable (and owe most to the efforts of Roach) in seeking a match between the aims and objectives of the national research and the specific issues of interest to the four local authorities. The library authorities were not untypical of authorities that might be found in other English geographical locations, and the case study work was informed by the focused postal audit of 12 (finally 11) local authorities. Yet typicality needed to be balanced alongside ease of access and funding implications in a project on a limited time scale. This is not to argue that the concept of typicality was used as if it were an "easy fix" to resolve practitioner or sponsor concerns about issues of generalizability. As Ward Schofield (1993) points out in relation to the various elements that comprise a case study:

> The solution to this dilemma cannot be found in choosing typicality on every dimension....This strategy gains less in the realm of generalizability or fittingness than it might first appear at a glance. More important, even if one could achieve typicality on all dimensions there would be enough idiosyncrasy in any particular situation studied that one could not transfer findings in an unthinking way from one typical situation to another (Ward Schofield 1993, pp. 201-210).

Rather, in a "thinking way," attempts were made to look cumulatively at the processes and practices of each case study and study these in association with the analysis of the documentation and the postal audit.

CONCERNING ETHNIC SYMMETRY

The two members of the research team were each lead researchers in two case study authorities. Where it was considered appropriate and/or pragmatic, for example, in some aspects of the focus group work, the team worked together. No attempt was made to confine the work of the "white" or the "black" researcher to case study authorities where black and ethnic minority respondents would be in the minority or majority. The terms black and white are in quotes in part to reflect the growing influence of post-structuralism, and an ongoing critique about the use of the term "black" as a political identity to refer to all minority ethnic groups (discussed for example by Modood 1992). Maynard (1994) also looks at terms like "white people" and "whiteness" arguing for "whiteness" to be recognized as a racialized identity which needs to be "deconstructed." Nor were attempts made, across the authorities, to racially match interviewers with interviewees. In this sense, the research team avoided the division of labor advocated by Brar (1992) that "white people" because of their "insider status" should focus on "white institutions," and "black researchers should focus on the black community as they are much more acutely aware of the nature and effects of racism on their lives" (referred to by Connolly 1998, p. 3). Instead, the research team opted for regular reflective conversations and report-backs on interview data that included discussion of interviewer-interviewee relationships. Had the research team followed Brar's advice, it would have faced an additional amalgam of research issues—since it was the "black" researcher who had a much more varied, and arguably, deeper experience of working in a "white" public service management arena—specifically public libraries—than the "white" researcher who, in contrast, had a more extensive research background of working in a variety of local and divergent communities. Pragmatic issues were also important. Gatekeepers preferred to work with one rather than two team members, and a straightforward relationship between the work of each team member and secretarial staff in each research center was maintained.

More generally, the preference was also to acknowledge the complexity of the field researchers' multiple identities *as well as* those of the research participants. This is not to ignore research tensions (an example is highlighted in a following section) but rather to recognize some of the more recent positions in ethnically-focused research highlighted, for example, by Rhodes (1994) who states:

> Arguments for the exclusion of white researchers from research with black people as subjects assume a congruence of interests between black researchers and subjects.... The only significant dimension of exploitation is assumed to be that between white investigator and black subject. [Yet] other dimensions of social inequality may be more significant to participants (p. 556).

For this research, it became increasingly apparent that the irrelevance of public libraries to the lives of some black and ethnic minority interviewees, in combination with the paucity of contacts with library users among the same, acted as an initial deterrent to interview, rather than the identit(ies) of the interviewer:

> To be honest when you first rang me I thought I'm not sure our group can help you with your research. I mean if we need information we wouldn't go to the library. We've got our own telephone lists, and we would just know who to contact. Just like the people who come here, well, they wouldn't go to...the big library at....I mean there was one locally but it closed. In any case they come here because we're not threatening (community service spokesperson to Morrison, Cityside, Roach and Morrison 1998a, pp. 43-44).

The marginality of the library to the lives of those with whom interviews were sought was expressed in another way by an interviewee who declared:

> The library exists up there on the hill, but down here we're getting on with the business of meeting the needs of the ethnic minority community (Roach and Morrison 1997, p. 433).

However, the stance taken by the research team also reflects a wider concern to question the singular reasoning that ethnic symmetry and ethnic identity *of themselves* could provide what Troyna (1998, p. 101) describes and contests as "a privileged access to the 'truth'." For example, the researchers' reflections included discussion about the extent to which the responses given to the black researcher were *especially* affected by respondents' concerns to give "politically correct" responses.

Moreover, team discussions frequently focused upon other aspects of our multiple identities, for example, gender difference, upon the collection and analysis of interview data, in conjunction with the locations in which our interviews took place, rather than upon the ethnic asymmetry of some but not all interview situations. Again, Troyna (1998) draws upon Gabriel (1994) to unpack the flaws of a "single, authentic perspective" and draws our attention to the complex ways in which researchers' identities are "constantly being negotiated in the course of research in ways which might attenuate or strengthen the insider/outsider status of the researcher" (Troyna 1998, p. 101). This is not to minimize or try to distort incidences where distrust of the involvement of a white researcher, or at least, a lack of empathy between myself and several respondents from the black and ethnic minority communities were discernible. An example is explored below.

"A WHITE CULTURAL FILTER?"

During the course of the study the research team undertook 120 interviews with citizens in communities of ethnic diversity—whether in their capacity as "representatives" or members of local community service organizations, as library users, members of citizens' panels, or focus groups. Half of those interviews were conducted by the author. On two occasions a mixture of distrust and/or scepticism of the project and the author's role in it were noticeable. If there were other occasions, then lack of awareness prevented any conscious reconsideration of the efficacy of the data collected. As Rhodes (1994) suggests, it may be the case that:

> communications will be passed through a white cultural filter....There are dimensions to black experience invisible to the white interviewer/investigator who possesses neither the language nor cultural equipment to elicit that experience (Rhodes 1994, p. 549).

While working in Midcentre City library authority, contact was made with community members who formed part of a standing consultative forum. The City Council's objectives were to consult with, and inform a range of communities about potential and actual developments in the city. Community members gave their time generously to the writer in order to support this research but within an overall framework where interviewees expressed views on both consultation overload and underload. This co-existed with perceptions that they were, on occasions, marginalized in the discussion of "important" information, and that consultations were part of a stage-managed *fait accompli* in which their influence upon practice was minimal. Not surprisingly then, my role as researcher was construed, on at least two occasions, as the role of a member of that city élite seeking yet more information about the quality of "their" life experiences, this time in the guise of interests in public libraries. As an interviewee from one organization—focused upon the specific interests of one ethnic group—said to me at the start of an interview: "what could you possibly know to write down that would express my experiences?" and "why didn't the Council employ someone who is [the same ethnic origin category as me, i.e. the interviewee]?" Nonetheless, the interview lasted 45 minutes, contributed important facets to the research overall, included data that was confirmed by other material, and was finally expressed in the national report and the report for that authority as follows:[2]

> *Consulting citizens* (an extract from the Midcentre City case study)
>
> The word consultation is open to a number of interpretations. In the research for this project, our interests have been to interrogate, through data collection, the extent to which the term "to consult" can be seen in terms of "to consider jointly" and "to look for information and advice" *rather than* "to take measures for the advantage of." The distinction is critical for a research project underpinned by interests to investigate moves towards a stakeholder or citizen's library in which citizens are actively engaged. [...]
>
> Five mechanisms [for formal and informal consultation] are discernible: consultations with the standing consultative forum; surveys and feedback from library users; library-focused research projects; library-focused events; and indirectly through the steerage provide by the Leisure and Services Committee of the City Council. [...]

With one exception, none of the community representatives interviewed could recall library services or library issues for young people being a matter of developmental interest or debate. This was not, they explained, a matter of disinterest on their part. Moreover, in two separate interviews with representatives from different ethnic communities, comments were made about what was perceived to be a relative invisibility of their contribution to city life. An interviewee pondered: "if someone came from Mars into the central library would they know that we existed?" Such comments leave partly unresolved the extent to which terms like "we" are representative views [or whether interviewees are "representative" of specific communities]. From another perspective, and in the absence of coherent consultative frameworks, the problem, considered a member of library staff, was being subject to the vagaries of political manipulation in contexts where the Council's position on separate provision for specific groups lacked clear articulation (Roach and Morrison 1998a, Chapter 4, pp. 85-87).

A POLITICAL ENDEAVOR

In research that is both policy- and ethnically-focused, discussion of the issues that pertain to the reliability and validity of the data collected have been frequently overshadowed by wider considerations that relate to the rationale for the research and its orientation. This is not to understate the importance of issues of reliability and validity for this study, and part of the ongoing discussion by the field researchers, centered on the ways in which their individual value positions were reflected in the processes of data collection and analysis. In all aspects, the research is an intensively *political* endeavor. Troyna (1998) documents, in particular, perspectives on the ways in which "the focus of (white) researchers' gaze on black communities is misconceived and an anathema to anti-racist goals" (p. 97). Building on earlier critiques of studies that have problematized black experience and emphasized an "otherness" that fosters "assimilationism" (Harris and James 1993, p. 1), James and Harris are among recent writers who berate (white) researchers whose "research gaze" is implicated in wider power structures that continue to pathologize the "otherness" of being black. How then might one interpret the gaze of this researcher?

PROBLEMATIZING LIBRARIES, NOT LIBRARY USERS

The research task in which the research team was involved was a social scientific exploration of the public library as a model of public service. The interrelations among public libraries, ethnic diversity, and citizenship were central to our concerns. In this important respect, it was the service and not the user that was problematized. Because ethnic minorities have been regarded as a "problem" for library service providers—requiring the deployment of specialist consultants and new funding formulas—the relationship between public libraries and ethnic diversity had not been explored previously. In this sense, the research presented a challenge to those who had assumed that the traditional paternalism of the local state was the appropriate base on which to define public policy. For the most part, the traditional public library service ethos had not been associated fully with direct public control or direct democratic accountability.

This did not ignore a central research task to explore the ways in which professional control of the service was maintained, or the need to interrogate whether and to what extent librarians' views about the diverse and heterogeneous claims on the library service were problematized by them. In the case study of an authority named Southparks, the notion that the community view had only limited import in the way the library service was delivered by those employed to do so, is expressed in the following way:

> My personal view is that we'd have no qualms about community groups actually suggesting additions to our stock, or suggesting new services or suggesting new ways to promote. But I suppose the professional in me would step in and say we are employed by the Council to provide the library service and we are accountable for the way that we run the service, and that obviously would need to be borne in mind. We'd always, by the nature of that, have to be the ones making the decisions (Roach and Morrison 1998a, Chapter 4, p. 117).

When the team asked how citizens saw themselves in relation to the public library, we raised issues of citizenship, of community and individual rights and responsibilities, as well as what is meant by "public" each of which, in sum or part, is undergoing transformation. Starting points focused upon new sets of library-focused questions; in doing so a re-examination of terms like ethnicity, inequality, and disadvantage was also critical. These constituted the conceptual frameworks that are highlighted in chapter 2 of the national report (Roach and Morrison 1998a, pp. 13-23). It was noted that writers on public libraries had, on the whole, been somewhat reluctant to theorize about their own practice and/or to probe the significance of libraries at the interface between micro-levels of practice and wider social, historical, and political structures:

> But, as Williams (1976) points out (albeit in other contexts), when certain forms of social organisation are seldom referred to unfavourably, the tendency is towards "functional ambiguity"; applied to the public library service, this has been accompanied by a desire to espouse the *cause* of public libraries *above and before* the meanings of the service are fully explored and implications for practice derived (Roach and Morrison 1998a, p. 13).

> Conceptual concerns were also directed at the competing demands on the public library service, and its role at the heart of understandings about civil society, where it has been seen as a vehicle for democracy through its facility to educate and inform. It was acknowledged that ethnic minority communities had experienced disadvantage and discrimination in access to public services (Skellington and Morris 1992) and that local government, had not, in general, been representative of ethnic minority communities, delivering services that were either inappropriate or inaccessible (Anwar 1994).

More than this, however, the team's opening stance was not only to note the paucity of critical discussion of these issues in library-focused literature,[3] but also to emphasize an emerging acknowledgment that "racism is present in many facets of the library service from staff recruitment and training to book selection" (Martin 1992, p. 26). The research team, therefore, sought answers to the larger question of whether in relation to its "grand" claims as central to democracy and citizenship, the public library service might be expected to exemplify pro-active, anti-racist approaches rather than mirror activities in other institutionalized forms. Such issues formed the basis to examine the challenge of ethnic diversity for public libraries.

In summary, the research posed the fundamental question: to what extent is the public library service open and accountable to ethnic minority citizens? In problematizing the public library service rather than its users, basic questions were also raised about citizen empowerment. Was it appropriate to pose our questions in terms of an empowerment framework for citizens? The researchers considered a number of perspectives.

CITIZEN EMPOWERMENT

In Troyna (1998) there is a forthright condemnation of white researchers who attempt to dispel "the distrust which 'people of color' have of the involvement of white researchers" (Stanfield 1994, p. 167) by framing the research task "in terms of an 'emancipatory' and 'empowering' discourse—a (disturbing) pattern which is also found in a growing number of empirical studies into 'race' and 'ethnicity' outside the USA" (p. 99). The stance taken by the research team for this study was to take the terms "citizenship" and "empowerment" as critical concepts for interrogating the scope and content of social rights as they apply to ethnic diversity, and also to the extent of participation by ethnically and culturally diverse individuals and groups in the organization and planning of national and local enterprises such as library services. The rationale was seen as critical to the research enterprise:

> In exploring the relationship between citizenship and public libraries, we needed to examine ethnic minorities as actors in their own right, in other words, to explore the issue of citizen empowerment. In relationships between the local authority, the public library, and ethnic minorities, the potential is for individuals and/or groups to make choices, and, in particular circumstances, become mobilised....Among the outcomes is the prospect that local government will/has become an arena where different interest groups engage in dialogue (or struggle) in order to ensure that their needs are met and that they receive the resources they feel they need. The tendency to increase ethnic minority use of libraries has been central to the library's general philosophy of accommodation...were some ethnic groups already empowered within the context of the public library service? As importantly, were some ethnic groups more empowered than others? Did ethnic minority groups "believe" they had a stake in what was provided by public library services? (Roach and Morrison 1998a, p. 21).

In the case study of Cityside the focus was upon the role of the library as a provider of information, and specifically its contribution to Cityside's attempt to promote multimedia initiatives as a means of encouraging more active participation in local democracy. Empowerment, it is more generally argued (Greenhalgh et al. 1995), emerges from access to information that assists in the translation of knowledge to the potential for economic, social, and political action. Such ideas draw on earlier principles of access to a "free" good. The term was interrogated among a range of actors. Library staff expressed support for this ethos in very similar ways. For example:

> One point about the library is that it is still perceived as a sort of neutral space and a sort of relatively welcoming place, and by and large, in [Cityside] most of the services are free so that [library users] can come in and get information on anything without feeling, you know, that they are being channelled down one course, or that we're trying to persuade them to do one thing or another (p. 41).

Other viewpoints beyond the library service were expressed more cautiously. Some assessments remained guarded about whether access to information, in whatever form(s), could easily be translated into empowerment for citizens, as in the following comment from a council employee:

> I mean a difficulty councils have is that we tend to sit here thinking we can give people power....I mean I'm not sure whether we [the council] are the right agency to be trying that because people have so many suspicions of our motivation...and you know we aren't always open (p. 42).

Again, another interviewee, who categorized himself as a member of an ethnic minority group, considered that:

> The thing about empowerment is that people are out there doing things. *They* might not be choosing to talk to *us* [local services] partly because a lot of *them* have given up on *us* because, you know, if you take black and ethnic minority groups *they* probably struggled a lot in the eighties for some sort of recognition from local authorities and now a lot of *them* are just off doing their own things. You know, *they* are not bothered what *our* policies are, you know *they* are running their own supplementary schools or *they* are running their own self-help groups, *they* are not looking to *us* (p. 44, my emphases).

In such ways, constructions of empowerment, and complex understandings about *them* and *us*, were embedded in findings that suggested that Cityside library services were among a number of information providers at the local level, and that for some ethnic minority communities, the network of ethnic voluntary sector organizations was much more relevant and appropriate as an access point to information. Moreover, while evidence pointed to the potential for multimedia initiatives to enhance local democracy, more work was needed to assess the extent to which such initiatives had become embedded into local participatory frameworks.

So, did this research and/or the deliberations that have followed it make a difference? And to whom? Some points can be made briefly. First, the time lag between the end of the project and opportunities for policy-focused action has been short. Second, we may need to consider Hammersley's (1994) doubts about the capacity of knowledge that is derived from ethnography to shape practice, a view he contends is based upon a misguided "enlightenment optimism." He gives two reasons for this. The first is described in terms of the nature of policymaking and practice:

> It is not just that policy makers do not make policy in this way [as the result of carefully constructed qualitative research], the point is that there are good reasons for policy makers not to do so...for instance it may be that no rational solution to the problems they face is possible within the time scale imposed....Moreover, policy making is a political process not a matter of intellectual problem solving (p. 146).

The second relates to the character of knowledge produced by qualitative research. He continues:

> When Herbert Blumer talks of different groups occupying different worlds...it does not take much of a leap of imagination to see that ethnographers are engaged in a process of "world construction" when they analyse data and construct research reports. One effect of these sceptical and relativist interpretations of social research is to undermine the basis on which researchers can claim relevance of their work to practice (pp. 147-148).

In what ways, then, have sponsors and policymakers responded to this project?

DISSEMINATION:
THE STORY SO FAR

Prior to the launch of this study, much attention and money had been given to the future of the library service. In contrast, this was the first major study to look at the relationship among public libraries, ethnic diversity, and citizenship. The report provides examples of effective practice within the field. Yet other aspects of the findings are starkly critical, yet have received widespread coverage and support in the public library world. In brief, the findings are that:

- The public library service has not managed to engage fully with ethnically diverse communities.
- A social distance exists between the public library and ethnic minority communities.
- There is a lack of clear vision and leadership on ethnic diversity and racial equality matters within the public library service.
- There is a lack of coherence in strategies to identify and track the changing needs of ethnic minority communities.

- The public library service is neither central nor sufficiently supportive of the social and community networks established by ethnic communities.
- The structure, culture, and ethnic profile of the public library service denies ethnic minorities a stake in the public library system.
- The public library service has failed to account for its progress while current systems are largely color-blind.
- The resource pressures on the service may present further challenges to ethnic minority engagement and inclusion.

The findings were presented at a national launch of the report in March 1998 that included recommendations for action at national, local, and institutional levels. One outcome was the allocation of further funding to Morrison and Roach to produce a baseline guidance document for circulation among service deliverers (Morrison and Roach 1998). This has received the endorsement of two national library organizations. Invitations to speak at major library gatherings have been frequent, although hoped-for attendance at the national launch by a government representative was not forthcoming. While given mainstream support by library professionals, one interesting "public" incident where a well-known library figure simultaneously applauded the research while maintaining a skeptical distance that was reinforced by reference to the qualitative and particularistic nature of the research (that the findings "were not necessarily a reflection of library practice elsewhere") has provided an example of "the undermining tendencies" referred to by Hammersley (1994), and noted in the previous section.

"WHITE" ON "BLACK": SOME CONCLUDING REMARKS

Of equal interest is the question of whether this white researcher did meaningful research on the reaction among public libraries, ethnic diversity, and citizenship, and for whom. A number of specific points have been rehearsed in previous sections and are not repeated here except to offer an overall assessment that, in relation to the study, any attempt to isolate the effect of a researcher on the basis of skin color alone would constitute a misinterpretation of the multiple identities brought to the research by the writer, the research team and the research participants. In relation to this, several points can be made.

First, while the research team *did* exhibit an overall awareness of the dangers of drawing attention to the "otherness" of black and ethnic minority groups, especially where "otherness" could be translated into "strangeness," there were some conceptual tensions. Research which focused on generic terms like "black and ethnic minority" populations, and issues of "ethnic diversity," ran the risk of collapsing and/or reducing the complex structures and experiences of different groups that are subsumed under such headings. Such issues were part of regular discussions about the research task. Despite our attempts to spell out "in detail" the conceptual underpinnings and complexities of the terms used, and our specific attention to the interests of each case study, our concluding text provides an all-inclusive framework in order to facilitate the translation of conclusions into ways forward for diverse research user communities.

Second, in combination, the framing of the research project drew on the perspectives of a black and white researcher who shared a mutual acceptance of the validity of what was understood by them to be "known" about issues of ethnic diversity. Thus while we regularly unpacked the "baggage" of values that we brought individually to the research, our combined professional knowledge and understanding of research on racism and on public libraries was prioritized over our racialized and gendered identities and experiences. Understandings were framed around perspectives on race and ethnic diversity, in particular its social and political constructions, and an acknowledgment of the disadvantage and discrimination experienced by black and ethnically diverse groups in relation to access and to use of public services. However, some identifications were not always deconstructed explicitly. Thus, in the field, there was always the tendency for the meanings of "whiteness" to remain implicit. Once the research team had articulated that the most influential members of public library services were white, the racialist identities of the "powerful" remained partially, though far from exclusively, implicit in the analysis. "Whiteness" was, then, in substantive as well as methodological terms, occasionally invisible and/or subject to the reader's interpretation of text.

Third, while the research endeavor is partly legitimized by making sense of the discourses and actions that ran counter to some prevailing library service orthodoxies, the research criss-crossed the binary divide between research to produce knowledge and research to achieve practical benefits. In this sense, while the term "empowerment" was deployed as an important conceptual tool, our study did not constitute the kind of "empowerment" research that is often aligned with collaborative action research. Whether or not this is perceived to be a weakness (or strength) of the research depends on the extent to which action research is viewed positively or negatively and by whom, and whether action research *per se* is interpreted as essentially "emancipatory" or "placatory" (Stanfield 1994, p. 167).

POSTSCRIPT

In the most recent publication arising from the research, the authors conclude:

> In the light of the findings and recommendations from the research there is now a further choice for librarians: how to respond to the research findings. For some, our research will prove harsh reading; for others it has confirmed what they already knew or suspected....We hope that libraries will seize the many opportunities presented in our report to support a new programme for change (Roach and Morrison 1998b, p. 360).

The research team is now disbanded, and the field researchers have subsequently moved to separate and different employment spheres. This might add fuel to the fire of writers who berate "careerist" researchers who, in their turns, enter the arena of research into ethnic relations and block the development of "knowledge and responsibility for consciousness" (Harris and James 1993, p. 2). Again, following a perspective developed by Troyna (1998) who draws upon Gabriel (1994, p. 4), this work took place within the context of contesting the generalization that the identity of any researcher, careerist or otherwise, could offer *the* "singular authentic perspective" (Troyna 1998, p. 101). As importantly, our strength was perceived in terms of a cross-center and cross-team combination of perspectives and talents rather than fragmentation.

Meanwhile, the collegial as well as pragmatic challenges are to maintain the momentum for further work when funding has ceased. As with most research, the momentum passes to the policymaker and practitioner. This paper provides a modest contribution to part of a story that constitutes the research study and, as yet, remains unfinished in its outcomes and aspirations for change. In telling an additional tale, it is hoped that the reader will be better able to consider one person's reflections on a research project, its processes and "what happened next." This might, in turn, inform those interested in developing further its substantive and/or methodological strands. The account remains a partial "white researcher's" story but one which would have been impossible to tell without the support, expertise, and insights provided by Roach, and the positive team approach that was constant throughout. Faults in this account remain entirely my own; many omissions remain, an aspect of the "reluctance" on the part of most researchers, for a variety of reasons, "to reveal quite all that occurred" (Walford 1991, p. 5).

ACKNOWLEDGMENTS

The author would like to thank Patrick Roach for his helpful comments and suggestions. The author acknowledges the encouragement given by the project directors Professors Zig Layton Henry and Robert G. Burgess, and thanks the British Library and case study authorities for the funding of, and support for, the study on which these reflections is based. The project would not have been possible without the contributions of the many participants who remain anonymous.

NOTES

1. The joint project directors were Professors Zig Layton Henry and Robert G. Burgess at CRER and CEDAR, respectively.

2. The extract is necessarily brief, but actors' constructions of the term "consultation" recur throughout the national report.

3. Dolan (1992) does exemplify an emerging critical stance.

REFERENCES

Anwar, M. 1994. *Race and Elections. The Participation of Ethnic Minorities in Politics.* Monographs in Ethnic Relations No.9, University of Warwick: Centre for Research in Ethnic Relations.

Bourne, J. 1980. "Cheerleaders and Ombudsmen: The Sociology of Race Relations in Britain." *Race and Class* 21: 331-335.

Brar, H. S. 1992. "Unasked Questions, Impossible Answers, the Ethical Problems of Researching Race and Education." In *Ethics, Ethnicity and Education*, edited by M. Leicester and M. Taylor. London: Kogan Page.

Burgess, R. G., C. Pole, K. Evans and C. Priestley. 1994. "Four Studies from One or One Study from Four? Multi-Site Case Study Research." In *Analysing Qualitative Data*, edited by A. Bryman and R. G. Burgess. London: Routledge.

Connolly, P. 1998. "The Introduction." In *Researching Race in Education: Politics, Theory and Practice*, edited by P. Connolly and B. Troyna. Buckingham: Open University Press.

Dolan, J. 1992. "Birmingham as a Whole." In *The Whole Library Movement: Changing Practice in Multi-Cultural Librarianship*, edited by Z. Alexander and T. Knight. Stoke on Trent: AAL.

Finch, J. 1985. "Social Policy and Education: Problems and Possibilities Using Qualitative Research." Pp. 109-128 in *Issues in Educational Research: Qualitative Methods*, edited by R.G. Burgess. London: Falmer.

Gabriel, J. 1994. *Racism, Culture, Markets.* London: Routledge.

Greenhalgh, L., K. Worpole, with C. Landry. 1995. *Libraries in a World of Cultural Change.* London: UCL Press.

Hammersley, M. 1994. "Ethnography, Policy Making and Practice." Pp. 139-153 in *Researching Education Policy: Ethical and Methodological Issues*, edited by D. Halpin and B. Troyna. London: Falmer.

Harris, C., and W. James. 1993. "Introduction." In *Inside Babylon*, edited by W. James and C. Harris. London: Verso.

Martin, B. 1992. "The Multi-Cultural Dimension to Education and Training for Librarianship." In *The Whole Library Movement: Changing Practice in Multi-Cultural Librarianship*, edited by Z. Alexander and T. Knight. Stoke on Trent: AAL.

Maynard, M. 1994. "'Race', Gender, and the Concept of Difference in Feminist Thought." In *The Dynamics of 'Race' and Gender: Some Feminist Interventions*, edited by H. Afshar and M. Maynard. London: Taylor and Francis.

Modood, T. 1992. *Not Easy Being British: Colour, Culture, and Citizenship.* Stoke on Trent: Runnymede Trust and Trentham Books.

Morrison, M., and P. Roach. 1998. *Public Libraries and Ethnic Diversity: A Baseline for Good Practice.* University of Warwick: British Library Research and Innovation Report 113.

Morrison, M., S. Band, R. G. Burgess, D. Costley, and K. Wardle, forthcoming. "Libraries for Lifelong Learning: The Contribution of Multi-Site Case Study Research." In *Case Studies in Educational Research*, edited by M. Dowling and B. Baldauf.

Patai, D. 1994. "When Method Becomes Power." In *Power and Method*, edited by A. Gitlin. London: Routledge.

Rhodes, P.J. 1994. "Race of Interviewer Effects in Qualitative Research: A Brief Comment." *Sociology* 28 (2): 547-558.

Roach, P. and M. Morrison M. 1997. 'The Place on the Hill?' *The Library Association Record* 99 (8): 432-443.

_____. 1998a. *Public Libraries, Ethnic Diversity, and Citizenship.* CRER/CEDAR, University of Warwick: British Library Research and Innovation Report 76.

_____. 1998b. "Pursuing the Wind of Change." *The Library Association Record* 100 (7): 358-360.

Skellington, R., and P. Morris. 1992. *Race in Britain Today.* London: Sage in association with the Open University.

Stanfield, J. H. 1994. "Empowering the Culturally Diversified Sociological Voice." In *Power and Method*, edited by A. Gitlin. London: Routledge.

Troyna, B. 1998. "'The Whites of My Eyes, Nose, Ears...' A Reflexive Account of Whiteness in Race-Related Research." In *Researching Racism in Education: Politics, Theory and Practice*, edited by P. Connolly and B. Troyna. Buckingham: Open University Press.

Walford, G. 1991. "Reflexive Accounts of Doing Educational Research." In *Doing Educational Research*, edited by G. Walford. London: Routledge.

Ward Schofield, J. 1993. "Increasing the Generalizability of Qualitative Research." In *Social Research: Philosophy, Politics, and Practice*, edited by M. Hammersley. London: Sage.

Williams, R. 1976. *Keywords*. London: Fontana.

EXPLORING THE WORLDS
OF CHILDHOOD:
THE DILEMMAS AND
PROBLEMS OF THE
ADULT RESEARCHER

Mari Boyle

INTRODUCTION

This chapter focuses on the methodological approach used during my doctoral research into the school experiences of a group of 18 young bilingual children. At the start of the research the children had only just begun school, and were aged five. I spent two years with the children, two days each week in the school during their first year, and one day a week during their second. The school the children attended served a multi-ethnic community, the main ethnic groups being Pakistani and Indian with a growing number of families from Bangladesh, and smaller numbers of African-Caribbean, Arab, Italian and white English families. The main aims of the research project were to study the theory and practice of teachers' approaches to teaching young bilingual learners; to consider the meanings

Studies in Educational Ethnography, Volume 2, pages 91-108.
ISBN: 0-7623-0563-0

FINDING AN APPROPRIATE RESEARCHER ROLE

There are a variety of ways researchers approach their role within qualitative research. For some researchers a detached observer role is preferred. Non-participant observation in educational research in Britain has been widely used, with researchers sitting at the back of classrooms and adopting "fly on the wall" techniques. King (1984), for example, during his research into gender differentiation in the primary classroom (1972-1975), undertook non-participant observation by maintaining a distance between himself and the five- and six-year-olds he was observing. He achieved this initially by remaining in a standing position—physical height, he felt, maintained social distance. He was careful to avoid eye contact believing that "if you do not look, you will not be seen" (p. 123) and through the use of this approach he maintained that the children ignored him in later visits. Further into his research he even hid in the Wendy House in an attempt to be unobtrusive. Corsaro (1981) used a method of concealed observation from behind a one-way screen during the initial stage of his research of kindergarten children. There are ethical questions to be raised about this form of covert observation. How far should we conceal our observation? On the one hand, if the subjects we are observing are not aware of our presence their actions will not be influenced by the researcher. On the other hand, covert observation could be interpreted by those under observation as showing a lack of respect and, as Woods (1986) points out, it may even backfire when discovered and both the project and the researcher's credibility could be jeopardized. I did not feel that either of these approaches were appropriate for my own research. I wanted to engage with the children I was researching, and maintaining any distance from the children themselves was impractical for two main reasons. Firstly, from the moment I entered their classroom many of the children came to talk to me, inquiring who I was, what I was doing, why I had a notebook and what was I writing? Secondly, as in many early years classrooms, there were often a number of activities going on simultaneously, and to remain seated in one area rather than being able to move around a classroom to see what children were engaged in more closely may have resulted in a distorted view of classroom life.

The alternative to non-participant observation is that of participant observation though there are varying degrees of participation. At its purest form this can entail full immersion into a research group, assuming a real role and contributing to the purpose or function of the group, and personally experiencing the group's life (see for example Parker's 1974 study of "The Boys" in which he adopted a marginal position within a group of "down-town" adolescents in Liverpool). For adults researching young children such a fully participative involvement is usually considered impossible. Fine and Glassner (1979) indicate that aspects such as physical size and perceived power prevent the researcher from taking on a completely participant role when researching children. Corrigan (1979), for example, being 6 feet 4 inches tall, felt his height made complete participant observation of 14-year-olds impossible. Fine and Glassner (1979) consider the issue of power differentiation as significantly important and one aspect which separates ethnographic research of adults and of children. With adults they claim it is rare that the researcher will hold a position of authority over the researched (though many feminist researchers would argue that in cases where women are researched by men there are unequal power relationships, and similarly where the researcher and researched are from different social classes or ethnic backgrounds, again there may be a difference in the power relationship). With children, the mere fact that the researcher is an adult immediately places them in a position of authority and power. Fine and Glassner suggest, therefore, that the researcher should adopt the role of friend with children, but warn of possible dilemmas which may face the researcher in such instances, particularly in situations of deviant behavior—should the researcher interfere or not? Knupfer (1996) points out that the role of friend may also in some instances be at variance with cultural norms, as she found in her study of Chinese kindergarten children in America. Her participation in games with the children was often met with laughter from the mothers, who would never have been asked by their children to participate, as this was not seen as an appropriate Chinese adult role.

Mandell (1988) adopted the role of least-adult, in her study of kindergarten children. She describes her role as fully participant, and argues that even physical differences can be minimized when participating with children. Mandell actively initiated conversation with the children she studied, and frequently joined in their games, acting as least like the other adults in the nursery as possible.

In my own research I developed two roles as a researcher, because of the different contexts in which I came into contact with the children. The first was that of least-teacher role, and the second was the least-adult role.

The Least-Teacher/Least-Adult Role

As most of my fieldwork research took place in the school environment, the context in which the research occurred had some effect on my role as a researcher. In many research projects based in schools, researchers have taken on the role of teacher as it allows the researcher to appreciate the strains of the teacher (see, for example, Lacey 1976 and Burgess 1983). However, as Lacey found, when the emphasis of data collection shifted from gathering information from teachers to pupils, the teacher role proved to hinder the data collection process. Lacey subsequently adopted an informal counsellor role when gathering data from pupils.

The children of this study initially viewed me as another teacher, in part because I was introduced to the class as "Miss Boyle." I attempted to play down this role by setting up boundaries, though I did not go as far as Mandell (1988), who rebuffed children's requests for help in performing adult tasks in the nursery by stating that she was not the teacher. I avoided acting too much like their own teachers; for example, I dressed more casually than their teachers. When children asked permission to do things after they had completed work I referred them to their teacher. In their first year at school children would ask me to mark work for them, which I did in pencil, not in pen as their teacher would, but opportunities such as this allowed me to discuss what they had been doing. They would then often go and ask the teacher to mark their work "properly." When they entered their second year of schooling I was never asked to mark work. On some occasions such as physical education, drama, art and science lessons, I joined in activities with the children, unlike their teachers who would either demonstrate activities or guide them through. In other situations, such as being placed in the Golden Book (a reward system used by the school), I refused to put forward names when children asked me. On occasions where the children felt I should act as the teacher, for instance whether they could change reading books, or requiring intervention with minor complaints about behavior from their peers, I would again refer them to the class teacher. (That is not to say that I did not intervene if children were causing serious disruption or physically fighting with other children but punishment for these offenses was given out by their teachers.) In this way, in the classroom context, I took on the role of least-teacher. As time went on, requests for "teacherly" acts lessened to the extent that I was no longer viewed as a "proper teacher." This was illustrated when I met one child, Manjid, playing in the street with her older brother who was at the school and her cousin who attended another school. Having stopped and chatted for a while, as I walked away I heard Manjid's cousin ask who I was. Her brother said I was her teacher, but Manjid replied "No. She's not my teacher, she comes in and talks to us and helps sometimes."

Adoption of the least-teacher role occurred in a classroom or an adult constructed learning context. In areas such as the playground or during free play activities my role changed from least-teacher, to least-adult, particularly at lunch-time, when I often went outside to talk with the children (their class teachers never went into the playground during lunch-time). Not wanting to be seen as more authoritative than the dinner supervisors who were on duty I employed similar strategies of deferral as mentioned above. As least-adult I joined in activities and games with the children, often by invitation, rather than standing on the outside and looking in. I have sat in the cushioned reading corner listening to children telling me stories, joined in "let's pretend" activities in the home corner or shop, participated in board games on the mat, built lego houses, threaded bead necklaces, been involved in "follow-my-leader" games in the playground, asked to adjudicate in races, and played clapping and rhyme games. Through this sort of activity I was able to talk with children on their level and on their territory. Like Mandell (1988), this enabled me to become accustomed to the language of the children and some of the rituals and rules in their own world beyond that of the classroom.

GAINING ACCESS

Negotiating access into an institution or school is a common problem in ethnography. In many ethnographic accounts the issue of access is often limited to discussions of ways of approaching institutions and teachers. Less consideration is given to access into pupil groups. Corsaro (1981) talks about the adult carers in his research as "gatekeepers," adults who had varying control over access to children's activities. Yet, as Mandell points out:

> So often it is assumed that if supervisors of children admit adult researchers into sites to observe children, then gatekeeping problems are resolved. This misconception stems from adult assumptions that children themselves are not a gatekeeping group, and that the usual unobtrusive role of adult researchers does not necessitate research bargaining with children. The least-adult role demands entry into children's perspectives, and thus necessitates negotiating an acceptable participant-observer role with children (1988, p. 441).

I found with the children of my own research that it was important for me to negotiate access with them rather than assuming that they would readily talk to me. I did this by informing the children about the research and developing a rapport.

Openness of the Researcher

When research involves adults, frequently the researcher will present some account of the project, its aims, what exactly the researcher will require and what will be required of the researched. The openness of the researcher in these instances can prove an important step in developing access. It may help to allay suspicion, which appears to have increased in recent years, about the researcher's motives and intentions, particularly in a school environment. Similarly, informing children about the aims of a project may also ease their fears regarding the strange person who keeps asking questions. How much detail of a project is given may depend on the age of the children. Some researchers have talked to children in terms they may better understand using concepts such as going to college, having to do work for homework, or in order to write a book (Fine and Glassner 1979). Corsaro (1981) responded to questions about what he was doing by the kindergarten children he studied, by simply stating he was "watching." There is of course a danger of patronizing children, by thinking they would not understand the aims of the research. When asked by the children at the start of the project what I was doing I would comment that I wanted to find out what children do at, and think about school. This was met with various responses from the children. Some accepted my explanation and commented straight away that they either liked or disliked school. One child commented that she thought it odd I was researching this because I should have been aware of what children did, as "didn't you used to be a child?" As the project progressed the children became more intrigued by my continuing presence in their classroom. Subsequently my explanations of what I was doing became more detailed and I introduced the concept of research, comparing it to some of the research activities that the children did at school. One child's response to this was to proffer some questions she thought I might wish to ask other children about, unfortunately this incident occurred close to the completion of the data collection stage and I was unable to follow up this potential line of investigation.

Rapport

Developing trust or rapport with subjects is often considered a prime way of gaining access to information which may otherwise be hidden from the researcher, particularly with children (Corsaro 1981; Fine and Glassner 1979; Mandell 1988). With adults the researcher may employ particular methods to get closer to their subjects, approaching initial meetings in a low-key way, finding mutual topics of interest and building up trust between the researcher and the subjects before approaching perhaps delicate issues (Woods 1986). In the same way it is necessary to build up rapport with children in order to elicit information from them. Pryor (1995) achieved this by being open to interaction with the children in his research, talking with them about subjects they initiated as well as those emanating from his research. Mandell similarly felt the need to be open to children's conversations, and to make them aware that she took them seriously:

> By perching on the edge of a sandbox, swinging beside children, or sitting on the climbers, I was invading the children's territory. This seemed different from children's regular experience of adults in those centres, but within the realm of normal adult behaviour. But by making myself continually available to the children for interaction (Cook-Gumpertz and Corsaro 1977) and by actually participating in the children's activities in childlike ways, I clearly distinguished myself from marginal or reactive observers. Children's initial responses to being taken as serious and worthy playmates were ones of joy and incredulity (1988, p. 443).

Within my own research, taking children's views seriously was an important part of gaining their trust and developing a rapport with them. It was particularly important as many of the children were learning English as an additional language. Trying to understand their views about school meant that the children needed to feel comfortable with me when I was inquiring about aspects which might have been culturally sensitive. This trust was built up over time, to a point where the children came to me rather than me going to them. With some children the development of trust took longer than with others, for instance one particular child was very unwilling to talk to me, and rarely came to me. I was careful to avoid urging him to talk, but by the latter stages of my research he began to show a curiosity in what I was doing with other children, and even came voluntarily to read to me. Allowing the children their own space shows respect, and providing opportunities for children to initiate conversations is in line with the concept of acting as a least-teacher or least-adult, in that adults and teachers need not be the main initiators of talk with children. Taking a genuine interest in what children want to say reverses the traditional role, particularly in the classroom of the teacher (or adult) as the main holder of knowledge. Furthermore I was open to personal questions the children asked me and told them my first name, where I lived, and what I did when I was not at school. In one sense the fact that the children asked such questions of me was perhaps an indication of how far from the teacher role they viewed me. The same questions were not asked of their teachers and personal information was usually disclosed by their teachers as anecdotal stories which related to lessons.

TALKING WITH YOUNG CHILDREN

In much ethnographic research, elicitation of views from subjects is often gained through the use of interview. Interviews range from unstructured to structured, and in most cases with adults, interviews are carried out on a one to one basis. Ball (1983) notes some of the linguistic skills that might be required of the interviewee. "The interviewee is asked to elaborate, illustrate, reiterate, define, summarize, exemplify, and confirm matters in his talk in ways that would be unacceptable in other talk situations" (p. 94). Woods (1986) also lists ways in which the interviewer might assist the interviewee once they have begun their discussion. These methods include checking on contradictions, playing "devil's advocate," searching for opinion, or requiring further clarification. Such "adult" techniques demand a great amount of linguistic skill and maturity which may not be suitable with young children. The following section examines my own approach to interviewing the children in this research.

Interview Setting

When interviewing the adults involved in my research, which included both teachers and parents, I would ask first if they would like to talk to me. Some said yes and others no. When I received a negative reply I chose not to pursue the potential interviewee. When the adult responded positively I would ask them to set a convenient place, time and date. I approached each interview in a different way depending on whom I was talking to. I tailored my dress to suit the interviewee, some interviews were conducted in a more serious way than others, and I frequently went with the headteacher for a cigarette in the caretaker's room when I interviewed her. All of this was done in order to achieve a sense of relaxation between myself and the interviewee, in the hope of creating a comfortable atmosphere for conversation (see also Measor's 1985 account of her interviewing approach). During my first interviews with the children far less consideration was shown towards them, partly because in essence they were a captive audience. In the initial stages of the project children were usually chosen for me by the class teacher because they had completed their work, and so it was convenient for them to do something else. On these occasions the date, time and place of interview was dictated by the researcher (and teacher) and not by the interviewee. Control was immediately placed in my hands and though the children were happy to comply, as the research progressed I began to ask the children directly if they wanted to talk to me, respecting the fact that they may not have wished to. Yet I still had control over what was to be talked about in these situations and in some cases the children picked up on this very quickly, as the following interview indicates:

> Me: Now, what I've been asking children about is, I don't think you're going to get
>   any closer (*to Sabida, trying to get as close as possible to me*)
> Sabida: I am.
> Me: Okay, what I've been asking everybody about...
> Sabida: What?
> Me: Is, what, what (*Sabida still trying to find a comfortable place*)
> Fouzia: Miss, can we choose what we like best in school?
> Me: Yeah, what, what are you good at in school?

In this particular situation I had been trying to ascertain from the children which areas of school work they thought they were good at. I had asked Fouzia and Sabida if they would like to come and talk with me and we went into an empty classroom. We sat on comfortable chairs all of the same height and I began my introduction to the subject. Fouzia had overheard me talking to other children about this subject earlier in the day and so immediately knew what information I was after. In part Fouzia initiates the conversation, this was something she was happy to talk about, it was an acceptable subject. Interestingly, the children prolonged this conversation on a number of occasions when I made indications that we should go back to class by protesting that they had more to tell me. Part of their willingness to continue may have been due to the fact that the children were in a situation where they had my undivided attention. One of the class teachers had commented how good it was for the children to have an opportunity to speak with an adult for longer periods of time. Robinson (1994) points out that teachers often feel guilty about not having enough time to give attention to individuals. An additional aspect which may have influenced the children wanting to remain was that this classroom had more toys in it for them to play with. Yet the children did have more information to share with me, and the conversation we had concentrated not only on what I wanted to talk about, but also subjects they initiated such as talking about friends and the Mosque school they attended in the evening.

The above was an example of a loosely structured interview; however, I frequently talked with the children in ad hoc situations, for example when two of the children had been racing outside in the playground, they came over to tell me about how they had both cheated in their race. This provided an opportunity to talk about cheating in other situations such as in class when they were working. Yet finding the right setting to talk with children was only part of the problem solved, the way in which interviews and conversations were structured were of equal significance.

Discourse Strategies

Davies (1982) noted how important it can be in child interviews not to approach subjects in a way which children perceive to be in lesson mode. In her interview-based study of 10-11 year old Australian children she illustrates the problems which can occur when children identify with this form of questioning as they attempt to "figure out what [they] *should* say and do in relation to adults" (p. 33). The danger is that the children identify the researcher as just another teacher, and therefore any information elicited from such interview situations will be limited, and could be suspect (Tammivaara and Enright 1986). A further problem with this approach is that the answers given can also be very short, and it can become difficult to gain any elaboration, as I found in some situations:

> Me: What sort of things do you think you're good at at school?
> Azmat: Maths.
> Me: Maths....Are you good at reading?
> Azmat: Yeah.
> Me: What other things are you good at?
> Azmat: Working.
> Me: What sort of things do you think you don't do very well?
> Azmat: Em, I don't know....I'm a little bit bad at listening.

It was not surprising that Azmat (aged six years) gave only one word answers in this situation. Young children are more likely to give "local" answers to questions (Robinson 1994), owing to far more concrete thinking strategies. The questions asked are relatively closed, abstract in nature and are obviously set around my agenda rather than Azmat's. The interview setting may also have had an influence on Azmat's responses as we were actually sitting in class at her work table when we had this conversation. By simply moving to another area a more valuable conversation developed in a later discussion. Although still within the classroom, Azmat and I were sitting together in the reading corner, rather than at a class table. Azmat read the story of Hansel and Gretel to me and we talked about the story afterwards, particularly about the feelings of the step-mother toward the children. The following conversation took place:

Me: Why do you think the step-mother wanted them to leave?

Azmat: 'Cos she's a step-mother.

Me: Oh! Is that what step mothers do?

Azmat: They do bad.

Me: Sorry?

Azmat: They do bad.

Me: They're bad. Are all step-mothers bad do you think?

Azmat: Yes.

Me: Is it just the step-mothers in stories that are bad, or is it real step-mothers as well?

Azmat: Real step-mothers too.

Me: Too? Why do you think that?

Azmat: 'Cos it's in films and stories.

Me: 'Cos it's in all the stories? What about step-dads? Do you think step-dads are bad?

Azmat: Dun know?

Me: Have you heard any stories with step-dads in?

Azmat: No.

Me: Just with step-mothers in. So which other stories have you heard with step-mothers in?

Azmat: This (*Hansel and Gretel*) and that's all. (*Azmat went off to find another book with a step-mother in but couldn't locate one*)

Although Azmat's responses are still short, she volunteers more information than in the previous transcript. She brings her own opinion to the conversation and needs to provide explanations for her views. She shows more interest in this conversation than the previous one, indicated by her eagerness to find another story which might prove her point. In this situation Azmat had been the one who had asked if I wanted to listen to her tell a story. She initiated the interaction and I was on her territory, as the reading corner was only ever used by the children. Azmat had chosen the time, the place, the setting and the subject of our conversation.

Shared Mediums

The previous example also shows how important materials are to conversation with young children. In the first example of Azmat, had I used some of her work as a focus for the conversation then perhaps this may have yielded more information. Providing a physical "*something*" to talk about in concrete terms, such as the *Hansel and Gretel* story book, I found to be a useful way of eliciting information. In an initial interview with a group of four children in their first term of school I used the book *Starting School*, by Althea, in order to generate conversation. Although in many ways I had been trying to avoid behaving as a teacher, the use of a story book to generate talk could be described as a popular teaching technique. However my objectives in this matter were not the same as those of a teacher. I used the story book approach because it was an activity the children were familiar with, but worked with only four children at a time, rather than a whole class, and in a separate area outside the classroom, in a comfortable reading corner. My use of books was not to develop the children's understanding of a particular subject or conceptual area, as might be the intention of a teacher, but merely as a prompt to ask children about their experiences of starting school. There were no requests for "hands up," though I made a point of asking each child the same questions. Additionally, the book provided some focus for the children, though they frequently wandered off the subject and in these situations my first reaction was to employ teacher/adult strategies to bring the children back to the point, though as time progressed I tried hard to avoid this. Woods (1986) terms this impulse to act as an adult or teacher in such circumstances as "reversion." The danger with such situations is that the researcher invokes the power difference between themselves and the children, and the children revert to pupil role, delivering answers which they think the researcher might want.

As my research continued I experimented with other materials to encourage the children to talk. Asking children to draw while they were being interviewed enabled some of the children to provide visual explanations of what they were telling me. I have a number of illustrations from the children of their families, best friends, teachers, the mosque and the temple, and samples of Urdu and Panjabi writing. I also used photographs to develop talk, some of the children in class and in the playground, others being pictures of children in other schools. Using these I would ask the children what they thought was happening in the photos and then to describe their own experiences of the same phenomena. For example a picture of a child crying in the playground led to discussions about children being hurt during playtime, discipline, rough games, gender differences and the child culture outside the classroom. I would also talk with the children while they were playing or working, asking for explanations of what they were doing. All of these strategies helped to build up a detailed account of the children's understandings and experiences of school.

Having discussed some of the interview strategies I used in my research I examine now the issues relating to the research of ethnic-minority children.

RESEARCHING ETHNIC-MINORITY CHILDREN

An important feature of my research project was the fact that many of the children were bilingual/bicultural which required particular consideration. Mandell (1988) indicated how important it was in her study to become attuned to the language that the young children used. She found that many of the two-and three year-olds she was studying did not enunciate in clear, adult ways, and as such she frequently needed to ask children to repeat themselves, which meant a disruption in the flow of interaction. One method of overcoming this which Mandell relied on was to note the non-verbal clues linked to the children's communication. Similarly I needed to rely heavily on non-verbal clues when talking with some of the children, as the following example illustrates. During a discussion with a group of four children using the story book approach mentioned earlier, we had been talking about the children's experiences when they first began school. One of the pictures in the book showed some children writing and I asked Simera (aged five years) if she enjoyed writing.

> Me: What about you Simera, do you like to do your writing?
> Simera: Em, three and a four and a five and a six (*drawing the numbers in the air*) and a this one and help, and a this and this and this and this and this and this ("*HELP" is one of the first words from the reading scheme, Simera also began to point to the lines of writing in the book*).
> Me: That's right, this is the writing isn't it, this is the writing on this book. (*me, pointing to the writing in the book also*).

Without the accompanying description of what Simera was doing while talking this piece of transcript would mean very little. Simera was able to show me what she had learned about writing in school both verbally and physically. Accompanying this visual display, my own knowledge, through observation in the classroom of the activities that the children did, allowed Simera and I to come to a shared meaning. In initial reading development at the research school, one of the techniques of the teachers was to ask children to point to writing or words in the books. Simera used this technique to show what she knew about writing. Additionally, the children were at times asked to draw in the air letters or numbers which were the focus of the sessions.

Where children had difficulty in expressing themselves in English patience was needed to understand what was said. Asria during her first year at school on occasions relied on the bilingual non-teaching assistant in class to help her communicate with her teacher. In her second year she relied more heavily on Axia, a close friend both in and out of school. When interviewing Asria I took advantage of this partnership and always talked with the two girls together. The following transcript shows how the two girls worked together.

> Asria: I'm good at, er Pakistan, always.
> Axia: In Pakistan.
> Me: You're good at Pakistan?
> Asria: Very, very good.
> Me: Did you go to school in Pakistan?
> Asria: Naa, naa.
> Axia: I'm not gonna go school then, because the people hurt them, in the school.
> Asria: The have, the have, the have something that hit it.
> Axia: Smacking.
> Me: They smack the children at school do they?
> Both: Yeah, yeah.
> Axia: If they be naughty.

Asria: No, if they does a (bab), eh yeah, if they does say a (bab) yeah.
Axia: If they say something wrong, yeah (*said to me*). You have to write it in English
or Pakistani (*said to Asria*).
Asria: Pakistani.
Axia: You have to write it in Pakistani or you have to draw in Pakistani.
(*Axia and Asria then start speaking to one another in Panjabi, Asria, explaining
something to Axia, which she relates to me.*)
Axia: Sometimes they speak and they writing in English, and sometimes they some of
them write in Pakistani.
(*Asria explaining more to Axia*)
Axia: But me I'm not, I'm not going to school then, because the teachers hurt them and
if you go Mosque they hit you hard, hard ways.

In this instance Asria and Axia worked together to explain something of which I
had no knowledge. Unlike the earlier extract with Simera, I had no prior knowledge of the children's experiences of school in Pakistan or at the Mosque.
Together, they were able to explain, Asria relying on Axia for translation, and
Axia checking her data with Asria. Had I not been in a position where I was talking with both girls then it may have been more difficult for us to come to any
shared understanding.

An advantage of undertaking long term research with bilingual children is that
one is able to get used to the way some children speak English. While the majority
of the children involved in the research spoke English with a high degree of flu-
ency, a few, such as Simera and Asria, were less fluent. Having spent a considerable amount of time in the classroom and playground talking with the children, it
became easier to understand what they were saying. I relied on the children's
knowledge of English, as I do not speak any of the children's first languages.
Being able to communicate with the children in their first language would have
been be an immense advantage in research of this nature. Yet even had I been fluent in Panjabi, I am neither Asian or Muslim as many of the children of this
research were. There are many who would question the validity of my approach
based on the fact that I am a white researcher, researching ethnic minorities.
Troyna and Carrington (1993), for example, argue:

First that white researchers cannot elicit meaningful data from black respondents because of
status and power differences between them…a second and more significant criticism is based
on the way in which the data elicited from black respondents are generally interpreted by white
researchers…the third and final element of this critique questions the white researcher's self
appointed role as ombudsman (pp. 107-108).

Earlier I examined the issues associated with power differences between the adult
and child, and illustrated some of the methods I employed which could serve to
lessen these. These same methods were also adopted with a view to lessening the
ethnic power differences. With regard to the interpretation of data I accept Troyna
and Carrington's argument that researchers from similar cultural backgrounds as

participants would have a much greater ability to collect and interpret data, but I feel that in some instances where the researcher is not of the same background as the researched then there can be advantage in the situation. Had I been of the same cultural background as the children in the last example, they may have assumed certain taken for granted knowledge on my part. In the example above the children needed to be explicit when talking about the Mosque school because they realized I knew nothing of this situation. It could be argued that studying groups of which one is not a member allows one to stand back from the culture in order to make the situation "anthropologically strange" (Woods 1986), one of the main functions of ethnographic research.

Yet within this situation the researcher must remain constantly critical of their methodology and interpretation of data. Sensitivity and awareness of linguistic and cultural differences is paramount within any research context or data will inevitably be misinterpreted. Tammivaara and Enright (1986) point to the fact that children, by the very fact of who they are, automatically live in two worlds, the world of children and the world of adults. When children attend school, they have to move in and out of these two worlds at an amazing speed, from interaction with peers to interaction with adults. For children who are bilingual/bicultural, they have to negotiate four worlds, that of the native (home) child culture, the native (home) adult culture, the second child culture and the second adult culture.

> For ethnographers studying linguistic minority children, it is necessary to avoid "adult-centrism" *and* "ethnocentrism'; to suspend age-related assumptions *and* culturally related assumptions; to ask themselves to participate in a fluid and confusing research milieu few would dare to hazard (Tammivaara and Enright 1986, p. 235).

Where the concept of childhood in the native culture differs significantly from that of the second child culture, researchers need to suspend their adult-centrism and ethnocentrism as the individualistic educationalist ideals of western models of family and childhood may run counter to some non-western cultures. The Chinese for example, view children's learning as contingent upon adult supervision and guidance (Knupfer 1996). Gregory (1994) found that in much of the research into the literate practices of different ethnic and social groups living side-by-side in the United States, the minority cultures viewed literacy in a utilitarian way rather than as a means of deriving pleasure, as is the dominant western view. Much of the "cult of childhood" (James and Prout 1990), can be ascribed to the view of childhood from a middle-class, westernized perspective (Knupfer 1996). This view has become prevalent also in many international associations concerned with children's "rights" and decisions are made on the basis of this one cultural blue-print (Boyden 1990). Knupfer (1996) outlines an additional dilemma faced by the researcher when he or she is perceived as a cultural model for both children and parents. In this sense it is not only that the researcher might be viewing the situation from a particular point of view, but their very presence might be violating cultural norms and expectations. In such situations the researcher might prefer a much more detached role as observer, though I would argue such a role might lead to misinterpretations of situations. What is needed is a critical awareness of the effect of the researcher on such situations (Haw 1996).

CONCLUSION

Children's worlds and their understanding of those worlds are an important area for research. It is noticeable that there are few ethnographic research accounts of young children, and even fewer of bilingual/bicultural young children (Knupfer 1996). Some of the reasons for this have been outlined in this paper. The adoption of an acceptable role in the research is vital if the researcher aims to avoid adult-centrism in situations of research into children's worlds. Tammivaara and Enright (1986) liken such researchers to tourists:

> ...invading the shores of exotic cultures only to find them quaint but clearly inferior. Ethnographers who insist on visiting and studying children from the rigid perspective of adulthood will in the end understand the reality of childhood no better than tourists who visit another land and do their best to bring their "home" with them. *Respect* for children and their knowledge about themselves, as well as the same willingness to suspend [adult] judgement and perspective in talking with *children* as in talking with adults are key components of the successful ethnographer's interviews and participant observations (p. 234).

Furthermore, I have argued that though in many situations researchers of similar cultural backgrounds to the participants may be best placed to understand and interpret data, where this is not the situation then the researcher should be aware of the limitations of their research, make those limitations explicit and be critical of their methodology, data and interpretation of that data.

Additionally I feel that researchers need to take risks, develop their sense of creativity and experimentation regarding role and methods of data collection if we wish truly to explore and understand the world of children. Part of that risk is to create spaces within research in which the voice of the child is also represented, as has been achieved in many ethnographic researches of adult experiences. As a researcher I do not want to speak for them, as I have found that they are capable of doing so themselves in a way which has a greater sense of authenticity. My role then is to provide opportunities through my methodology for the children of this research project to find appropriate ways in which to express themselves and importantly to reflect their expression through any subsequent reporting of the project. It seems a difficult task when many research reports which claim to reflect what occurs in the world of children appear to discount their perspectives in favour of adults. If the child's voice is omitted, how then can we say that what we write reflects their world?

REFERENCES

Ball, S. J. 1983. "Initial Encounters in the Classroom and the Process of Establishment." In *Pupil Strategies*, edited by P. Woods. London: Croom Helm.

Boyden, H. 1990. "Childhood and the Policy-Makers: A Comparative Perspective on the Globilization of Childhood." In *Constructing and Reconstructing Childhood: Contemporary Issues in the Sociological Study of Childhood*, edited by A. James and A. Prout. London: Falmer Press.

Burgess, R. G. 1983. *Experiencing Comprehensive Education: A Study of Bishop McGregor School.* London: Methuen.

Cook-Gumpertz, J., and W. Corsaro. 1977. "Social-Ecological Constraints on Children's Communicative Strategies." *Sociology* 11 (3): 411-434.

Corrigan, P. 1979. *Schooling the Smash Street Kids.* London: Macmillan.

Corsaro, W. A. 1981. "Entering the Child's World: Research Strategies for Field Entry and Data Collection in a Preschool Setting." In *Constructing and Reconstructing Childhood: Contemporary Issues in the Sociological Study of Childhood*, edited by J. Green and C. Wallett. Norwood, NJ: Ablex Press.

Davies, B. 1982. *Life in the Classroom and Playground: The Accounts of Primary School Children.* London: Routledge and Kegan Paul.

Denzin, N. 1989. *Interpretive Interactionism.* London: Sage.

Fine, G., and B. Glassner. 1979. "Participant Observation with Children." *Urban Life* 8: 153-174.

Fine, G., and K. Sandstrom. 1988. "Knowing Children: Participant Observations with Minors." *Qualitative Research Methods* 15.

Geertz, C. 1973. "Thick Description: Towards an Interpretive Theory of Culture." In *The Interpretation of Cultures: Selective Essays by Clifford Geertz*, edited by C. Geertz. New York: Basic Books.

Gregory, E. 1994. "Cultural Assumptions and Early-Years' Pedagogy: The Effect of the Home Culture on Minority Children's Interpretation of Reading in School." *Language, Culture and Curriculum* 7 (2): 111-124.

Haw, K. F. 1996. "Exploring the Educational Experiences of Muslim Girls: Tales Told to Tourists—Should the White Researcher Stay at Home?" *British Educational Research Journal* 22 (3): 319-330.

James, A., and A. Prout. 1990. "Re-Presenting Childhood: Time and Transition in the Study of Childhood." In *Constructing and Reconstructing Childhood: Contemporary Issues in the Sociological Study of Childhood*, edited by A. James and A. Prout. London: Falmer Press.

King, R. 1984. "The Man in the Wendy House: Researching Infants' Schools." In *The Research Process in Educational Settings: Ten Case Studies*, edited by R.G. Burgess. London: The Falmer Press.

Knupfer, A.M. 1996. "Ethnographic Studies of Children: the Difficulties of Entry, Rapport, and Presentation of their Worlds." *Qualitative Studies in Education* 9 (2): 135-149.

Lacey, C. 1976. "Problems of Sociological Fieldwork: A Review of the Methodology of 'Hightown Grammar'." In *The Process of Schooling*, edited by M. Hammersley and P. Woods. London: Routledge and Kegan Paul.

Mandell, N. 1988. "The Least-Adult Role in Studying Children." *Journal of Contemporary Ethnography* 16 (4): 433-467.

Measor, L. 1985. "Interviewing in Ethnographic Research." In *Qualitative Methodology and the Study of Education*, edited by R. G. Burgess. Lewes: Falmer Press.

Parker, H. J. 1974. *View from the Boys.* Newton Abbot: David and Charles.

Pryor, J. 1995. "Hearing the Voice of Young Children: Problems and Possibilities." Paper given at British Educational Research Association, September.

Robinson, H. A. 1994. *The Ethnography of Empowerment: The Transformative Power of Classroom Interaction.* London: Falmer Press.

Tammivaara, J., and D.S. Enright. 1986. "On Eliciting Information: Dialogues with Child Informants." *Anthropology and Education* 17: 218-238.

Troyna, B., with B. Carrington. 1993. "Whose Side Are We On? Ethical Dilemmas in Research on Race and Education." In *Racism and Education: Research Perspectives*, edited by B. Troyna. Buckingham: Open University Press.

Woods, P. 1986. *Inside Schools: Ethnography in Educational Research.* New York and London: Routledge and Kegan Paul.

Woods, P. 1996. *Educational Research in Action: Study Guide, E835.* Buckingham: The Open University.

Woods, P., M. Boyle, and N. Hubbard. 1999. *Multicultural Children in the Early Years: Creative Teaching, Meaningful Learning.* Clevedon: Multilingual Matters.

IMAGE AS A SYMBOLIC GIFT

Angela Xavier de Brito and Ana Vasquez

This paper will try to show the advantages and disadvantages of the use of a video-camera in the ethnographic observations we have been developing since the 1980s. The idea that the research process is underlined by a permanent process of negotiation made us decide to analyze it from the point of view of the theory inspired by Mauss's "Essay on the Gift" (1950). It shows the progressive establishment of a relationship of trust between the researcher and his or her subjects is constructed within the broader framework of an exchange system, a complex system where the circulation of symbolic gifts contributes in a decisive way to the quality of the data collected and to the pertinence of their analysis. To demonstrate this point, we will analyze the multilevel negotiations which took place in the context of observations we made over two years—with the help of two video-cameras—in two high schools (in Paris and its near suburbs).

First, we intend to emphasize the complexity of the negotiations involved in gaining permission to observe and to film each of the actors (administrators, teachers and pupils). Second, we show how the particular interactions with teachers—using rushes and short research films—helped us establish relationships based on trust. We were thus able to discuss teachers' practices with them and also understand the complexity of their pedagogic choices. Finally, the dynamics of this research helped us examine in depth some concepts that have lately been

Studies in Educational Ethnography, Volume 2, pages 109-125.
ISBN: 0-7623-0563-0

receiving a great deal of attention from the media in France, such as "culture," "original culture," and "cultural identity."

ON MAUSS'S "ESSAY ON THE GIFT"

According to Mauss, in a great number of primitive civilizations exchanges and contracts took the form of gifts, in theory voluntary, but in fact obliged to be given and returned. The voluntary and free character of these gifts is their most important feature—even when, in the gesture that accompanies the transaction, there is nothing but empty formality and the action is motivated by obligation and economic interest. Various features highlight the systematic character of the gift:

1. Three obligations structure the offering of the gift: the obligations to give, to receive and to repay. The obligation to give is the essence of the gift: if we do not give, we lose face. To refuse to give or to receive, to neglect to invite, is to declare war, as it means a refusal of alliance and of communion. But the object given must be acceptable to the recipient: that is why it must be shown before being given. The obligation to receive is equally compelling. We do not have the right to refuse a gift; the clans are not free not to demand hospitality, not to receive gifts, not to trade, not to contract alliances. To do this would be to show that one is afraid not to be able to repay: one loses face. The obligation to repay a gift is the logical counterpart of the first two: one accepts a gift because one will definitely make a return gift one day. The repaying of a gift does not have to be immediate—it even requires a certain amount of time. It is, however, imperative both that it is repaid and that this is done in a dignified way.

2. In primitive societies, it is groups—clans, tribes and families—that oblige each other, that exchange and make contracts, as they confront and oppose each other. Individuals take part in this process according to their social position and their social prestige, but in a collective spirit.

3. Groups exchange not only goods, riches, or objects of economic value but, even more, forms of politeness, feasts, rites, military services, women, children, dances, festivities and so on. The market is transitory and the circulation of riches is only one of the terms of a broader and more permanent contract.

4. Gifts are made in a voluntary way, presented without stipulations. But, in the long term, it is rigorously obligatory to give and return gifts, under the threat of a private or a public war.

5. One of the most important mechanisms of these exchanges is, of course, that a person is compelled to repay a gift offered, in a spirit of emulation that requires that the clinching gift—the one that seals the transaction—be always superior to the opening gift—the one that begins the transaction. These principal gifts are surrounded by all sorts

of intermediate presents. In the end, it is the mechanism of obligation, and of obligation by exchange of objects, that is at stake.

6. The gift is not inert: even after being released by the giver, it retains something of his or her person. That is why a tie established through material objects is a linking of souls: to give someone something is to give him or her a part of oneself, and accepting something from someone is to accept a part of his or her essence, or "soul." If people give and return things, they are giving and returning respect to each other. We give ourselves when we give something and, if we give ourselves, it is because we owe ourselves and our possessions to others.

7. Two other notions must equally be emphasized: one is that of credit or term; the other, honor. Regarding credit, the nature of a gift is ultimately to oblige the recipient. The return gift, even in the form of a show of mutual respect, requires a certain delay. As for honor, the nature of prestige requires that we give without limits, without counting. It is necessary to spend all we have without reserve, sometimes to the point of destroying gifts in front of one's allies. Gift-giving and repaying is founded on a principle of antagonism and rivalry: everything is conceived of as a contest of riches, as if one were not willing to receive anything in return. Such trading is thus noble, full of etiquette and generosity.

8. Material objects possess a virtue, a magical force, which obliges them to circulate. One must not keep them for long; one must not be too slow or too reticent in passing them on. So, although one does actually possess the gift one receives, it is a particular kind of ownership: the gift is made only on the condition that it be transmitted to, or used on behalf of, a third person. Nevertheless, all these acts have multiple underlying motives such as competition, rivalry, display, or a quest for greatness and interest.

9. All social life is thus impregnated by this system of exchanges. There is a permanent round of giving and accepting, with social life sustained by a continual and manifold stream of gifts offered, received and repaid, out of obligation and interest, for greatness and for services, as a challenge or as a pawn.

10. This system of perpetual giving and taking (from clan to clan or from family to family) evolves towards a system where the individual gains power, though without arriving at an individual contract. In this context, the form of the gift counts as much as its value. It is something other than what is useful that circulates, because of the multiple ties which are formed from these relationships. The notions of market, sale or price are thus irrelevant, as the end result of this cycle is an abstract one, that of producing a friendly feeling between the persons involved.

Some authors think that Mauss's "Essay on the Gift," although based on an analysis of primitive societies, remains very up to date. Lévi-Strauss (1950, p. xxxiii), for one, says that it establishes the basis of "a modern theory of reciprocity" because of the relational character of symbolic thought.

> Exchange is a synthesis immediately given to, and by, symbolic thought which, in exchange as in any other form of communication, surmounts its inherent contradiction which seizes things as elements of a dialogue, simultaneously underlying the relationship between myself and the other, and destined by nature to go to and fro from one to the other. Whether these things belong to one or to the other represents a situation derived from the initial relational character (Lévi-Strauss 1950, p. xlvi).

More recently, Jacques Godbout and Alain Caillé (1991) go so far as to think that the gift is everywhere in modern society: they define the gift as "every exchange of goods and/or services between two persons made without a return guarantee, in order to create, nourish or recreate social links between them." That is why we must think about gift-giving not as a series of unilateral or discontinuous deeds, but as a relationship, a social tie, the social relation in its very essence. Gift-giving and repaying constitutes a system of social relations, which cannot be reduced to economic and/or power relations.

We believe that an ethnographic approach inspired by gift theory allows us to analyze social interaction in its complexity, as a "total social fact"—to employ Mauss's terminology. The gift exists in every kind of social institution, be it religious, juridical, economic, political, familial or aesthetic, allowing us to seize their historical, social and psychological dimensions. Mauss's "Essay on the Gift" emphasizes complexity when he suggests that we can find simultaneously in the gift generosity and selfishness, community and market laws. As we have said before, the things given symbolize the respect due to others. Moreover, his suggestion that all social relations must be civil has allowed us to found a research ethic, which guides the researcher's attitudes towards his or her peers and towards his or her research subject.

LESSONS FROM OUR EARLIER RESEARCH PRACTICE

Our earlier research practice was mostly done in the context of French and Spanish[1] primary schools. It was very close to classic ethnography: a long time spent in the field, an attempt to establish a "thick description" (Geertz 1990), the effort towards the recognition of the researcher as a good person (Foote-White 1943) and an attempt towards interdisciplinarity.[2] Our approach to educational institutions took into account the "school culture," that is to say, a specific structure of values and norms which included time and space (Vasquez and Xavier de Brito 1996), as well as specific power relations, interpersonal relations and everyday rituals (Erickson and Mohatt 1982; Hammersley 1990; Hammersley and

Atkinson 1983; Spindler and Spindler 1982; Woods 1986). According to Goffman (1973) and Devereux (1980), this institutional life shapes a specific idea of the Self, establishing a set of appropriate life goals and specific defense mechanisms. Moreover, the standardization of schooling has transformed schools into a powerful socialization universe (Chombart de Lauwe and Bellan 1976; Vasquez and Martinez 1996), where the new generations share similar experiences. Our approach also tries to take into account the complexity, imprecision and uncertainty of social reality (Morin 1990), to introduce a historical dimension (Julia 1995; Ludke 1994; Rockwell 1997) and to put into practice in the ethnographic analysis the multilevel approach proposed by Ogbu (1981).

As for research methodology, experience showed us that classic ethnographic procedures such as taking exhaustive notes did not produce the information we needed to reconstruct the atmosphere of the institution and the dynamics of the actors in action. Much precious information (gestures, expressions, tensions, colors, and so on) was thus lost. Members of the research team[3] who were not present at the observation site could not form a precise idea of the context and meaning of the different interactions. Moreover, teachers often did not understand why we spent such long periods in their schools without producing at least "some useful conclusions" for their practice. The academic papers we produced from the research were clearly of little practical use to them. Not only was our written language too distant from that of teachers, but the teachers often admitted not having the time to read papers, which some of them considering boring. Besides, as we did not want to be seen as if we were "judging" the teachers, we tried to avoid criticism when discussing their practice—which may not have been the right choice, as we then seemed to be neither clear nor sufficiently comprehensive enough in commenting on their work. So, at first, it was above all the issue of communication—with teachers, with our research fellows and also with students—that made us explore the methodological possibilities of the use of a video-camera in our research work.

THE SIGNIFICANCE OF PRELIMINARY NEGOTIATIONS

We began this new research on high schools having decided not only to observe "everything that happens in a school-day" (Wilcox 1982), but also to record it thoroughly on film. We were not totally prepared, however, for the difficulties presented by the use of video-cameras in the context of schools: spatial problems, bureaucratic problems, participants associating us with journalists and problems arising from the imagination of the actors.

Filming conditions are far from ideal in this context: actions cannot be planned and some technical devices are precluded. If the mere presence of the researcher changes the observed situation, even more so does the conspicuous presence of a camera in a classroom. Our primary intention was not to disturb the interactions, but this of course meant that we could not move freely, or position the camera in the best spot. We were often limited to the teacher's discourse, as we could use only the camera's microphone. At other times, the unusual presence of a camera triggered curiosity but also rejection and fear. In addition, school spaces are not designed for filming, being sombre, narrow and over-crowded. These human and technical difficulties limited the practical possibilities open to us as well as hindering access to negotiations.

Administrative Negotiations

The first official contact established was with the principals and administrators of the schools concerned. Even in a school more open to research, the use of a camera arouses some suspicion. In using a camera we were likened to television journalists, whose reputation is to distort the reality of what they record. But the reaction was not the same in each school. In the suburban school, we had to promise from the outset not to show on television the films we made. This was not so in the Parisian school, where the principal was not worried by this aspect of the filming but insisted, however, on written permission to film from the Ministry of Education (which never came, as the negotiations had been made by telephone). Moreover, we knew from the start that many schools complained of some researchers who, after obtaining their data, never returned to the schools to communicate their results. We therefore introduced in our research project an undertaking to report back the results, not only in the form of a final film and a report, but also in intermediate research films which could serve as a starting point for discussion between the school actors and the researchers.

Negotiations with Actors

The use of the camera provoked different reactions from teachers and pupils, from curiosity to outright hostility. Pupils always asked us if we were filming for "Channel J," a popular television channel among young people. As for teachers, the elements which led them to give us access to their classroom were not always explicit. Some of them agreed immediately, without even reading the research project; some were happy to have access to material which might help them improve their pedagogic practice; others did not even want to discuss their refusal with us in person, transmitting it to us via the vice-principal. One of the teachers of the Parisian school refused access to her classroom on the grounds of her mistrust of television and of the use we were going to make of the images. It took her a whole year finally to accept the presence of the camera. Moreover, the school hierarchy made direct negotiations with pupils difficult. Teachers did not see any need to ask for pupils' permission to be filmed, perhaps because they thought that would put in question their authority in the classroom. They had already opened their classroom to us: on these grounds, they were reluctant to leave us alone with the children. This attitude did not surprise us much because, in our previous experience at the primary level, we had never seen the teachers requesting their pupils' agreement. A teacher's authority was such an obvious fact that no pupil could conceive of not accepting something the teachers had already agreed to. When we arrived in a primary school class (with the teacher's previous agreement), the teacher introduced us and we explained briefly what we were doing. Pupils very often asked questions about the project, showing curiosity rather than mistrust. Perhaps this previous experience distorted our view of the pupils' agreement; the fact is that we made several mistakes in this respect. In the first place, we neglected to negotiate with the pupils in some classrooms, and were clumsy in trying to circumvent the overt opposition or even the aggressive reactions of some suburban pupils. Interestingly, as we will discuss later, it was their reaction that pushed us to mount a short film about their classroom—our first return-gift to the gift of their image.

On the issue of parents' permission to film their children, the Parisian school suggested loosely that we should ask for it but, as they did not insist, neither did we. The relation between school and home is still not clear; in general, schools view with disfavor any intervention by parents in what they consider their sphere of authority. Moreover, we proposed to observe the whole school, and it would have been very hard to have the permission of all the children's parents. In this same school, however, the researcher had established a good relationship with the Parents Association and regularly attended their meetings. The president of this association, a psycho-sociologist, was quite interested in our work: no parent belonging to this association raised any objection concerning the filming of their children. Nevertheless, the researcher was aware that they were not necessarily representative of all the parents.

Things went differently in the suburban high school, where the research was based mainly on the observation of one teacher and her classes. On her first meeting with the principal, the researcher stated her need for the parents' agreement, as it was usual to do at the primary schools she had observed earlier. She obtained the written agreement of some, and at least no opposition from the others, within two weeks. She was also invited to a small meeting with the parents from one of the classes she was following, where the parents, mostly working class, were above all interested in their own child's school performance. Again, there was no opposition to the filming.

Negotiations about Showing the Films We Made

It was not just the school administrators who were suspicious of the use we were going to make of the images; some teachers also wondered about this. Perhaps this is somehow linked to the primitive belief which sees the capturing of the image by photograph or video-camera as stealing a part of oneself; as Tournier (1986) puts it, perhaps it was the fear of being ridiculed in front of others. But the teachers and administrators were distrustful not only of the outside public: there was also reticence about films being shown to the school's partners (such as the Parents Association) or even to the pupils in the same school. Some teachers preferred to show their images only to teacher friends. Nevertheless, they agreed to let them be shown to other teachers in general, or at academic meetings. According to Mauss (1950, p. 180), "the gift is only made under the condition that it will be used on behalf of another person, or transmitted to a third person, a faraway participant." In our case, this would mean that the film would be shown only to those with whom the persons filmed have some affinity, be it personal or professional. The researcher is thus seen as a mediator between the given thing (the biography, the everyday life and/or the image of the research subject) and the other, their brother, the one they want to reach. But most of these arguments remain unspoken and/or implicit.

Theoretical Elements for Discussion

Some researchers do not fully take into account the significance of the preliminary negotiations needed for entrance to the field. The use of the video-camera made us particularly aware of the significance of these negotiations for the research process and of their contribution to the quality of the data collected. According to Mauss, it is at this moment that the respective status of the participants is fixed and the positions and/or intentions of each person are made clear.

Negotiating with administrators to observe and to film is not enough in itself to conduct research. There is a concrete gift—the permission to enter the school and to observe the common spaces, such as the restaurant, the recreation court and the corridors—and a conditional gift—the permission to negotiate with the teachers access to their classrooms. On the researchers' side, only a conditional promise could be made, as the filming depended on the agreement of the teachers to open their classrooms. Thus, our gift depended on theirs. The real research link—the "clinching gift" (Mauss 1950, p. 184), the one that confirms and seals the transaction—begins with the negotiations to impose on the teachers the presence of a "stranger's eye" in a space they consider their own, and where any kind of evaluation is seen with distrust (Vasquez and Xavier de Brito 1993). Our practice shows that often the way to make teachers change their minds is to make our intentions clear by showing them what we are doing. In this sense, presenting the first rushes/short films to teachers and pupils was very useful in convincing them of the worth of our research practice.

FILMED MATERIAL AS GIFT

Our filmed production in this research consisted mainly of three types of films: (a) broad rushes, without editing; (b) short "cut-and-tape" research films edited by ourselves; and (c) a few broadcast films, quite hard to produce because they were expensive, we lacked either technical resources or knowledge to edit them ourselves and the administrative steps for receiving technical help were very long and complex.

It was almost by accident that we decided to show the first filmed images to our research subjects, before having the time and the money to edit our rushes properly. It took the hostile reactions of some suburb pupils to the filming activity to prompt Ana Vasquez finally to make a short research film with the few rushes we had of them—in order to show pupils themselves in action.[4] Before viewing the film, the pupils were quite anxious, as if their own image could deceive them, but they were also curious to see themselves through the eye of an external observer. In both high schools, the reaction to viewing the films was a mixture of excitement and amusement, which led us to film them seeing themselves. They asked to see the films again and again. In the suburban high school, it had a double effect: first, it served to seal a tacit agreement to continue the research and second, it created a sort of complicity between the pupils and the researcher, which could be felt afterwards, during the filmed interviews.

This first viewing session led teachers from the suburban school to demand also "to see what we were doing"—which we did, showing some of them rough rushes of their classrooms. These rushes—unfinished material, cheap and easy to prepare in a short time—had a certain impact on teachers, some even asking to see them again at home. We think this demand was twofold: there was a narcissistic motivation, as they wanted their family or friends to see them in their professional surroundings; but they also wanted to analyze our work in a freer way. These rushes opened to us the possibility of discussing the practice of some teachers without the difficulties we have already stated. They were also useful at academic and special training seminars,[5] where they helped us focus on particular aspects of the socialization process, classroom dynamics, or key incidents (Wilcox 1982). For instance, in the suburban high school, we proposed to one teacher we had been following that she analyze with us three key incidents we had observed and filmed. Her prompt acceptance led us to edit a first cut-and-tape version that we viewed together, and to discuss its contents with her, filming her reactions. A later version was then edited with her permission, introducing her comments, which opened the possibility of a freer discussion with her and her colleagues about their everyday practices, which often had to involve dealing with unexpected incidents—"our real problems," as they called them.

The dynamics of the research process at the Parisian high school were not the same (Xavier de Brito 1994). Seeing and analyzing the rushes at the regular meetings of our research team brought to our attention some contradictory aspects in the organization and use of classroom space, as well as of the school space as a whole, which seemed invisible to the institutional actors. Our question was, why could school actors not see that the mere disposition of tables could handicap their pedagogic style, or that corridors were the only real free space for pupils? We then sought institutional help to make a broadcast film on this subject (Xavier de Brito 1995). The film was shown at a teachers' informal meeting, where their enthusiasm and their excitement (even among those teachers who did not participate in the research) towards our findings surprised us. Unfortunately, the effort to edit a finished film made us lose a great deal of time, and we could not continue working with this group, as we had reached the end of the project.

WHAT CHANGED AND WHY?
AN ESSAY OF INTERPRETATION

By this time, it was quite evident that showing the films to the actors had an impact on their attitudes to our research and to ourselves. As stated above, our initial interpretation was that the pleasure of seeing themselves in action, or hearing/viewing themselves in the course of an interview, triggered a sort of narcissistic reaction. People rarely have the chance to see their own image in movement, particularly within a professional framework. Whatever the reason, something had happened that touched our own relationship with them as individual, autonomous actors.

We tried to understand this unexpected link of empathy, always from Mauss's standpoint. We found that, during ethnographic observation, we were surrounded by a context of exchanges very similar to those described by Malinowski (the *kula*) and by Mauss (the *potlatch*)[6] where the actors (the researcher included) were led to respect the triple social injunction of giving/receiving/rendering. This context of exchanges, which began with only a few teachers, extended itself with time to many other teachers and even to other school actors, as we became familiar with the institution, and as they learned to identify us. Moreover, our deep involvement in the research process, the making, projecting and discussing of the films, constituted a gift they recognized and accepted—wakening even the spirit of emulation of some teachers who did not want, at first, to participate and who felt afterwards bound to open their classroom to observation. As Mauss (1950) puts it, "the force of the gift obliges the other to give, to rivalize in generosity with the one who has already given."

In reality, the gift is a very difficult thing to interpret; it all depends on the dynamics of the exchange process. Does the meaning depend on the view of the one who gives or of the one who receives? For instance, the giver may think he/she is fulfilling someone's need out of generosity. But the receiver can see it as a return-gift which puts him/her out of debt; or as an excessive gift, which he/she feels unable to repay; or even, as an insufficient gift, not up to his/her expectations as a partner in the transactions. In our research, there was still a "silent mob" who saw us as strangers, even if carrying a camera singled us out in a certain way. "We fraternize but we remain strangers; we communicate and we are opposed...in a constant tournament," says Mauss (1950, p. 205). What are the limits of this acceptance? Would we be accepted only by some people and never by others? Is there a gender effect which makes our acceptance by the women teachers easier? The gift exchanges are simultaneously the fact of "clans and individuals" which, let us not forget, are "divided by ranking, gender and generation" (Mauss 1950, p. 164). But time has certainly broadened these limits. Which of our personal qualities and/or institutional characteristics could have contributed to it? Teachers changed, but so did the researchers. Goffman (1973) emphasizes the importance of what happens "behind the scene" of the ethnographic research and Foote-Whyte (1943) points out that the researcher's personality and "the personal relationship he/she could establish" in the field could be more important for his/her acceptance in the community he/she intends to study than any intellectual explanation. In any case, the degree of acceptance by each actor will always be different, according to the interplay of the researcher's methodological choices with the interests and needs of the actors observed, to our personal characteristics, and to the strategies each of us employs.

THE EPISTEMOLOGICAL ANALYSIS OF SOME CONCEPTS

The final part of this paper will center on how the use of the camera contributed to the examination of concepts such as "culture," "original culture," and "cultural identity." The central hypothesis of our research was that the "integration" of "foreign children" to a French school could be handicapped by the distance between their parents' original culture and the French one. The observations showed that the concept "French School" does not work as a homogeneous term, either in respect of those who work in them nor in respect of a supposed national cultural unity. Some teachers and administrators have lived and worked for several years in foreign countries and some of them, as well as many of the blue collar workers, come from old French colonies (Algeria, Antilles, and so forth). The filmed interviews with these persons helped us to understand their differences in relation to the school culture.

The expression "French culture" is rather a political term, reinforced by the media. In the same way, "integration" is a notion usually accepted and employed by teachers and school actors, in opposition to "assimilation" (which supposes the loss of original culture). The notion of "integration" is based on a largely diffused static concept of culture, as if migrants could keep intact forever the norms and values of their original culture. From our standpoint, culture is practised in everyday experience, and migrants succeed in using simultaneously two cultural codes and in selecting the norms and values appropriate to each circumstance, according to their needs and interests. Inevitably, the original culture changes throughout its practice in a different cultural context, especially when foreign workers have been out of their country of origin for a long time. The majority of the children observed were born in France; those born in a foreign country usually came to

France when they were very young. Thus, practically all the pupils had been socialized in France and their accents, when they spoke French, were very similar to those of French children from the same social class. The rushes, moreover, showed that there was certainly a visible difference in their skin color, which was "not seen" by the teachers, on the grounds of the Republican ideology of "equality," but which had a certain unconscious influence in their everyday practice. The rushes also made clear a relationship between color of skin and a certain kind of streaming.

Finally, the data analysis shows no particular differences in the behavior of children from foreign parents and children from French parents (and even grandparents). The actual differences—not necessarily between French and (supposed) foreign pupils—rather suggest the interplay of several complex causes.

A PROVISIONAL END: CONTRIBUTIONS, DISILLUSIONS AND NEW RESEARCH GROUNDS

Using Video: Limitations and Possibilities

The main goal of the researcher—the apprehension of social reality—certainly poses to him/her quite a few methodological and epistemological problems. Much has already been said about the illusion of obtaining "neutrality" and "objectivity" from the use of the classical repertoire of quantitative research instruments instead of the qualitative one—which implies the recognition of the influence of one's subjectivity in the research process. In the course of an interdisciplinary observation inspired by an ethnographic approach, the realization of our own limitations made us aware that it is impossible to seize everything that is going on in an ethnographic scene. Even if our field diary was very exhaustive, there is a limit to what we can note about an observed scene, and we are certainly bound to favor one aspect or another. If the observed phenomena are repetitive, we are given a chance to complete our notes, to reorient our eyes towards another aspect of the reality, to add some more details to our first perception. But this is not the case when we are observing interactions which are, by nature, ephemeral. So the question is, how can we absorb, in a single and unique observation, a maximum number of details, in order to arrive at a "thick description" of the scene observed? The awareness of these limits led us to try using another eye—the camera as a research instrument—to make up for the gaps in our observation. The mechanical eye indeed seems, at first sight, more trustworthy than the fallible human eye, as it can fix an image, permitting its reproduction as many times as we need, giving a new potency to the power of observation. But, like all research instruments, the camera also has its inconveniences, presenting some pitfalls of which we must be careful.

The first risk concerns the illusion of seizing "reality" in an "objective" and "neutral" way. For us, reality—like the research object—is something that is constructed by the researcher. In this context, the camera is just another instrument added to the repertoire of research instruments—no better or more reliable than any of them. We must never forget that, behind the camera, there is always the human eye and mind—carrying its subjective, cultural and ideological representations (Banks 1998). Our experience proves that the use of the camera to observe what we call, after Wilcox (1982), an ethnographic scene, does not escape the partiality of the observation, just as it does not prevent the influence of the researcher's subjectivity. There is an implicit bias in what we choose to focus on that is inspired by both our scientific and our cultural assumptions.

The second problem is more technical. Even a very elaborate camera cannot capture all that happens, even in the reduced space of a classroom. The use of technical devices is not enough: the wide-angle lens can distort the image as much as the use of a zoom, the first one giving us an overall perception with no relief, the latter catching some details with no direct relation to the whole of the scene. It would take so many cameras to capture all the angles of the space we want to observe that their introduction would completely disturb the observed scene. We can, nevertheless, establish a most accurate parallel between the construction of reality and the editing of a film: the researcher plays with the images in order to reconstruct his/her conception of what has happened while shooting the scene.

The third risk concerns the changes in attitude of the actors before the camera. As times goes by, some actors get more used than others to the presence of the camera: pupils, for instance, behaved more naturally, stopped making funny faces and grimaces. But there is always a kind of awareness of the camera's presence, which is revealed by participants" sly looks at it (and at us). The camera never became entirely "invisible" to some teachers: their body postures, the rigidity of their backs, betrayed the fear they had of seeing their actions recorded on film. So the presence of the camera changes the observed situation, but we cannot be certain that its influence is greater than that of the presence of the researcher herself.

In spite of all these problems, we agree with Harper's position (1998) that it is certainly possible, and even desirable, to develop a visual ethnography within a theoretical approach that takes into account the above-mentioned factors, illusions and nuances.

First, we certainly do not make a claim to objectivity. But surely the film can help us to broaden the scope of observation by capturing some broader phenomena and by allowing for the repetition *ad infinitum* of recorded images? Repeated analysis allows us, on one hand, to refine the researcher's perception and, on the other hand, to put emotions at a distance, when we are far from the actors (Peixoto 1993). It can also contribute to a reflection about our own way of looking at the research scene.

Second, the filmed documents are certainly helpful when we write about the research results. In the writing of our book, they allow us to review and compare the scenes, in order to avoid the tendency we felt in previous research to forget, confuse or distort observed facts.

Third, the filmed documents make the collaboration between researcher and the subjects studied more intense. As the latter can see themselves in action and analyze, together with the researcher, their own practices, the interpretation of their experience is more spontaneous, allowing the expression of emotions and feelings that otherwise might not come out.

Fourth, the use of rushes and cut-and-tape films has permitted us to create a forum for discussion with the actors themselves. The simultaneous analysis with the actors (especially teachers) of filmed classroom scenes generated some interesting dialogues, in particular when the observed teacher accepted the participation of some of his/her colleagues. Some of them suggested that we contact the education authorities to propose the use of this method in high schools. For many years, the Ministry of Education have promoted continuing education as a way to update teachers' methodological and pedagogic knowledge. Several programs have been organized but teachers saw them as too theoretical, certainly interesting from a general cultural point of view, but having little or no bearing on their everyday practice. Teachers found that our method—viewing oneself at work and analyzing that particular experience with an outsider (under the condition of mutual trust and empathy)—might allow them to overcome the limits of the continuing education programs and broaden their awareness of the limits and positive aspects of their practice.

The "School Ethnographer":
Video as a Tool for Professional Development

These remarks have helped us imagine a new job: the "school ethnographer," a person specially trained to observe and film the teachers' everyday practice and then to discuss it with them. The people most qualified to be those "school ethnographers" would be the teachers themselves; the fact that they have experienced the same problems facilitates empathy and a trusting relationship. A study of teachers' professional meetings, carried out with Spanish colleagues, showed that teachers prefer spontaneous informal meetings because they can choose the subject and the "significant others" (Mead 1934), that is to say, the persons whose opinions are important for them (Martinez and Vasquez 1988). Along the same lines, Hargreaves (1988) states that teachers create a sort of non-official collegiality with some of their trusted colleagues, in order to analyze the specific problems they come across in their everyday work. In fact, a "normal" teaching day can include many an unexpected event, from funny or doubtful jokes to personal stress or crisis, gang rivalries, physical or verbal aggression. Teachers have to deal with all these problems while at the same time carry on with their teaching (Woods 1990, 1993). School ethnographers could be very useful in improving both the pedagogical methods and the socialization process within schools, as their practice would be founded on Freire's assumption of self-awareness; by discussing their findings at length with people who share the same experiences teachers can arrive at a critical vision of their own practice (Freire 1996). The attempts we made in this direction were well accepted, but we have never been able to go beyond small experimental groups with a very short life span. A centralized education system, like the French one, does have some disadvantages, among which is its bureaucracy. It must be said that our attempts to introduce the idea of school ethnographers in French high schools have so far failed.

This research experience also led us to see that another of the major problems in educational research (in France) is a conceptual confusion arising from the acritical transformation of notions used by the media into sociological concepts, with no screening for media and political influences. The need for epistemological work which can examine in depth our "problématiques" and our tools of analysis is paramount. That is why the next stage of our ethnographic research will take the form of a more theoretical work.

ACKNOWLEDGMENTS

We would like to thank Simone Bateman and Jayme Porto Carreiro for their excellent help in the revision of this paper.

NOTES

1. Ana Vasquez had a research agreement with a research team from Barcelona (Spain), where we first saw the results of employing video-cameras in ethnographic research.

2. A. Vasquez is a psychologist/psychoanalyst and A. Xavier de Brito is a sociologist.

3. Our research team was composed of four persons. In addition to the authors of this paper it included Sandra Macedo and Ana Cristina Leonardos, both Brazilian sociologists working temporarily at our research center.

4. Vasquez, A., *Quand la quatrième T fait les maths, film SECAM, 12'*. This film was edited with the help of Ana's son and nephew, both video specialists.

5. We have shown them at doctoral seminars in Brazil, Chile, Spain, Switzerland and France and at quite a few scientific meetings, including the Summer University for teachers recently organized by the École Normale Supérieure de Fontenay-Saint Cloud (France).

6. According to Mauss, the *potlatch* is a system where clans and families from the American southwest exchange material and/or symbolical gifts, mixing the economic, juridic, politic and symbolic levels of society. The *kula*, as analyzed by Malinowski in his book *The Argonauts of the Western Pacific* (London, 1922, mentioned by Mauss 1950) is also, according to Mauss, "a kind of great potlatch, a sort of inter-tribal trade which extends to all the Trobriand Islands and their environments."

REFERENCES

Banks, M. 1998. "Visual Anthropology: Image, Object and Interpretation." In *Image-Based Research: A Sourcebook for Qualitative Researchers*, edited by J. Prosser. London: Falmer Press.

Chombart De Lauwe, M. J., and C. Bellan, C. 1976. *Enfants de l'image*. Paris: Payot.

Crozier, M., and E. Friedeberg. 1977. *L'acteur et le système*. Paris: Seuil.

Devereux, G. 1980. *De l'angoisse à la méthode dans les sciences du comportement*. Paris: Flammarion.

Erickson, F., and G. Mohatt. 1982. "Cultural Organization of Participation Structures in Two Class-Rooms of Indian Students." In *Doing the Ethnography of Schooling*, edited by G. Spindler and L. Spindler. New York: Holt, Rinehart and Winston.

Foote-Whyte, W. 1943. "On the Evolution of Street-Corner Society." In *Street Corner Society*, edited by W. Foote-Whyte. Chicago: University Of Chicago Press.

Freire, P. 1996. *Pedagogia da Autonomia. Saberes Necessários à Prática Educativa*. São Paulo: Paz e Terra.

Geertz, C. 1990. *La Interpretación de las Culturas*. Barcelona: Gedisa.

Godbout, J.T., and A. Caillé. 1991. "Le don existe-t-il (encore)?" *La Revue du Mauss* 11, 1st trimester, Nouvelle Série: 11-32.

Goffman, E. 1973. *La mise en scène de la vie quotidienne*. Paris: Minuit.

Hammersley, M. 1990. *Classroom Ethnography: Empirical and Methodological Essays*. Buckingham: Open University Press.

Hammersley, M. and P. Atkinson. 1983. *Ethnography: Principles in Practice*. London: Routledge.

Hargreaves, A. 1988. "Artificial Collegiality: A Sociological Analysis." Paper presented at the XX World Congress of the AIS, Madrid.

Harper, D. 1998. "An Argument for Visual Sociology." In *Image-Based Research: A Sourcebook for Qualitative Researchers*, edited by J. Prosser. London: Falmer Press.

Julia, D. 1995. "La culture scolaire comme objet historique." In *The Colonial Experience in Education: Historical Issues and Perspectives*, edited by Novoa, Depaepe and Joahnningmeier. Gent: Pedagogica Historica.

Lecompte, M. D. 1987. "Bias in the Biography: Bias and Subjectivity in Ethnographic Research." *Anthropology and Education Quarterly* 18: 43-53.

Lévi-Strauss, C. 1950. "Introduction à l'oeuvre de Marcel Mauss." In *Sociologie et Anthropologie*, edited by M. Mauss. Paris: PUF.

Ludke, A. 1994. *Histoire du Quotidien*. Paris: Maison des Sciences de l'homme.

Martinez, I., and A. Vasquez. 1988. "À quoi servent les réunions d'enseignants?" *Revue Internationale de Pédagogie*: 47-58.

Mauss, M. 1950. "Essai sur le don. Forme et raison de l'échange dans les sociétés archaïques." (1923-1924). In *Sociologie et Anthropologie*, edited by M. Mauss. Paris: PUF.

Mead, G. H. 1934. *Mind, Self, and Society*. Chicago: University of Chicago Press.

Morin, E. 1990. *Introduction à la pensée complexe*. Paris: Esf.

Ogbu, J.U. 1981. "School Ethnography: A Multilevel Approach." *Anthropology and Education Quarterly* 12 (1).

Peixoto, C. 1993. "À la rencontre du petit paradis: Une étude sur les rôles des espaces publics dans la sociabilité des retraités à Paris et à Rio de Janeiro." Ph.D. Thesis in social ethnology and anthropology. Paris, École des Hautes Études en Sciences Sociales.

Peshkin, A. 1982. "The Researcher and Subjectivity: Reflections on an Ethnography of School and Community." In *Doing the Ethnography of Schooling*, edited by G. Spindler and L. Spindler. New York: Holt, Rinehart and Winston.

Rockwell, E. 1997. "Ethnography and the Commitment to Public Schooling." In *Educational Qualitative Research in Latin America: The Struggle for a New Paradigm*, edited by K. Anderson and Montero-Sieburth. New York: Garland.

Spindler, G., and L. Spindler, L. (Eds) 1982. *Doing the Ethnography of Schooling*. New York: Holt, Rinehart and Winston.

Tournier, M. 1986. *La goutte d'or*. Paris: Folio.

Vasquez, A., and I. Martinez. 1996. *La socialisation à l'école: Une approche ethnographique*. Paris: PUF.

Vasquez, A., and A. Xavier de Brito. 1993. "L'oeil de l'étranger: La méthode ethnographique dans l'étude des processus de transculturation." In *L'individu et ses cultures, qu'est-ce que la recherche interculturelle?* Vol 1: 40-50, edited by F. Tanonand G. Vermes. Paris: L'Harmattan/Ecole Normale Supérieure De Fontenay-Saint Cloud.

Vasquez, A. and A. Xavier de Brito. 1996. "Il était une fois le temps et l'espace. Recherche ethnographique sur deux variables souvent oubliées à l'école." *L'Année de la Recherche en Sciences de l'éducation*: 169-184.

Wilcox, K. 1982. "Methods in Ethnography." In *Doing the Ethnography of Schooling*, edited by G. Spindler and L. Spindler. New York: Holt, Rinehart and Winston.

Woods, P. 1986. *Inside Schools: Ethnography in Educational Research*. London: Routledge.

———. 1990. *Teacher Skills and Strategies*. London: Falmer Press.

———. 1992. "Symbolic Interactionism: Theory and Method." In *The Handbook of Qualitatative Research in Education*, edited by M.D. Lecompte and J.P. Goetz. London: Academic Press.

———. 1993. *Critical Events in Teaching and Learning*. London: Falmer Press.

Woods, P., and P. Sikes. 1994. "The Use of Teacher Biographies in Professional Self-Development." In *Planning Continuing Practitioner Education*, edited by F. Todd. London: Croom Helm.

Xavier de Brito, A. 1994. "La relation de don dans la construction de l'objet de recherche." *Revue du Mauss,* 2nd semester: 160-175.

———. 1995. *Espaces Scolaires et Socialisation,* Film Pal/Secam, 17'. Post-Production M-F. Deligne: Maison des Sciences de l'Homme.

THE CR/EYE OF THE WITNESS

John F. Schostak

The desire of the witness is not merely to see but to see the truth and to be the bearer of a truth others can only accept. Does the power of ethnography only reside in the status provided by witnessing? Is it undermined by the power of authoring and hence stage-managed? And what happens at the edge of seeing and beyond the reach of the eye where neither consciousness nor rationality can provide desire with any certain object? And by adding the term "educational" to "ethnography," what does the witness desire then? Indeed, what is "educational" seeing and witnessing? I want to pursue these questions by considering the act of witnessing as it is mediated through symbolic structures that pre-exist any act of intersubjective witnessing. To do this I will introduce a little theory from the standpoint of Lacan and then follow it through with examples from interview- and document-based research into a city-based newspaper in Canada. The purpose is to develop an ethnography that is also educational. I locate education at the heart of freedom. Education, for me, is the process and perspective (acts of "seeing," witnessing) that one adopts in order to challenge that which is taken for granted, to "draw out" opportunities for exploration, to reflect upon experience, to generate and evaluate alternatives in order to develop oneself in relation to others and to inform decision making and action in ways that are creative and mutually enhancing. Education, like ethnography, can take place anywhere and at any time.

Studies in Educational Ethnography, Volume 2, pages 127-143.
Copyright © 1999 by JAI Press Inc.
ISBN: 0-7623-0563-0

Whether it is people in a pub or in a classroom disputing each other's claims, or working out possibilities for alternative ways of living, or whether it is a journalist attempting to discover the "truth" of something, or an ethnographer exploring different cultures, trying to understand and map the lives of different groups of people, there is the ever present possibility of education. Critical to each process is the act of "seeing" and in particular, "witnessing."

In this chapter, a newspaper editorial office serving a Canadian city is the concrete focus. The way in which the newspaper presents itself is as a kind of seeing agent, a witness, for the people of the city. The task is to represent the city to the readership. Its credibility depends upon the trust the readership give to the acts of witnessing claimed by the journalists. The texts that they produce result in what I argue to be a curriculum of the city which has at least the potential of being educational. Through their acts they can challenge the views of their readership, they can challenge the versions of "truth" proclaimed by governments, the rich and the powerful in all walks of life. Alternatively, a newspaper can be a powerful medium through which an illusory knowledge of the world is constructed. An ethnography of newspaper practices, if it is to be educational, does not merely describe and re-present the processes, culture and practices of the newsroom but does so in a manner that further explores and challenges the taken for granted—the sources of illusion through a form of "seeing" is constructed in the minds of a reader. In what way may ethnographic seeing challenge and serve as a counter to the construction of deceit and illusion?

ETHNOGRAPHIC SEEING

Ethnography is a much abused term, its meanings stretched to fit the occasion. I want to continue this tradition. Rather than immediately focusing upon any principle of "reflexivity" or of "naturalism" as being essential to the methodology of ethnography (Hammersley 1983, pp. 3-10)—both dubious terms—I intend to locate ethnography more squarely upon the "graph," the writing, the processes of signification through which an "ethnos," a "people" appears as the signified of the writing/signing/signifying process. For a newspaper these "people" can be conceived in various ways, as a "readership," as a "community," as "interest groups" and so on, or broadly as a symbolic facilitating myth. However, the newspaper cannot simply be described as the center—reflexive/reflective center—of the process through which the conception takes place. What is conceived/produced as "people" is not mainly done by a given agency but is rather more an unintended consequence. The "newspaper" is always ex-centric and the reflective and reflexive processes always de-routed and re-routed. Its function may be described as producing the illusion of a reflexive and reflective community through naturalistic news gathering, being faithful to the "facts" of the case. However, the illusion is just that. An ethnography which has the intention of naturalistically reflecting or *re*presenting this is missing the point—it is deceived. In the shift to the eye (from the rational Cartesian or scientific I) truth is no longer simply monogamously opposed (and thereby attached) to falsity but plays faithlessly through falsity and fiction with desire, pleasure, hate, fear in a realm as much of the aesthetic as of the rational. So what is the intention? As with many such questions without an answer, asking is the point.

Since ethnography is formed through writing, its methodology is already under sentence. Lacan wrote:

> Notre recherche nous a mené à ce point de reconnâitre que l'automatisme de répétition (*Wiederholungszwang*) prend son principe dans ce que nous avons appelé l'*insistance* de la chaîne signifiante. Cette notion elle-même, nous l'avons dégagée comme corrélative de l'*ex-sistence* (soit: de la place excentrique) où il nous faut situer le sujet de l'inconscient, si nous devons *prendre* au sérieux la découverte de Freud.

> *Our research has led us to this point of recognising that the automatism of repetition...takes its principle from what we have called the* insistence *of the signifying chain. We have drawn this very notion as a correlative of ex-istence (that is: excentrically located) where we have to situate the subject of the unconscious, if we should take Freud's discovery seriously* (Lacan 1966, p. 19).

There is an important methodological issue here for the writers of folkways. Signifiers, not signifieds,[1] insist from a point that is eccentric to the self defined through the agency of the ego, the conscious. The repetitive insistence of signifiers, the drum beat which exists outside, but by which we formulate meanings, frames the possibility of witnessing. That is to say witnessing, as distinct from the passive reception of sensual stimuli, is always to be mediated by a symbolic and cultural system.

As adults familiar with language not simply as a tool but as the breath of life, the very substance of identity, of selfhood, of reality we too readily overlook its strangeness until confronted by alien languages or unfamiliar uses of familiar words. Any word means what it means, it acts as a simple unassuming witness of things named or described or states of being expressed. That this is nonsense is confirmed with some critical reflection. Yet the seduction of the signifier to seem faithful to its conventionally associated contents is more often than not too powerful to resist. Indeed, as Geerz (1988) argues, ethnography has too much relied upon the authorial voice of the ethnographer to produce a naïve realism, or better, a truth effect (cf. Baudrillard 1990) where authorial seduction produces an appearance of the real. Taking Baudrillard out of context, if "*seduction represents mastery over the symbolic universe, while power represents only mastery of the real universe*" (italics in the original, p. 8), there is then a battle between two orders of representation.

The witness cannot be a passive observer in the clashes or alliances formed between the masters of the symbolic and the masters of the real. The witness accuses and demands to be heard and believed. The observer may withdraw into an indifference or may walk away. Witnessing trembles between desire and fear in order to make something heard and known.

What is the role and status of truth in witnessing?

THE TEXTUAL PRODUCTION OF THE WITNESS—THE CASE OF THE NEWSPAPER

All experience, if it is to be related, must pass through a process of symbolizing. For another to understand there must be some degree of sharing the process through which symbolization takes place. There must be a way of unlocking the code of the witness as author. Is there some universal key? Or is it the case that the truth of the witness is forever at one remove, removed from immediacy by the very process through which it is told?

A newspaper takes its authority as a credible witness from the extent to which it is accepted as being a reliable reporter of facts, reported facts that are merely the mirror of "what happened." The witness in this sense is a guardian of memory. To be a reliable teller and guardian involves some sense of trustworthiness (see the later discussion by the editor-in-chief).

Memory, in the sense being explored here, is far from the passive writing of traces onto a hard disk and more like the strategic play between analyst, "clues" and personalities that are essential to the detective genre stemming from Poe and Conan Doyle. But with a difference: where the detectives imagined by Poe and Conan Doyle could rest their conclusions upon the irresistible force of logic, public memory is constructed through the ambivalent play of signifiers organized rhetorically by the masters of the symbolic. The difference is between a univocal logic and a plurivocal play of reasons, images and covers. Where the univocal constructs a linear melody, the plurivocal has its multiple layers of chords and discords. It is a multiplicity which never quite covers what it means to say. It is a place where fact, memory, imagination and desire collude in the fantastic production of the real, as reality effects in the way that (a) a *trompe-l'oeil* produces the effect of a real object on a painted surface, and (b) the half-light of dawn or dusk shows nothing with a clear and distinct value, and thus imagination works to fill in the gaps or draw the boundaries of objects which then emerge as fantastic beings. Upon the deceptive surface and in the half-light what can be witnessed and what can be taken as having been witnessed?

Such witnessing is dangerous; it releases too much of what can no longer be contained and yet entraps by other means:

> J'attire l'homme vers plus de lumière; vers une zone frappée par un rai lumineux qui vient de la surface, traverse un soupirail et projette sur le mur la forme d'une grille. Nous allons jouir dans une cage fictive, une cellule aux barreaux seulement fabriqués par l'ombre et la lumière.

I attract the man towards more light; towards a zone struck by a ray of light coming from the surface through a basement window and projecting on the wall the form of a grill. We are going to come in a fictive cage, a barred cell made only out of shadow and light.[2]

Cyril Collard (1989, p. 89) writes of his life and of his impending death through AIDS through the light of fiction. He writes of the ambivalent pleasures in a world "entre chien et loup," where in the shadows it is no longer possible to tell the difference between the dog and the wolf, between friendship and danger, a place however, intensely seductive with intense emotions and uncontrollable drives, a place created through a dynamic of the fictional and the real. This place is the borderlands of the imaginary:

L'imaginaire est tout d'abord la fiction qui s'installe du seul fait de parler. Le patient parle et sa parole crée la place d'un pouvoir fictif que le psychanalyste aura ou non a occuper.

The imaginary is first of all the fiction that takes hold from the fact of speaking alone. The patient speaks and his word creates the place of a fictive power that the psychoanalyst will not have to occupy (Nasio 1987, p. 51).

From the fact of the newspaper "speaking out," reporting upon a world, a realm of the imaginary is created in the mind of the reader, a fictive cage constructed of the newsworthy attracting the reader within its columns to take pleasure there (cf. Anderson 1983). By taking on board and thinking or speaking this fictional realm into existence the reader creates what is essentially a fictional power possessed by the newspaper as a place of "truth," a "place of knowledge," a place of believable or at least plausible realities. Where a psychoanalyst or some other may choose whether or not to occupy such a place in the imaginary[3] of the reader/listener, the newspaper sells itself precisely in terms of occupying a space which witnesses truthfully, in the best interests of the reader.

The fantastic production of the real, whether private or public, is never entirely personal (meaning unique, eccentric, located in the individual) and never entirely impersonal (meaning distributed across a system of information and independent of any given individual). The newspaper deploys its fictive power over the imaginary of readers by being a guardian of public memory (as what really happened), present circumstances and the fantastic production of the real. In doing so it must represent itself as a known "personality," that is, not act out of character in the imaginary community. It thus mimics the relation between personal and impersonal, individual and distributed: the individual who is *in character* and in relation to the distributed sense of what constitutes a *civilized character among others*. Through positing and being a vehicle for the distribution of the *character who acts*, memory and the fantastic production of the real constructs a sense of the normal, how things are normally dealt with, how decisions are normally made, what news is normally presented and so on. In this way the newspaper presents a social mirror within which people who stand before it can see their own faces as being normal or otherwise. This confirmation or lack of confirmation is itself a kind of witnessing of the self and has all the liberating and alienating effects that people such as Lacan (1977) have described. The educational issue then is when and to what extent a newspaper challenges or reinforces the normal and under what conditions; and whether it should do so by invoking a sense of continuity or discontinuity, or a sense of Us-ness or Them-ness, a sense of unity or fragmentation and so on.

STANDING BEFORE THE NEWSPAPER

The first impulse is to tell the story.[4] Then it falls into the usual patterns of locating the gatekeeper who would provide the name (of who to contact next) and lend authority to the ethnographer who wants to "get in." Then making contact, "Professor x suggested that I contact you, I want to look at the ways a newspaper 'stories' a school, a city, its people." And so on. This story was learned from the years of doing research, talking to others, reading. The ethnographer becomes subject(ed) to the story which distributes its characters across the stage. The intention of making an ethnography already targets a "people," throws a loop around them and pulls it tight.

The people in question work for a newspaper. The newspaper is circumscribed by job contracts, legal definitions of incorporation, financial documentation, mission statements, memos, timetables, and as a result the "people" become in question; such questions as "what is my job?" "what do I do next?" "how do I make a good story?" "My" and "I" designate a responsibility, a place to be filled, and a potential guilt and thus an anxiety about the impossibility of being fully adequate to the demand. The newspaper is in this sense a structure of demand, obligation, guilt, anxiety, through which an "I" and an "other" get to be positioned in all their concrete realities. Of course, that is not all. Remaining in question, the I leaves its trace in a biography/autobiography which is split at source, both personal and impersonal, both in here and out there. In the story not everything is told, nor can be told; out in the cold these residual "bits"—these off-cuts—wait to have their day.

The reflexivity of the biographical/autobiographical I is split, its memory a tombstone to some sort of reflexive identity held, not securely, between the I and the Other. This I is thoroughly intersubjective at its limit in the Other, being located nowhere as such since its nature is to be distributive (and thus virtual rather than actual) across a system. It is not the reflexive "I am I" of narcissism: the I that is conjured out of a loving reflection on an image presumed to be the I of the eye's gaze into the mirror, a witnessing marked by a celebratory cry of recognition and anguish. The joyful image of the I that stands before the eye of the "I am I" entails also a desperate reflexive struggle to draw up an exact correspondence between the I as felt and the I as ideally reflected (cf. Lacan 1977). The biographical I may be thought of as the collision between narcissistic reflexivity and intersubjective reflexivity. Or at least the illusion of a collision.

Standing before the newspaper is not quite like standing before a mirror. Although no such bystander is innocent in either case, the reflection of light by the mirror is real and in real time, whereas the light and the time of the newspaper is virtual or symbolic. The newspaper is not the little bit of paper with its ink markings but is that mirror of reality which is conjured into symbolic existence taking for its metaphorical authority the dumb reflective surface of real mirrors everywhere: seeing is believing, I read it in the news. Standing before the newspaper to read therein the reality of life is the first step in construing a people with a folk memory and their unique auto/biographies which form the routine bases of "stories." This relation between a symbolic reality and the presumed "real" reality standing behind it (or before it—in both its locational and temporal senses) gestures towards the key transformational work of the newspaper. The time before newspapers and mirrors is long gone. Now standing after them, I want to tell the story of this transformational work. It is a project of "seeing," "witnessing," "cr(eye)ing."

THE TRANSFORMATIONAL WORK OF THE NEWSPAPER

What do people do or say they do, in working for a newspaper? The editor-in-chief talked about his role in a way that seemed to unify a past and a present into a story of increasing sensitivity to and inclusion of the voices of both staff and the community:

> Well, it has certainly changed in the eight years that I've been here. I had an earlier meeting today with an editor from another newspaper and we were talking about how that job has changed. Traditionally the editor's job had been, sort of, the person who was the, I guess, final arbitrator, or principal decider about what was important in the community and saw what was really news or what was really new. Everywhere (I think) in the, certainly in the newspaper business, certainly at this newspaper that's a much more collaborative process today and one that involves much more the community than it did 20 years ago or 30 years ago when I first got into this business. And even eight years ago when I came here it is much different than it was then. It's collaborative in the sense that the hierarchical rules that used to be imposed, that is that the person with the most experience or the biggest gun um the editor-in-chief, was the person who made all the key decisions. And those things were made more or less on the basis of what I knew or believed to be true, and what was most considered as a result of what I knew or believed to be true, or best for the community. That whole notion has started to change but that's the way it was ten, at least ten years ago. The editor of then, and even when I came to this newspaper, the editor made those decisions when the system or the process itself was unable to, based on (sort of) whatever knowledge the person brought to bear. Today lots of people are involved in that process. And they're involved both on the basis of their connections to the community, their experience in life, their understanding of their community and the world around them, their place in it are all factors today that are brought into consideration. We make a decision about what we're going to do. We are much more today likely to ask the community what it thinks about that than we ever have been before. And so today our decision to

pay attention for example to the budget process that the city has just been going through is as much a function of our believing and my believing that it's an important news story as it is a function of the community having told us that it thinks that it's an important news story. And indeed I think increasingly the fact that the public has told us that is becoming more and more to outweigh whatever I might think or whatever my peer group might think is really important. It's not necessarily true that the public edits this newspaper, there is in this country—I presume in all Western countries where there are free news media—in this country it is thought to be sort of sacrosanct that the newspaper retains the freedom to decide what it does and in fact is deemed therefore to be heresy that the public in any way would be part of that process. I don't think that. We don't think that. We always retain the right to do whatever we choose to do whether that's right or wrong or indifferent. But we believe today here that the process of infor- mation provision is a business and that part of being successful in that business requires that you're providing something useful and meaningful and relevant to your customers—to enable you to do that they have to have some hand in helping you shape what it is you do. You need to have the experience to monitor and prevent one particular group becoming more important or having an opportunity or an edge that some other group might not have. But you do need to provide some vehicle in the community or vehicles in the community that are mining con- stantly some sense of what it is that the community wants to get, and that's today how our job has changed and my job has changed in the last ten or 15 years. You just would not have thought that necessary ten years ago, eight years ago.

There are many distinct propositions in this lengthy extract from an interview last- ing about an hour and a half.

1. There has been a change in the editorial role, newspaper management style and relationship to the community.
2. This change is towards more collaborative decision making.
3. Involvement in decision making is founded on: (a) personal experience, (b) connections to the community, (c) understanding of community, world and own place in community and world.
4. Newsworthiness is a function of: editor's, journalists' and public's opinion that it is important.
5. The freedom of the press to print whatever it wants is not compromised by public involvement in decision making.
6. Information provision is a business: this provides a motivation for the inclusion of the public's demands in terms of what they find useful and meaningful and hence appears to be a rationale for proposition "5."
7. Experience in monitoring contributes to the prevention of one voice dominating another due to undue influence.
8. To accomplish the collaborative work of the newspaper, information mining vehicles are necessary.

The list is not exhaustive and is not yet refined. In the usual course of qualita- tive research this first analytic description may be tested, refined and elaborated by searching out other voices, watching proceedings as they take place and ana- lyzing the final text of the daily paper. The work might add to the discourses on the social construction of news and opinion. What, however, would be an explicitly educational turn.

A beginning might be made by remarking some superficial resemblances. First, during this century there has been generally a move in the teaching professions around the world away from traditional, autocratic, transmission models where "knowledge/facts/information" was hierarchically passed from the teacher to the taught. Second, parallels may be made with the world of business where the move has been from vertical to "flattened" systems of management. Indeed, third, a comparison may also be drawn with longer term political moves from autocratic to democratic involvement. Arguments may be made about the success, consistency and "reality" of these changes. Finally, comparisons may be drawn with the gradual moves towards democratic forms of evaluation research and collaborative forms of action research. There is, of course, nothing essentially "educational" as distinct from say "fashionable" or "politically manipulative" about any of this. It is certainly in the interests of a government or a business to have its citizens or workers compliantly consultative and creatively problem solving in the interests of greater power, privilege and profit for the ruling groups who have effaced themselves behind a smiling face of benevolence and soothing words of worker, consumer and community empowerment.

What is educational is the extent to which people as individuals and as members of communities in a local-global context can break through what might simply be called the social constructions through which they are led into an unthinking or uncritical or unaware complicity in reproducing the structures and processes of their own or others' alienation, exploitation, violation, drudgery, or despair, or poverty. When a newspaper identifies as its purpose—or at least a major purpose—being the vehicle for the representation of the views and needs of a community there is at least the possibility that it may do more than simply act as a mirror. It moves towards the position of educating—drawing out—by "mining" and "monitoring" views in order to "prevent one particular group becoming more important" than another in that process. There is just the flavor of the old Humanities Curriculum Project here which, directed by Stenhouse in the late 1960s and the early 1970s, provided a model for the rational debate of controversial issues in schools that was not teacher dominated, focusing upon the processes through which knowledge and opinion are constructed rather than the rote learning of "facts." At its other extreme there remains the possibility of schooling through a sifting of views and needs to spin them into a common core web of received canons of wisdom which may perhaps be called a national news curriculum, the ideological purpose of, say, a *Daily Express*, *Mail*, *Telegraph*, *Sun* or *Daily Mirror*.

By focusing on the processes through which facts are generated, ordered and disseminated, a tentative or provisional formulation of the transformational work of a newspaper, in common with other agencies through which knowledge, information and opinion is disseminated, can be made. It is a process that moves from "facts," through "ways of arranging facts"—whether autocratically, democratically or aesthetically—to produce an ordered understanding or grasp of "reality," to "breaking through" this ordered understanding in order to grasp otherwise hidden connections or hidden disconnections. It is the "breaking through" that is one mark of the educational as distinct from the "schooled" and points towards an explicitly *educational* ethnography.

WITHIN THE FIELD OF VISION:
THE CUTTINGS FROM GLOBAL TO LOCAL

There has to be some means of cutting up the world, shedding light upon places, people and events so that friends and foes may be distinguished, placing it all into manageable portions in order for a newspaper to handle the vastness, the diversity, the ephemeral nature of things and events. This cutting up is the manner in which a newspaper develops a "curriculum," that is, a course of affairs, events, reflections, debates, commentaries that are disseminated to a readership. How the world gets to be "cut up" into curriculum parcels—such as sports, business news, current affairs, opinion pages, local, national and international politics and so on—is thereby important to the vision that readers construct of themselves, their world and their place in it. But how important?

Twenty years ago, 30 years ago, the newspaper was the dominant provider of all kinds, all forms, of current information in this community. Thirty years ago there was one other local television station or one local television station which coincidentally then we owned. And people with cable probably had access to six or eight other channels, each of which would have had a small suppertime and maybe late evening newscast. And 30 years ago ask the question—where do you get most of your national and international information?—most people would have said probably the newspaper. Asked that question in 1987, which was the first time in a national study in Canada it was asked, and asked that question again in 1993, a vast majority of Canadians said, I get my, most of my national and international news off television and an increasing number of people—a slim majority in 1993 and a large minority in 1987—said I get most of my national and international commentary and background off of television. What's happened in 30 years is that this market place has gone from cable access to five or six television stations to cable access to 40 or 50 television stations. We've gone from there being, you know, relatively short suppertime or late night newscasts to television stations offering—two of them—24 hour a day news and one, another one, offering 24 hour a day sports. We've gone to almost every television station providing some extensive degree of national and international news and public affairs programming. That provides our customers with a huge variety of things that we could never ever begin to duplicate. So the notion that we would be competitive in providing national and international information in 1996 is just ludicrous. What we do still own and probably long will, because currently it's very expensive and it requires probably some degree of residency in London [Ontario], is information and news about our community. We have more than 100 news-gathering assets who actually live here. We have a long sense of history with this community, we understand it, we grew up in it. We have, we know many people here, we have lots of people who live here and lots of trained professionals, therefore, who have tentacles into the community that allows us each day to gather the largest collection of local information that anybody can muster. This is our competitive advantage. It's something that the Canadian Broadcasting Corporation can't duplicate. It's something that the local television station can't duplicate. It's something that, at the moment at any rate, information pretenders like the telephone company or the cable company cannot duplicate. So it's because it's our competitive advantage, it's the part of what we do and do best that we need to exploit and and the part therefore that over time strategically we are moving to reinforce, to promote and to accentuate in our product

(Editor-in-chief).

The shift has been from being the monopoly provider of the vision of the whole world to being a monopoly provider of local news. In fact, the view that the newspaper has of itself in its mission statement is to be the monopoly provider of news, information and advertising, but "there's no indication in our corporate strategy as to why we we want to do that." However the editorial department has a statement of intentions for itself:

We see our role as being a community connector, of providing information that helps people make better choices about the way they live, about how they live, that otherwise they would be unable to make, because no other entity—public or private—provides that kind of community connection.

This community connection is a particular kind of work through which a grounded curriculum, a process of tapping into a community to form an agenda of concerns that reveal otherwise hidden connections, is created as a basis for making choices. There is in this an emergent image of a reflective citizenry which is produced through the work of the newspaper.

So we see our role now being the community connector, being an agent therefore of community, ongoing community change and improvement; of being part of the process by which this community comes together, stays together, grows together and part of the system therefore that makes London different than Toronto or different than some other place.

The conceptual work of the newspaper is to form then to cut up the body of the city. Parallel to this is organizing the newspaper as a machine for gathering and representing according to the conceptualization of the city as being a whole and as being parts or cuts/slices of the whole. The categories exclude, act as if invisible and hence render invisible at the symbolic representational level the prior acts of conceptualizing into unities and cutting into parts.

THE FAIR MIRROR AND TRUE

The editor-in-chief considers that there is a "constant requirement" from customers to "provide information that is fair and balanced and accurate." Because of this the newspaper is split into two sides: (1) the news gathering and (2) the editorial, that is the opinion forming or commentary side.

> Unless our customers can be ensured that what we are doing is sort of straight up there's no reference point on which you can evaluate any of the ideas that we may subsequently attempt to pile onto that. The way to, we believe, to ensure that our information is as fair as we can make it, is as balanced as we can make it, or is as accurate as we can make it is to separate anything else that might be layered on that, from that process. And that process in fact, of just trying to be fair and accurate and balanced is the larger of all of the things that we do. So we provide that first of all. And then we reserve the right based on our experience and our knowledge to—from time to time—pile on top of this information some critiquing of it, some prioritising of it, some assessment of it—provide some additional depth to it, provide some connectivity to it. We do sort of all of those things in varying degrees on top of that base line of information. And the sort of—the farther we get away to—or the farther we get to what is sort of purely our own invention, our own ideas based on that information, our own criticism based on that information, the closer we get to what we describe the opinion part of the news-paper and at a certain point and it's not very far away from the base line we start to label things as such. So if it's an analysis of the fact we label that, if it's an out-and-out rant on the facts which would appear on the opinion page we call that in big letters our opinion. If we don't do that then it's—then it would always be—a question of whether this was a fact that was somehow unassailable or if it could be assailed would be in the next day's paper. Or whether this is just sort of our own invention or our own opinion upon that. People need to be able to know which is which.

The staffing of the newspaper follows this conceptual distinction between news gathering which provides the "factual" base line and the editorial side which generates commentaries and opinions.

OF BRUTE FACTS, STORIES AND WITNESSES

A story emerges from an act of unifying particulars scattered through time and space: it is the dominant framework for "arranging facts," for recalling them and designating them true as distinct from false memories. It is a kind of boot-strapping where the particulars and their truth do not exist outside a story, nor do stories exist apart from particulars and their status as "true." Yet something must play the part of a brute fact (or brute mirror) which is the subject/object of mastery: the mastery of the I of the witness constructing a kind of total vision, a panoptica. Mastering the facts, being in command of the details—it recalls that dialectic which has served philosophers well: the master and slave who are locked into a mutual struggle of self-survival that depends on the one never annihilating the other. Equally, it recalls the transition from raw to cooked that Levi-Strauss saw as the cultural process itself. Moreover, it recalls another kind of mastery that results from war, the exercise of brute power to root out and destroy and hence replace in its entirety. All such forms of mastery as these seem implicated in or co-opted by "desire" and by "pleasure" if the various contemporary discussions informed by psychoanalysis and Hegelian perspectives are to be believed.

The innocence of facts falls away in the play of desire. Memory and the witness are both constructions of this play, a play rather like that which builds enough flexibility into a suspension bridge for it to bend with the wind but not so much that it snaps out of shape and crumbles into the water below. It is a play of tensions. Memory signifies a something that is claimed to have or have had existence. The witnessing subject who puts forward his or her memory of a particular experience as crucial becomes a key source of brute facts, the news as witnessed by....However:

> Psychoanalysis...acknowledges that no fact is unequivocal. This is so because no fact exists outside a signifying chain and no signifier is unequivocal. And since this is so, psychoanalysis reasons, the subject, affected by the facts of its life, is affected by meanings that it never lives, never experiences. This is what psychoanalysis means when it speaks of the overdetermination of the subject: the subject is subject to the equivocations of the signifier. It is for this reason that Freud was led to defend constructions of analysis, those analytic imaginings of events that affected the subject even though they never happened *as such*, were never experienced and thus could never be remembered *as such* (Copjec 1995, p. 68).

The witness as subject to the entire signifying network in the above sense is never in a position to see anything except as reflected by something acting like a mirror. Yet this is not the sense of the witness who returns from some trauma so far beyond any containing mirrors that seek to cover it with explanations that all words fail, that understanding is itself an obscenity (Lanzmann 1995). These two notions of the witness render problematic any straightforward concept of the role of any observer whether witness as ethnographer, witness as reporter, witness as evidence (talking head, smoking gun, hard documentation). When the witness witnesses—who/what is doing the talking? And what is the nature of that which is being talked about? There is such a loss of the real in much of contemporary theory and day-to-day discourse—who can call the difference between the image and that which it is supposed to reflect?

> Between the subject and the real, civilisation—the social order—is interposed. This order is now conceived not only as that which, in equipping the subject with a fantasmic body, satisfies its desires, but more, as that which produces the desires it satisfies. Happiness is thus defined no longer as subjective, but as *objective*. For all the mirrors, cameras, telephones, microphones, planes, passenger lists, and statistics can be seen as so much social paraphernalia of surveillance by which alone the subject is made visible—even to itself. If we cannot judge immediately what measure of pain or pleasure belonged to a historical individual, this is not because we cannot project ourselves into her subjective position, her private mental sphere, but rather because we cannot so easily project ourselves into her objective *social* sphere in order to discern the categories of thought that constructed her expectations, narcotized her against disappointment, made her obtuse to her own suffering (Copjec 1995, pp. 40-41).

Between the subject and the real, what is borne by the witness if it can no longer be expressed in the "objective social sphere" of a given readership? What is born(e) is the traumatic rift itself that can never achieve closure without obscenity. The trauma/real remains, impossible to be taken up and explained and hence exhausted of its power to generate rifts in the social order or civilizing mirrors that mediate between the self and the real. The social order can be conceived of as a strategic play between warring factions to sew up the rifts, erase the sutures to create a world that is always remembered *as such*. Key to this operation is the relation between my opinion and our opinion and how the one gets subjugated by the other to produce a world remembered *as such*.

WITNESSING *AS SUCH* IN EXCESS

Where is the ethnographer in witnessing *as such?* One choice is that the *as such* may be taken as the empirical/brute facts upon which to build second order explanations and theorizations. As such, the ethnographer is drawn into the imaginary of the *as such*. To witness beyond is to enter the ob/scene (the becoming scene/seen which is often reacted to in disgust or horror by those whose vested interests it challenges). It is at this point that the witness enters the realm Collard referred to as the realm of the *chien-loup*. It is the cross over point between day and night, between tame and wild, between conscious and repressed and indeed between local and global in the postmodern games played by multinational capital to exploit difference, location and political powers in playing off one nation or region against another.

To frame the boundaries between self and other, us and them, here and there, local and global, the senses of the body create the only bearings we have in the world—and yet they are as untrustworthy as our faith in them is strong. The more we realize the sense of being on the edge—the edge of the solid, the permanent in truth—the more we slip to the extreme, where the abject haunts experience, taking the place of the objects derived from our realities mediated by bodily perception. Whatever constitutes bodily perception of a world of innerness and outerness is the perceptual eye/I/aye—the I that must affirm what is given by the eye. Its flickering light of consciousness projects about and within the bars of the fictive cage which in containing also places a measure upon the bounds for its restless pacing. Disturbing this affirmation of the real of perception creates a rift and a sense of an excess—that which is beyond and access to which is forbidden (Schostak 1993).

Educational ethnography is, firstly, the process of witnessing the emergence of the "gap" through which a "beyond," an "excess," an "obscene" and "abject" may be glimpsed. Such a witnessing slips from the center ruled by some master ego (whether the master ego of science, or the autocratic ego of a leader or god). Witnessing then slides off stage and out of frame and becomes eccentric to the world of the commanding ego which rules the stage of mirrored representations. Witnessing, by occupying a position of Otherness to the contemporary framework which holds together and "performs" the stage calls into question the primacy of the frame and the stage. The witness offers an alternative view and hence frame for viewing and for staging. It is not necessarily the case that this alternative is "true" or "truer." Rather, different viewpoints mean different ways of constructing otherness, excluding, and of generating waste and residuals. Essentially, this deconstructive witnessing is that which unglues social or symbolic identity, transforming it into an unsayable brute real. In perceiving anew the world and the self, the eye re-constructs the reflective center, the I of experience which in its exstatic standing out from the undifferentiated affirms existence in crying aye to the truth of the real, the real world of the self. The creation of bars (or barriers) is necessary to the witnessing aye. Perception and affirmation without limits can have no meaning, no edge, no durability, no manipulability. And so the world *as such* is reconceived as the truth of the witnessing is assimilated to a new world order until, of course, there is another cry of the witness who sees beyond the new limits to an obscene, an abject that has no name.

The witness is thus essential in driving the dialectic of education as a focus of challenge to the prevailing order, schooled into existence by the contemporary frameworks for staging the political, social, cultural and personal lives of individuals, groups and communities (Schostak 1996, 1998). If there is a crisis in contemporary theoretical and methodological responses to the postmodern scene it is because witnessing has been reduced to either naïve scientific empiricism or consumerist lifestyle sampling where "anything goes" or a nihilistic retreat into depression and madness. If the old concepts of mass, solidarity and social justice can no longer be employed as motivators of social change it is because the witnessing eye/aye to change is looking elsewhere at a world conceived quite differently along global-local axes. If the witness is to project alternatives that are persuasive for change in the global-local context of contemporary life then the gaze must create those projects in the spaces overlooked by modernist and postmodern visions alike. It is a vision that no longer gazes out from a center in order to create a common stage ruled by a leader.

This witnessing is always unassimilable to a commanding center of any kind. Its space is always off center. Educational ethnography involves a confrontation between a supposed center and an ex-centric witness which draws out and thus "graphs" the emergence and processes of confrontation, the dissonance and the possibilities for alternative forms of personal and social being and thus of conceiving alternative folk ways seen only through the cr/eye of the ethnographic witness.

NOTES

1.   A sign is composed of two "sides": the signifier—the material mark or vehicle (such as the ink mark or sound waves which can be perceived); the signifier—the content such as a concept. The system of signifiers employed in the construction of written language, for example, pre-exists any single individual and does not belong to a given individual but exists in this sense outside all individuals. The grammatical rules together with the conventions of language contribute to a law-like structure external to the individual which organizes his or her thinking processes symbolically.

2.   I have translated *jouir* as "come" in its slang meaning of sexual orgasm, which is precisely the meaning intended by Collard describing a place where people go to meet partners for casual sex. His book is a story of a man in his thirties, ravaged by AIDS, torn between his desire for casual sex with men and his desire for a particular young woman.

3.   The word "imaginary" is used here and elsewhere in a sense quite different from the word "imagination." Lacan in his theoretical writings distinguishes between three realms: the Real, the Imaginary and the Symbolic. The imaginary refers to a particular dualistic relationship between a self and an other where the self constructs his or her identity through the agency of the other. Metaphorically it is like looking in a mirror and obtaining an idea of one's physical appearance through the reflection. Similarly, Anderson described how a newspaper constructs a sense of an imagined community of people like one's self: British like me, or middle-class like me and so on, who have values and beliefs like mine or who have strengths I envy and would like to be like. The imaginary then is not imagination although it may draw upon processes of the imagination and may draw upon perceptual images through which to construct a sense of the real. The Symbolic expands the dualistic relationship into wider social relationships which may pronounce judgement upon the dualistic relationship forbidding its development, as in the classic Oedipal relationship described by Freud. Here the imaginary relationship (or dualistic and reciprocal relationship of need or demand for satisfaction and love) between mother and son is threatened by the appearance of the father. Through the father the child is introduced to the wider laws of society which in this instance forbids incest. These laws interpose between mother and child breaking the dualistic relationship and allowing the emergence of the laws of the symbolic domain to begin to organize future development of the child's potential in relation to others. The Real may be conceptualized in many ways, but in this instance it is useful to think of it as that which all our symbolic systems attempt to cover and represent but which must ultimately fail to do so. The Real cannot be reduced to the symbolic. People may say they know who I am and can call me by name and describe me in many different ways. However, none of these names and descriptions are adequate to "contain" me. Something is always left out. If I reduce myself to the names and descriptions people have for me then I am essentially "alienating" myself in language.

4.   The journalist needs to be able to identify the story in the events that have been witnessed. It is the story which makes it marketable. I am using story here in a wider sense of the repertoire of ways of organizing what has been seen into events, actions, actors, structures, processes and so on. Many may object to comparing so-called scientific methods of making sense of the world with the process of storying whether by fiction writers or by journalists. When I employ the term "story" I am not suggesting that there is only one possible story, or one unified story. The word acts rather like the variable "x" in a formula. Asking the question, "what's the story?" is rather like asking, "what's the value of "x" in this instance?" which will then help me solve the riddle for this particular case. However, there is a trap here. By accepting the story that is told, I become subject to its organizing frameworks. The role of the educational ethnographer then is neither to accept nor to reject the story but to explore it. Hence there are many stories here: the story of the journalist who has constructed the story from those of informants. And there is the story of the ethnographer who learns the stories of doing ethnographies in order to construct his or her own way of storying (as methodology, as an account of, a study of, and so on) the stories of the people being studied. Each story is an "x" in the complex nest of stories. The

question is: how can all this be unpacked? Or, how can the loop that pulls them tightly into "the story" be undone?

REFERENCES

Anderson, B. 1983. *Imagined Communities: Reflections on the Origin and Spread of Nationalism.* London and New York: Verso.

Baudrillard, J. 1990. *Seduction.* Montréal: New World Perspectives.

Collard, C. 1989. *Les nuits fauve.* Paris: éditions J'ai lu Flammarion.

Copjec, J. 1995. *Read My Desire. Lacan against the Historicists.* Cambridge, MA, London: MIT Press.

Geerz, G. 1988. *Works and Lives: The Anthropologist as Author.* Cambridge: Polity Press.

Hammersley, M. (Ed.) 1983. *The Ethnography of Schooling: Methodological Issues.* Driffield: Nafferton Books.

Lacan, J. 1966. *Écrits I.* Paris: Éditions du Seuil.

_____. 1977. *Écrits. A Selection.* London: Routledge.

Lanzmann, C. 1995. "The Obscenity of Understanding: An Evening with Claude Lanzmann." In *Trauma: Explorations in Memory,* edited by C. Caruth. Baltimore, London: John Hopkins Press.

Nasio, J.-D. 1987. *Les Yeux De Laure. Le Concept D'Objet* a *Dans La théorie De J. Lacan.* Paris: Flammarion.

Schostak, J. F. 1993. *Dirty Marks: The Education of Self, Media and Popular Culture.* London, Boulder: Pluto Press.

_____. 1996. "Teacher Education: Notes Towards a Radical View." Pp. 257-274 in *Teacher Education Policy: Some Issues Arising from Research and Practice,* edited by R. McBride. London, Washington: Falmer Press.

_____. 1998. "Developing under Developing Circumstances: The Personal and Social Development of Students and the Process of Schooling." In *Images of Educational Change,* edited by J. Elliott and H. Altrichter. Buckingham: Open University Press.

ETHNOGRAPHY IN THE HANDS OF PARTICIPANTS:
TOOLS OF DRAMATIC DISCOVERY

Jim Mienczakowski

It is sometimes hard to discern where ethnographic practice might currently be heading and how we will, or should, reconcile the growing move to disestablish methodology through what may be described as the new or contemporary ethnographic movements. Denzin (1997, p.7) refers to contemporary movements as being part of a response to a crisis of "legitimation." Within this crisis it is claimed that the authors of ethnographic texts are invoking authority from their texts through claims of methodological and theoretical validity made to the reader. Such notions of methodological and theoretical validity are, consequently, used to conceal the researcher's semblance of authority in order to evoke recognition of a given order of truth amongst readers (Denzin 1997; Lather 1993).

Throughout the 1990s the ways in which ethnographers make representation through research have been the focus of much debate, and in my own work the development of consensually agreed and performed representations, validated by informants and audiences, has been central to various authority claims. Part of my response to this crisis of legitimisation has been to move towards the polyphonic

Studies in Educational Ethnography, Volume 2, pages 145-161.
Copyright © 1999 by JAI Press Inc.
All rights of reproduction in any form reserved.
ISBN: 0-7623-0563-0

voicing of informants and their concerns and to contest repeatedly the research representations made through public performances and post-performance forum debates. This response has not been predicated upon a desire solely to satisfy trends in theoretical preference but to explore new methodological approaches which offer practical solutions to the production of cultural insights and further offer the potential to impact upon the lives and understandings of readers and audiences. However, rather than re-working here the theoretical notions of how public voice representation (Agger 1991) and vraisemblance (Todorov 1977)[1] may be combined in order to overcome problems with legitimation and to find currency as texts which facilitate emancipatory change, I shall concentrate upon the practical application of ethnography which has both emancipatory and educational potential.

First I shall discuss a practical and achievable project in which senior-school students use ethnography to establish new understandings of their community before describing my own current contemporary practice which opens the discussion and determination of particular social issues for school and tertiary student audiences. I shall concentrate upon the practical application of educationally focused ethnography simply because, for me, involvement with applied ethnography has been a process of validation in its own right. That is to say, having in my earlier days produced a number of lengthy ethnographic texts in order to satisfy the requirements of both research and the academy[2] I have little confidence that the arguments I endeavored to produce have ever been widely read. Conversely, the contemporary texts I shall describe, which have been constructed by school students and by other researchers for in-school and community use, have enjoyed far wider recognition and consequently have "currency." Part of this suggested currency must lie in the notion that students involved in the approaches I describe are the constructors, not subjects, of ethnographic practice and use ethnography as a reflexive tool.

EXAMPLE 1

Situated within the urban belt of Queensland's Gold Coast, Coombabah Senior High School is an established co-educational school which caters for students from widely diverse social backgrounds. Within a mile of the legendary "Surfer's Paradise" the school and its host community are part of the pageant of events and competing cultures that make the Gold Coast unique. Host to major car races and international surfing events the area has one of the most rapidly expanding populations in the southern hemisphere. Often likened to Miami, it is a melting-pot of cultures and nationalities and is also a major Asian tourist destination and a popular venue for American and European film production. However, the local community is beset with a high degree of unemployment and between 1990 and 1997 the vast migration of a reported 1,500 people a week from economically depressed states and neighboring countries to Queensland's south brought a rise in social problems and placed the local health and education infrastructures under considerable pressure.

In response to the difficulty of gaining ingress and acceptance amongst a socially diverse and fluid high school population, Anna Zantiotis of Coombabah State High redefined the year 12 English syllabus to include an ethnographic report and research section. Herein, students participate in a ten-week research and writing project which hones their writing skills and fosters a high degree of participation among students who may have been otherwise "non-participatory" in formal curricular activities. Zantiotis describes her reasons for encouraging this form of research approach as multiple:

> The students are able to undertake fieldwork which has the potential to relativise social and cultural life and reveal the underlying taken for granted world of one's own and other cultures. In addition, doing an ethnography involves a theoretical component, social skills in dealing with interviewees, note taking and organisational skills and of course reporting what is found. Above all, the understanding of ethnographic techniques and logic and the successful completion of ethnography requires a good understanding of verbal and non verbal cultures, especially logic (Zantiotis 1998, pp. 1-3).

Students are further invited to present their researches in seminars at nearby Griffith University so that parents, teaching students, lecturers and peers will, it is proposed, be further involved in discussing the student representations of research. It is here that students who are considering tertiary education might be given insight into how research is constructed and construed in tertiary environments and may be able to experience further, through participation, the practices and language skills integral to undergraduate academic life.

Zantiotis lays the foundations of this year 12 work with a sequenced year 10 junior school unit called "Spy School" in which students approach the challenges characteristic of observational research methods which study non-verbal communication. Following a prescribed route of tasks, students are assessed on the written accounts of their observations. In the senior school work, students spend two weeks on "field work," a further two weeks in "writing up" and are given a total of two weeks to prepare for and deliver their seminars.

In the last few years the production of students' research has become a highlight of the school calendar. With 1998's trawl of research reports ranging from studies of an élite businessmen's "Breakfast Club," Physicians and their Medical Culture to Digital Software Pirates, Bikers Clubs, Ravers, Born Again Christians, Council Road Workers, Teachers who Smoke at School, Trolley Boys, Racing Sailors, Carers of the Aged, Teenage Drinkers, Cyberchatters and the inevitable Australian Body Board Surfers the students' reports have been the source of much local interest and interaction. Interestingly, it is the students themselves who are most vociferous about the value of this approach to study. Student comments relating to the worth of this enterprise include the following:

Before I began my study of check-out operators I thought it would be boring and uninteresting....My original view of them was changed by my findings.

I enjoyed this assignment, I enjoyed being with grungers,[3] questioning myself with and against them, but most of all I enjoyed the fact that I've grown to dismiss stereotyping, to see the truth for myself.

My first impression of bikers was that they were loud mouthed, beer swilling drunken vagrants. What I found was a group of very responsible men, whose code of ethics were better than most politicians....

Of real significance in Zantiotis's approach is the inclusion of theoretical and methodological approaches to the construction of reports which allow senior school students to frame their own research and conduct studies in communities of their own choosing. Of equal significance is the regularity with which students report that the research has given them insight into the cultural worlds of others and how they have re-visited and reformulated stereotypical and prejudicial personal understandings as a result of the eth- nographic interaction. Students also frequently talk of an improvement in their personal communication skills and self-esteem gained through such work.

I personally get quite embarrassed and nervous when I speak in front of people, but since performing my ethnography talk I have sort of become more relaxed when talking in front of people....

I really, really enjoyed doing the ethnography and I felt I put in a good effort due to the fact that I liked it and was interested in what I was studying which makes a big difference....

The assignments we were given are somehow related to our future after school....

At a methodological level we are not here dealing with anything other than the foundation of a traditional approach to anthropologically based ethnog- raphy. What may be important to realise is that ethnographic practice is being valued not for its research product alone but for the aggregation of skill training and personal development that complement other areas of learning and social development. These areas of observation, reportage, social skills, theory, logic, personal organization and analysis are often the "taken for granted" prerequisites of research at a tertiary level. Implicit in being a researcher in education or any other discipline is that we have already accrued a sufficient skill base to conduct adequate research. It may be worth keeping in sight the fact that ethnographic practice need not be valued for its end product alone but for the unique location and potential offered through the research process. Leading on from this school based work, I now draw comparison with the goals of ethno-drama and its student based processes.

EXAMPLE 2:
ETHNO-DRAMA

The body of work described as critical ethno-drama in this chapter seeks to provide reflexive insights for teachers, students, counsellors, care givers, health agencies and others into the worlds of particular health consumer and social communities. In telling the stories of groups of health consumers, health professionals and social workers to social work, health and student communities via the agency of ethnographically derived theatre (in which the meanings and explanations of the performances are negotiated with audiences in forum discussions at the close of performances) it is hoped that an opportunity to share insights and negotiate explanations and meanings (Bakhtin 1984) is created.

As an ethnographer and sometime teacher of the performing arts, I am aware of how responsive and yet seemingly *unchallenged* the audiences of the majority of theatrical productions remain. Given that it is also uncommon for the informants of many ethnographic researches to be able to access and comment upon the ethnographic account *to which they have contributed* once that account has been constructed and objectified as an academic report (Cherryholmes 1993), the ethno-drama process seeks to offer scope for continuous informant validation beyond the report writing stage. Consequently, the processes of critical ethno-drama attempt to offer emancipatory insights by telling informants' stories, largely narrated in their own words, to wide audiences inside and outside the confines of the academy. Furthermore, by combining the research process with theatrical narratives constructed by informants, performed by students and updated and informed through post-performance audience discussions, it is hoped that research becomes relevant to both informants and students as well as those outside the academy.

The explanations, meanings and insights generated by ethno-drama performances are consensually controlled and created by informant groups. As informants validate not only their own data but the scripted and performed scenarios generated by the research, the ethno-drama process represents not only an opportunity to voice informant understandings, explanations, experiences and emotional location within the circumstances of their experiences of health or society but further gives rise to opportunities for student nurses, guidance counsellors, teachers and health professionals to reflect, as participants or audience members, upon their own professional practices (Coffey and Atkinson 1996).

Specifically, the ethno-drama is not indicative of a desire to see the restoration of an idealised form of critical-emancipatory practice nor does it signify an overt embracing of postmodern fragmentation. The polyphonic voicing of our informants' agenda in a "public voice" (Agger 1991) to wide audiences who might otherwise be disadvantaged or inhibited from accessing and interpreting the micro-minutia discourses of research data presented in traditional academic forms is not an attempt to return to a meta-narrative or to lionise the worth of individual mini-narratives. If, in effect, we view the postmodern fracturing of meta-narratives not in Lyotard's (1984) terms of "shattering" but more in Bernstein's (1996) terms as dislocation, specialization and localization then we might see postmodern stories not as a limiting rupturing of human understanding but as a tenable micro-minutia discourse on what is going on (Mienczakowski 1997; Mienczakowski, Smith and Sinclair 1996).

BACKGROUND

Throughout the 1990s major ethno-drama productions have involved funded research shared between the Faculties of Nursing and Health Sciences and Education and the Arts, Griffith University. Usually two-act, full length performance pieces, these have entailed casts and production teams of around 35 and have been used as coursework elements for student assessment for the nursing, education and theatre students involved in them. As part of the research process, the ethnographically derived scripts are published and circulated to health authorities and community groups for comment and amendment; they are also made available to audiences throughout the performances.

After careful validation of contents and representations made, the scripts are performed to invited relevant groups of health consumers, health professionals, counsellors and social services groups and health agencies. Here expert informants assist in determining the accuracy and validity of the representations made—the performances will not be open to public scrutiny until a form of consensus has been achieved with informants. Expert informants are usually health consumers, health professionals working in relevant fields, carers of health consumers and support services, and their testimony and advice is used to interrogate and balance the report findings and scenarios drawn from observation, interview and other standard data collection devices. The overall intention is to depict the lived realities of particular health groups and illuminate their experiences of health issues in order to better inform service providers, health professionals and the general public of how the experience of health consumption (i.e., schizophrenia, alcoholism, acquired brain injury, and so on) impacts upon individuals and families and is dealt with by service providers and communities.

All validatory performances are also forum workshopped (Boal 1979, 1985) in order to add data continually to the research process and script/report. Performances, often sponsored by health education agencies, are also shown to general audiences of school and tertiary students and interested others as part of an overt attempt to influence understanding and attitudes towards given health and social issues (Mienczakowski, Morgan and Rolfe 1993). Consequently, validation implicitly implies validity and consensus for specific informant groups in a collective expression (or performed statement) of lived realities at a given point in time. The validity of the ethno-drama is not intended to be generic, enduring or universal—though undoubtedly commonalities (and hopefully relevance) of experience will be uncovered in the stories of, for example, persons with alcohol dependency in Australia and perhaps those in similar health circumstances elsewhere.

The formative work in this field involved the full length plays *Syncing Out Loud* (Mienczakowski 1992), an ethnographically based play concerning experiences of schizophrenic illness, and the later *Busting* (1993), which describes experiences of institutionalized alcohol detoxification processes. These were performed by nursing and education students and student actors in theatres and residential psychiatric settings to health informants and health professionals and to student and school audiences. The *Busting* and *Syncing Out Loud* projects were used to develop vicarious training experiences, through the role-play of real life scenarios, for nursing students. By dramatizing informants' life experiences and involving student nurses and others in both the characterization and researching of the roles, student nurses not only played the parts of professional nurses in the scenarios but were also engaged in the characterization, research and prolonged representation of the experiences and perceptions of target health consumers and their families. Student actors further took responsibility for their performed representations during (Boal 1979)[4] forum interactions. The forum sessions are engineered in order to provide opportunities for informants to be able to reflect upon the actor's interpretation and representation of self (Conquergood 1988, 1991; Turner 1986) and so that audiences may realize how particular social and mental health issues are experienced (Mienczakowski 1996, 1997). Moreover, student participants, in role, may be able to gain insight into informants' lives. This mode of vicarious training has been used in other health settings concerned with understanding patient perceptions (Cox 1989; Watkins 1990).

FORUM ELEMENTS

Essentially, forum elements involve audiences questioning and debating the representations made on stage with the actors, informant representatives and project writers and directors. Forum validation sessions, which supply each audience member with a copy of the script and a supplementary questionnaire, are recorded on audio tape. Data drawn from the forum discussions may be added to the performance script which is periodically revised and amended as the representations given during performances change meaning. In this way the script is always under revision and remains open to amendment and change. It is never finished and the meanings generated within it are never closed.

THEORETICAL BASIS

The guiding principle governing this critical theory[5] based ethnographic approach is to attempt literally to give voice to groups within society who otherwise consider themselves to be, to an extent, disempowered or disenfranchised. In voicing their concerns in, largely, their own words we intended to compare and contrast their explanations of the circumstances surrounding their worlds with the impressions and perceptions of their life-worlds interpreted or received by the general public and relevant professional bodies. At all times consensus with the contributors is vital (Habermas 1971, 1984, 1987) and the scripts are constantly subject to amendment and revision to ensure that the representations made are recognizable to, and offer the insights desired by, informant groups.

The emancipatory agenda of these projects involves a theoretical relocation of Habermasian (1971, 1984, 1987) communicative consensus within Alberoni's (1984) vision of "the nascent state." Within this conception emancipation is signified by, in all likelihood, little more than the creation of a nascent moment in which insight and critical reflection impel individuals towards objectivity or even *latent* objectivity. Nascency, in Alberoni's terms, is the advent of an advent, the moment in which an individual first fully comprehends their self-conscious location within the circumstances of oppression. Conversely, Marxian critical theory, according to Alberoni, is alleged to mobilize the masses "in the name of their interests, their resentment, and their desire for revenge" (Alberoni 1984, p. 229) and hence to perpetually construct new enemies against which to move. Accordingly, Alberoni redefines the search for truth and enlightenment as the *individual* discovery of a form of self-consciousness "which appears at a certain point as consciousness of one's own historicity" and gives rise to the individuals' ability to acritically moderate his or her understanding of the past into prehistory.

CURRENT WORK

Having in recent years established both a viable methodology and an audience for this type of research, we are currently constructing a project to help interpret and promote the work of the Sexual Assault Services in our local region. This current work, *Stop! In the Name of Love,* which traces the trajectories of recovery of victims of sexual assault, is being constructed in partnership with the local Sexual Assault Services and with contributions from the Police Sexual Assault Squad and officers of the State Legal Services and Department of Public Prosecution. Unlike our earlier work, which involved intensive fieldwork stages in detoxification and psychiatric settings, much data have been provided for this study through secondary interview. Direct interviews with counsellors, lawyers and police officers have taken place but no victim of sexual assault has been interviewed *directly* by our research team—sexual assault service counsellors have acted as the medium through which we have gathered victims' testimony via interview tapes, correspondence and other data. Rather than illuminating the circumstances of assault, informants were asked, through counsellors, to describe their "trajectories of recovery," and although this approach inevitably entailed some informants further voluntarily describing the nature of their experiences of assault, the focus has been upon the personal strategies through which some victims of assault may have moved towards recovery. This change of approach, of course, is a direct response to the sensitivity and confidentiality involved in this area of research.

The project's remit is, above all, to demonstrate publicly that there are those who have discovered trajectories of personal recovery from sexual assault and that discrete support services exist to offer help to those who wish it. In identifying such recovery trajectories it is proposed that the role and functions of the Sexual Assault Services, Police Sexual Assault Squad and even the Department of Public Prosecution will also be explored and explained in a *no holds barred* narrative which prompts reflexive thought and action from within those agencies. In order to open the discourses of trajectories of recovery from sexual assault and abuse to wide audiences, the ethno-drama script and educational information support packages are to be provided to the senior years of local high schools and a small touring performance will be taken around participating schools.[6] Forum post-performance sessions therein will consist of debate with accompanying representatives from the Sexual Assault Services and possibly Police Services, as well as with teachers and the actors of the plays. It is through such debate that school students will be able to question the representations made and contribute to or amend the script data. In this way the script and research will be an ongoing interpretation.

FICTION

That the scenarios and characters within the script are based upon the actual words and lives of others has repeatedly proven to have significance for our earlier ethno-drama audiences. However, it would be unlikely that a cohesive, informative and stimulating performance could be seamlessly constructed without resorting to bridging plot and action gaps with "filler dialogue" or "fictional occurrences." Consequently, all aspects linking scenarios or characters together that are not based upon actual recorded events are fictionalized—but in a very limited way. That is to say, fictional events are constructed only where necessary and all fictional account work is agreed as *real* and *plausible* by counsellors and other expert informants before being inserted into the script. To date, work involving police officers' accounts of how they professionally and personally perceive victims, offenders and the route towards conviction has been completed and performed as a one-act, one-hour play, *Baddies, Grubs and the Nitty-Gritty* (Mienczakowski and Morgan 1998a). Two further acts are near completion. A

performance of the above play in America in February 1998 confirmed that the
scenarios depicted had wide inter-cultural "currency" and "authority," as police
officers and social workers in the U.S. audience immediately claimed strong identification with the events and characters portrayed. This element of the project is
intended to demonstrate problem areas relating to judicial and legal interactions
with victims and to highlight the experience of reporting sexual assault to police
services.

Act 1. Scene iii. The Senior Officer briefs a new recruit. (Baddies, Grubs and
the Nitty-Gritty)

> Col: Robert, in my experience the system supports a woman best by finding a
> perpetrator guilty which means we have to get the evidence and quickly.
> The special room for this stuff is downstairs. It's got a video and triple
> deck tape recorder. I like to get them giving evidence on video—so that if
> we can get that as evidence we can *see* her give her story....See the
> expression on her face—see how she feels about it—see if she breaks
> down and cries. When that goes to a jury....See?....It can be the clincher.
> We will also have to ask about the *nitty-gritty*. Get the blow by blow
> details. So, Robert, what did they tell you on your two week training
> about the way we conduct interviews?

In taking such work into schools the overall intention is one shared with McLaren
(1997, p. 9); that of creating "critical citizens who are no longer content in occupying furtive spaces of private affirmation but who possess the will and knowledge to turn these spaces into public spheres." Rather than leaving the worlds of
victims, the police and counsellors unspoken, unexplored and uncontested we are
seeking to open them to debate and redefinition. This is done at the request of our
informant groups in order to reduce misunderstanding and stereotypical identification of these issues. Although this approach might be described as "emancipatory" and be further labelled as part of a practitioner research approach branded
by Hammersley (1992, p. 151) as all too often utilizing a simplistic concept of
emancipation and ethnography, there is no overwhelming or cogent evidence to
believe that the approach is unrealistic. To the contrary, there have been numerous
moments when the recordings of forum discussions and written comments of
audiences, informants and participants in our work have revealed "critical events"
(Woods 1996, p. 118) or epiphanal moments (Denzin 1989). At such times, audience members and participants have claimed that they have been able to revise
their emotional and personal location with an issue because of the insight and
emotional impact of an ethno-drama.

It has been argued elsewhere that ethno-dramas may be capable of producing limited or latent emancipatory effects for audiences and participants, effects which are largely unrelated to any uniform audience
interpretation of a given performance or to any political aim. The perfor-

mance of a research narrative undoubtedly impacts upon performers and audiences at both an intellectual and emotional level. The following quotation (gathered during a post-performance discussion of a confrontational ethno-drama production dealing with acquired brain injury)[7] indicates the cathartic potential of such research-based performances to induce "change" through intentional emotional location with the social and/or professional lives of audience members.

> The doctor (in the audience) was sort of excited and shaky, emotional. She didn't know where to begin. "That was me!" she said. You know? Really surprised. "I've been doing that, doing that for years...". She was devastated. She described it as a sort of realisation, like she knew that she was talking to a person but because they'd had a bash on the head or a tumour and couldn't reply to her she assumed they were vegies[8] even though she was working in the hospital to prove just the opposite (Cast Member, *A Good Smack in the Head*, 1995).

Earlier work (*Syncing Out Loud*, 1992) noted a distinct pattern of emotional and unpredictable audience and participant responses which led to the production team later establishing firmer guidelines for preparing and subsequently de-briefing audience and cast members for the potential emotional impacts of ethno-drama performances. During a performance of *Syncing Out Loud* to patients of a residential psychiatric hospital some audience members later reported a range of strong emotional responses varying from deep empathy to "spinning out."[9] Moreover, as that particular performance became unexpectedly interactive, with patients joining the actors on stage in unplanned for and impromptu debate or otherwise shouting from the auditorium to complain about their own experiences of institutional treatment, cast members and producers also experienced a range of unplanned and unpredicted emotional responses and recognitions (Mienczakowski and Morgan 1997, 1998b; Morgan, Rolfe and Mienczakowski 1998). These numerous responses included one cast member fleeing into the night believing she had been spoken to by "the devil" and another professing *aggressive* and *potentially violent tendencies* towards audience members because of their unsolicited interruptions to the performance. More moderate responses included others who were highly excited by the challenge or conversely intimidated by the audience's unpredicted interactions.[10]

In general it is supposed that ethno-drama performances offer the potential to make extreme empathetic connections with audience members because it is tacitly understood that the stories being told are *research based* and are not essentially fictional. Moreover, the productions seek to establish credibility with expert and informed audiences by accurately depicting the lived realities of certain medical conditions or institutional experiences.

Enter Sally: Sits on chair center stage.
Scene 2. Baddies, Grubs and the Nitty-Gritty

Sally: Well, when I was initially sexually assaulted it was around the Christmas
         period and I couldn't get help. I don't think funding was very good at the
         time but eventually, I did speak to somebody in the city, um....I rang as
         many different organisations as I could—people were either on breaks or no
         one was available—so in the end I was forced to ring the police.
           It was very intimidating, and the police officer I saw, er, whilst he befriended
         me, um...he actually eventually crossed the line of his professional role,
         ah....Started to come around....(Long pause) We eventually had a relationship
         for a while. I think he found my vulnerability and dependence, all of those things,
         he found them erotic.
           When I went to the police...I wasn't....It wasn't offered to me to see a woman,
         and retelling the whole saga took eight hours. The first four hours....Oh shit....
           Finally I saw him. I think I saw him about a week after it had occurred. He
         took me into an interview room and ah...didn't record anything or anything.
         The door was open. I had to come back the next day and make my statement in a
         public office and you could have heard a pin drop. So...it was quite intimidating
         really. Everyone could hear and there were lots of interruptions. He very kindly
         came in on his day off, the next day, to take my statement 'cause he saw my gen-
         uine distress. Ah, it was still pretty intimidating. I would have much preferred to
         talk to someone...a woman in an office in a sexual assault clinic.
           Look, the first positive thing I did after the assault was to go to the police, well
         before that the first positive thing was to physically run away and hide from my
         assailant. The second positive thing was to go to the police. That was a really big
         step because it was putting all of my eggs in one basket and publicly saying "it's
         not my fault" in front of a lot of uniformed men. So I think it was a big step in the
         healing process...and going through with the stalking charges was a big step too,
         because it meant that I was saying that I count and have rights and the law should
         protect me.

Exit.

The engendering of empathetic and emotional audience responses (Ellis, 1991;
Ellis and Flaherty 1992) through performed representations is intended to connect
and confront audiences (Conquergood 1992, 1993, pp. 342-343) and participants
with the realities of informant lived experiences. The move to emotionally engage
audiences is fostered by the audiences' understanding that the staged representations they are seeing are largely documented, informant-worded research narratives based upon real lives. Hence, the above extract of data drawn from the character Sally, for example, demonstrates the potential of the ethno-drama process to
allow informants to voice, in their own words, their experiences and concerns of
being disenfranchised, or subordinate (Fraser 1990). This "voicing," to audiences
of police, relevant professionals and others, is essentially reflexive and reflective

in nature. In essence, it informs those officially responsible (Apple 1993) for determining legal redress or provision of care of their clients' needs and experiences.

Social service agencies, police, government representatives, health professionals and health educators are all invited to ethno-drama performances, and surveying of our audiences (and audiences of other research-based plays) has revealed that health theatre and issues-based theatre predominantly attract audiences interested professionally or otherwise in the subject of the research. Health theatre attracts health consumers, health practitioners and members of support services, and issues-based performances attract audiences from co-related support services, etc. The implications strongly suggest that, at the least, such research-based performances hold the potential to offer insight and provoke change amongst those who play a part in the construction of health and social provision (Mienczakowski 1997).

ETHNOGRAPHY: CONTEMPORARY TRENDS

The development of ethnographic narrative into a full scale performance vehicle is clearly an elaboration and enhancement of ongoing, world-wide interest in evolving ethnographic constructions and practices (Ellis and Bochner 1996, pp. 26-31). Ethno-drama sits within an extant school of theatre which searches for social change (Epskamp 1989) but differs from other forms of similar theatre in that it adheres to the principles of a formal and recognizable ethnographic research methodology, above and beyond the artistic demands of aesthetics, in its attempt to produce cultural critique (Denzin 1997). This is a route which has now been further explored by some high school and college practitioners (Diaz 1997; Fox 1997).

Contemporary ethnographic research is also written and disseminated in formats which have embraced poetry and biography (Ellis, 1995; Richardson 1991, 1992, 1993, 1994) and interpretative interactionism (Denzin 1989, 1995). Such moves are part of developing methodologies which attempt to use ethnographic and social science practices to question the usefulness of boundaries between literature, arts and social science explanations of the world (Ellis and Bochner 1996). The recognition that explanations of the world made through literature and the arts are closer to understandings gained through anthropology and the social sciences than those made via the physical sciences (Rorty 1980) is of significance here. Turner (1986) envisaged ethnographic practice in which the *performance* of ethnography could be seen as a means of investigating channels of reception and human understanding. Critical ethno-drama seeks to meld the traditional values of textual, academic presentation and those of performance in its investigation of human understanding. In constructing research as script and performance, we are exploring a position which Conquergood (1991, p. 190) sees as "deeply subversive and threatening to the text bound culture of the academy."

The proposition is that performed ethnography may provide more accessible and clearer public explanations of research than is frequently the case with traditional, written report texts (Mienczakowski 1996). The public performance of ethnography in the argot of its informants may be argued to de-academize the report construction process. Significantly, ethno-drama also returns "the ownership, and therefore the power, of the report to its informants as opposed to possessing it on behalf of the academy" (Mienczakowski 1996, p. 255).

CONCLUSION

The element linking the approach offered by Zantiotis and that of ethno-drama is that both value the processes for student participants as well as the final outcomes. Student ownership and participation are the key to the success and relevance of both these ventures. For Zantiotis, students engage in practices which develop social skills alongside academic ones. Similarly, ethno-drama impacts upon audiences of school children as well as acting reflexively upon informants, government agencies and the student nurses, teachers and social workers who make up the casts. In many ways, the earlier health related ethno-dramas were overtly concerned with giving vicarious experience and professional insight to nursing students as well as opening representations of common illness to public debate. Our current work seeks to influence school audiences with the wide dissemination of ethnographic practice.

All experimentation and development of ethnographic methodology is potentially fraught with theoretical dilemmas and problems of application. That we continue to explore and contest the viability of emergent methodologies must be an indication of a continuing desire and need to interpret and investigate the social world ethnographically. That the exploration of ethnographic methodologies now takes us into the realm of practical application in school settings (with the adoption of students as participants and practitioners who develop personal, professional and academic skills through their ethnographic interactions) may be an avenue of exploration which is worth fostering and expanding.

NOTES

1. Todorov's notion of textual verisimilitude suggests that written researches may evoke emotional responses in readers according to their credibility as "real," "plausible," or "likely" representations of perceived truths.

2. Such as Mienczakowski, J. 1988. "The Conditions of Service for Secondary School Teachers within a South London Division of the ILEA." MA Dissertation, King's College, London, or "Waterways Down Housing Project: Report on Potential Community Social Impacts." 1994-96. Commissioned by Warren Morton and Associates—Report to State Government.

3.   Grunge is a form of drab and uncoordinated fashion and music. The fashion involves dull, baggy clothing and, in Australia, is often described as a youth sub-culture of the "grotty" or "daggy." (Dag is a common term for dung which has adhered to the rear of a sheep's fleece. Need I say more!)

4.   Augusto Boal is the founder of a form of emancipatory theatre in Brazil which allows participants to reconstruct and overcome the circumstances of their political and social oppression. In "forum" theatre the themes are devised by audiences who participate in the construction of solutions to their given problems.

5.   Critical ethno-dramas reinterpret not only ethnography but critical theory. Within our context of health education drama, critical theory seeks to be emancipatory by giving its subjects the means by which they can politically and socially locate, understand and influence the conditions of their existence. We have specifically chosen to work with the victims of sexual assault, persons with schizophrenia and persons undergoing detoxification for alcohol dependency, in order to voice their opinions.

6.   All previous ethno-dramas have involved educational packages and services made available to audiences or schools. These have ranged from counselling services related to alcohol awareness and mental health to free alcoholic drinks to adults and penalty-free breathalyzer tests provided to audiences by community police and health services.

7.   *A Good Smack in the Head* (Appleby 1995). Student performance involving clients from Headway Incorporated, Gold Coast.

8.   Australian colloquialism meaning "vegetable" or "basket case," that is, an incapacitated person.

9.   "Spinning out" is a term frequently used by persons with schizophrenia to describe the onset of an episode of psychotic/dysfunctional thought or behavior.

10.   The cast consisted of theatre, education and nursing students. Of note here is the observation that cast members who were nursing students were not intimidated or phased by the audience interactions and proceeded (in role) both to continue to perform and to assist in returning patients to their seats. Performers who were theatre students appeared less able to deal with patient interruptions to their performances.

REFERENCES

Agger, B. 1991. "Theorising the Decline of Discourse or the Decline of Theoretical Discourse?' Chapter 5 in *Critical Theory Now*, edited by P. Wexler. New York and London: Falmer Press.

Alberoni, F. 1984. *Movement and Institution*. Translated by P. Arden Delmoro. New York: Columbia University Press.

Apple, M. 1993. *Official Knowledge: Democratic Education in a Conservative Age*. New York: Routledge.

Appleby, P. 1995. *A Good Smack in the Head*. (Acquired Brain Injury Performance Group) Headway, Gold Coast, Pty. Gold Coast: Griffith University.

Bakhtin, M. 1984. *Problems of Dostoevsky's Poetics*. Edited and translated by C. Emerson. Minneapolis: University of Minnesota Press.

Bernstein, B. 1996. *Pedagogy, Symbolic Control and Identity: Theory, Research, Critique*. London: Taylor and Francis.

Boal, A. 1985 [1979]. *Theatre of the Oppressed*. Translated by C.A. and M. L. McBride. New York: Theatre Communications Group.

Cherryholmes, C. H. 1993. "Reading Research." *Journal Of Curriculum Studies* 25: 1-32.

Coffey, A., and P. Atkinson. 1996. *Qualitative Data Analysis*. London: Sage Publications.

Conquergood, D. 1988. "Health Theatre in a Hmong Refugee Camp: Performance, Communication and Culture." *TDR—The Drama Review—A Journal of Performance Studies* 32 (3): 174-208.

———. 1991. "Rethinking Ethnography: Towards a Critical Cultural Politics." *Communication Monographs* 58 (June): 179-194.

_____. 1992. "Ethnography, Rhetoric, and Performance." *Quarterly Journal of Speech* 78: 80-123.

_____. 1993. "Storied Worlds and the Work of Teaching." *Communication Education* 42: 337-348.

Cox, H. 1989. "Drama in the Arts Lab." *Australian Nurses Journal* 19(1): 14-15.

Denzin, N. 1989. *Interpretive Interactionism.* London: Sage.

_____. 1995. "Performance Texts." Paper delivered to the American Education Research Association, April, San Francisco.

_____. 1997. *Interpretive Ethnography: Ethnographic Practices for the 21st Century.* London: Sage.

Diaz, G. 1997. *Turned On/Turned Off (a clarion call).* Qualitatives '97 OISE. Toronto: Desktop Publication. Edited by L. Muzzin et al. August.

Ellis, C. 1991. "Sociological Introspection and Emotional Experience." *Symbolic Interaction* 14: 23-50.

_____. 1995. *Final Negotiations: A Story of Love, Loss and Chronic Illness.* Philadelphia: Temple University Press.

Ellis, C., and A. Bochner. 1996. "Talking Over Ethnography." Pp. 13-45 in *Composing Ethnography: Alternative Forms of Qualitative Writing,* edited by C. Ellis and A. Bochner. London: Sage.

Ellis, C., and M. G. Flaherty. 1992. *Investigating Subjectivity: Research on Lived Experience.* London: Sage.

Epskamp, K. 1989. *Theatre in Search of Social Change: The Relative Significance of Different Theatrical Approaches.* The Hague: Centre for the Study of Education in Developing Countries (CESO).

Fox, K. 1997. "First Blood: Rituals of Menarche." OISE. Toronto: Desktop Publication. Edited by L. Muzzin et al. August.

Fraser, N. 1990. "Rethinking the Public Sphere: A Contribution to the Critique of Actually Existing Democracy." *Social Text* 25/26: 56-80.

Habermas, J. 1971. *Knowledge and Human Interest.* Translated by T. McCarthy. London: Heinemann.

_____. 1984. *The Theory of Communicative Action.* Translated by J. Shapiro. Boston: Beacon Press.

_____. 1987. *Philosophical Discourse of Modernity: Twelve Lectures.* Translated by F. Lawrence. Boston: Beacon Press.

Hammersley, M. 1992. *What's Wrong with Ethnography?* London: Routledge.

Lather, P. 1993. "Fertile Obsession: Validity after Poststructuralism." *Sociological Quarterly* 34: 673-694.

Lyotard, J-F. 1984. *The Post-Modern Condition: A Report on Knowledge.* Minneapolis: University of Minnesota Press.

McLaren, P. 1997. "Unthinking Whiteness, Rethinking Democracy: or Farewell to the Blonde Beast; Towards a Revolutionary Multiculturalism." *Educational Foundations* (Spring).

Mienczakowski, J. 1988. "The Conditions of Service for Secondary School Teachers in a South London Division of the ILEA." MA Dissertation, King's College London.

Mienczakowski, J. 1992 [1994]. *Syncing Out Loud: A Journey into Illness.* Brisbane: Griffith University Reprographics.

_____. 1996. "An Ethnographic Act: The Construction of Consensual Theatre: Ethnography in the Form of Theatre with Emancipatory Intentions." Pp. 244-264 in *Composing Ethnography: Alternative Forms of Qualitative Writing,* edited by C. Ellis and A. Bochner. London: Sage.

_____. 1997. "Theatre of Change." *Research in Drama Education (RIDE)* 2 (2): 159-171.

Mienczakowski, J., and S. Morgan. 1993. *Busting: The Challenge of the Drought Spirit.* Brisbane: Griffith University Reprographics.

Mienczakowski, J. and S. Morgan. 1997. "An Evening With the Devil: The Archaeology of Emotion." Society for the Study of Symbolic Interaction, August 11-12, Colony Hotel, Toronto.

Mienczakowski, J., and S. Morgan. 1998a. *Baddies, Grubs and the Nitty-Gritty.* Act 1, from *Stop! In the Name of Love.* Performed to the SSSI, Houston, February 17, 1998.

Mienczakowski, J. and S. Morgan. 1998b. "Finding Closure and Moving On: An Examination of the Challenges Presented to the Constructors of Research Performances." *National Drama, ND (UK)* 5(2): 22-29.

Mienczakowski, J., S. Morgan, and A. Rolfe. 1993. "Ethnography or Drama?" *National Association for Drama in Education (N.J.)* 17 (3): 8-15.

Mienczakowski, J., R. Smith, and M. Sinclair. 1996. "On the Road to Catharsis: A Framework for Theoretical Change." *Qualitative Inquiry, USA* 2(4): 439-462.

Morgan, S., A. Rolfe, and J. Mienczakowski. 1998. "Exploration! Intervention! Education! Health Promotion! Reviewing the Application of Ethno-Drama to Mental Health." TasTHEMHS. September 7-11. Casino Hotel, Hobart.

Richardson, L. 1991. "Post-Modern Social Theory." *Sociological Theory* 9: 173-179.

_____ . 1992. "The Consequences of Poetic Representation: Writing the Other, Rewriting the Self." Pp. 125-137 in *Investigating Subjectivity: Research on Lived Experience*, edited by C. Ellis and M. G. Flaherty. Newbury Park, CA: Sage.

_____ . 1993. "Poetics, Dramatics, and Transgressive Validity: The Case of the Skipped Line." *The Sociological Quarterly* 35: 695-710.

_____ . 1994. "Nine Poems. Marriage and the Family. *The Journal of Contemporary Ethnography* 23: 3-13.

Rorty, R. 1980. *Philosophy and the Mirror of Nature*. Princeton, NJ: Princeton University Press.

Todorov, T. 1977. *The Poetics of Prose*. Ithaca, NY: Cornell University Press.

Turner, V. 1986. *The Anthropology of Performance*. New York: Performing Arts Journal Publications.

Watkins, P. 1990. "All the World's a Stage." *Nursing Times* 86(21): 47-48.

Woods, P. 1996. *Researching the Art of Teaching: Ethnography for Educational Use*. London: Routledge.

Zantiotis, A. 1998. "Ethnographic Evaluations, AST." Coombabah State High School Curriculum.

DISTANCING RESEARCH OBJECTS
THROUGH INVOLVEMENT OF THE SELF

Bob Jeffrey

The suspension, or bracketing, of values feelings and prejudices is not now considered to be viable in qualitative research (Richardson 1990; Rose 1990; Woods 1996). It is also argued that the researcher's subjective and imaginative activity is an essential part of the analytical process (Eisner 1979; Ely et al. 1997; Woods 1996). The researcher's main instrument is him or herself (Woods 1986), as observer, interpreter, constructor and recorder of contexts and interactions. If the subjective creative approach is to be supported, is it still possible to satisfy demands for plausibility and credibility (Hammersley 1992)? Woods argues that both involvement and distance are necessary features of qualitative research and that,

> To guard against the dangers of going native, one is advised to cultivate some social distance. The researcher is, after all, different from the subjects of the research. She or he is there to research, to plumb the depths and "get to the bottom of things" certainly, but of all groups involved in any specified interaction and in the way that recognises put-ons, power positions, "line shooting" and fairy tales. She is also there to analyse, to advance explanations, and to represent material in ways that might not otherwise occur to the inmates. Establishing comparative bases in and among groups, cultivating rap-

Studies in Educational Ethnography, Volume 2, pages 163-182.
Copyright © 1999 by JAI Press Inc.
All rights of reproduction in any form reserved.
ISBN: 0-7623-0563-0

port with other groups, triangulation of methods to increase validity, reflectivity outside the situation, the consideration of material post hoc, the writing up of field notes
and diaries all aid the process and enable the researcher, if involvement and distance
are cultivated in a judicious mix, to have the best of both (Woods 1996, p. 62).

It is not detachment that is required for this implies an objectivity which would
run counter to the theory that involvement is necessary to understand research
contexts. Detachment also implies an objective representation whereas the methodology used in much qualitative research, including my own, accepts the theory
that the researcher constructs the representation.

The methodological concept of distance accepts that the researcher is part of
the research frame. Film and theatre audiences and readers of books engage
with the plot and character interactions as a "reality" while also recognizing the
role of the director and writer in selecting and shaping their experience of the
construction. In qualitative social science the researcher's subjectivity is recognized as a central part of the representation of research contexts (Richardson
1990; Wolcott 1990; Woods 1996) and through methodological explanations
researchers account for the ways in which their subjectivity influences their representations. Distancing is achieved by comparing and contrasting the
researcher's close involvement with alternative research material of similar sites
and comparing analysis with other perspectives derived from relevant theoretical models. The research site is also considered and analyzed within its geographical, social and political context.

The club golfer, like the involved researcher, knows the various undulations
and slopes of his or her course or research context in great detail and has a personal experience that contrasts with other club members or researchers. The
golfer gains another perspective of the course in terms of its own internal construction and its relation to the wider environment when they either see it dis-
played on a map or are able to view it from a high point in the locality. They
gain new perspectives in the twists, turns and undulations of each hole and how
the eighteen holes fit together. The researcher uses other perspectives—triangulation—to gain a more distanced view of the research site. Golfers' experiences
of playing other courses add to the conceptualizations they have of their own
course and new analyses are carried out in terms of quality, difficulty and interest. They are also part of a wider international golfing frame experienced
through magazines and television and one in which they are able to make connections and comparisons with their own golfing experiences and the characteristics of their own course. In similar fashion, researchers employ other theories
and models to compare and contrast their own experiences. Golfers are also part
of an even wider frame of general life. They are able, if they so chose, to consider the value of golf compared with other leisure and social activities. They
are also able to consider issues concerning the use of the land for golf instead of

agriculture, the use of a wide range of pesticides and what might be considered extravagant water consumption.

The distancing of the researcher is only a distancing within a wider frame of involvement but nevertheless it ensures that the researcher uses other experiences and perspectives in the analytical process. Distancing is, in social science terms, the collection of subjective observations and analysis, the comparison of these with other research, perspectives and theories, alongside temporary withdrawals from the immediate research site to consider the wider environment. The process of distancing is mainly achieved through writing, for it is in this process that conceptions are formed and articulated. Written texts are then put alongside each other, alongside the other collected material and reconstructed by the researcher until an "authentic" (Guba and Lincoln 1994) version is constructed. The process does not deny the researcher's engagement or involvement. The latter is necessary for insight and imagination but it is put alongside other analyses and re-analyzed through the researcher's cognitive reflections. The manifestation of this activity is in the writing process where thoughts, ideas, feelings and insights are not just recorded but stances are discerned (Ely et al. 1997).

Writing memos is one of the recommended features of qualitative analysis. For Strauss and Corbin (1990) memos are "written records of analysis related to the formulation of theory...They represent the written forms of our abstract thinking about data" (pp. 197-198). For Woods (1996) they can be "free writing memos, one aim of which is to explore our own feelings in relation to what we are discovering" (p. 97). These different memo forms have been distinguished as analytical and reflective (Ely et al. 1997), yet these distinctions are blurred as reflections can also involve analysis. Attempts to respond to the creative use of subjectivity in my research, and the demands of distancing for social science analysis have resulted in the use of two particular forms of free memo writing, the reflective and the vignette (Ely et al. 1997). The former are overtly analytical and may contain some description and the latter are overtly descriptive and may contain some covert analysis. Both display subjectivity for creative and analytical purposes and at the same time they are part of a longer process of distancing the object. Description is the starting point of research and bias is "entry level theorizing" (Wolcott 1995, p. 186). Two main questions are addressed:

- How do the memos evolve and what use are they?
- How far do memos assist in distancing the object?

Written memos from two projects (see below) are used to show how the involvement of the self through identification, playful writing and the engagement of life interests begin the process of distancing.

BACKGROUND

I accept the theory that there is a "reality" to be understood (Hammersley 1992), but that it can only be partially discerned through the constructions created by the researcher. Even interviews or conversations are constructions by both respondent and researcher as they engage in an interaction (Jeffrey 1995). In symbolic interactionist terms the "I" is the creative, interpretative part of the research process and the "me" is the social science form (Woods 1996) that I reflect as I work.

The research sites have been primary schools and classrooms involving two research projects, over the last six years, entitled, "The Effects of the National Curriculum on Creative Teaching" and "The Effects of Ofsted Inspections on Primary Teachers." Professor Peter Woods directed the projects and I conducted fieldwork and initial analysis and writing. Both projects used qualitative methods extensively and within that approach we used ethnographic methods which incorporated depth of involvement over long periods of time. The first project was conducted in five schools and involved about 20 teachers and the second project involved six schools and 80 teachers.

IDENTIFICATION

The self has a past and a future (Woods 1996) and identification with the respondents at the research site was an expression of the self that I could not eradicate. I identified emotionally, experientially, appreciatively and humanely.

Emotional Identification

The memo, *Swans*—stimulated by a visit to *Swan Lake*—led to a sympathetic description of all the teachers at one school.

> I left the school, on that Friday before the inspection, at 5:30 to go to *Swan Lake* at Covent Garden and I found out later that Cloe was the last to leave at 9:45. As I enjoyed the invigorating and delightful music of the first Act of *Swan Lake* with its party atmosphere I began to feel quite close to the Trafflon teachers and felt angry that they were not part of this very jolly and uplifting environment. Later, over the weekend and on the first day of the inspection, I put together some thoughts about why I really liked these people....I am moved by the pain of it all, by the stress, by the plummeting of self esteem, by seeing how their cherished values in terms of pedagogy are being marginalized, by their fear of failure, and by the tensions created. I am particularly moved by the way these people, who have committed themselves to their pupils and gained over the years some measure of confidence about what they do and what they can contribute to society, find themselves to be no more than units to be examined, observed, scrutinized and assessed. This particular week was the lowest time for them as they entered into the fringes of the central spotlight of power—the Ofsted inspection.

I ended the memo with two questions:

> Does this approach—impressionistic/subjective—have a place in ethnography if it goes alongside the respondent's perspectives and is triangulated by other testimony within the context? Is it actually our responsibility to make public our subjective involvement?

The subjective expression of my feelings towards the teachers assisted with the empathy I needed to gain (Woods 1996) in seeing the context of an Ofsted inspection from their perspective. These were not the last words that were written about this school and these teachers but they helped me get closer to them, to immerse myself for a while in their lives. What was more relevant was the support I gained from the director of the research:

> The aim of this particular memo is understanding rather than validity (cf. Wolcott 1994), relevance rather than rigour (Stake 1981), pursuing the idea that research "should rely more on personal experience and personal meaning as its data, and more on participant observation and introspection in its method" (Woods 1996, p. 106).

My subjective writing was welcomed by my colleagues, and considered to be an integral part of the process of data collection and analysis. It encouraged me to speak more forthrightly. The articulation of my feelings was in contrast to my ideological constructs of primary teachers. "I like all of them, all those I engage with, in spite of the fact that I know we often differ in terms of educational practice, educational values and political biases." My feelings and reflectivity developed awareness (Rowland 1996).

Experiential Identification

My experience affected my interpretation. In the same *Swans* memo I alluded to the class connections between us. I failed the 11 plus examination and came from a single-parent family living in a low-rise council flat until I went to college.

> Most of these teachers are what I would call working-class teachers. I have not gathered all the statistics yet but it has become clear that many of them have had a struggle to get themselves to their position. Carol, the reception teacher went to secondary modern school after failing her 11 plus, gained one A level and went straight to college and then to this school where she enjoys her language post and never has wanted a managerial role, for class teaching is her main interest. Clare the part-timer did have a middle-class father who was a French fashion designer but he died when she was 20 and left only debts. She went to grammar school and then college. Tania trained in Cyprus and began teaching here in the 1950s and has used this job to support her family, who as immigrants haven't had it easy. Toni, the deputy head, came from a family who were interested in education but she failed her 11 plus. She has a couple of A levels and went straight from college into teaching which she enjoys and she feels that she makes a valuable contribution as deputy head. Veronica left home at 17 and worked full time while studying part time to obtain qualifications for entry into college. All she ever wanted to be was a teacher and she loves school. She downplays her academic potential but waxes lyrical about her teach-

ing and her children. Vicky, the Nigerian teacher, was concerned that she didn't understand the primary system that her children were to enter, so she decided to get a job in a primary school. She has grown to enjoy the enthusiastic children and the close relationships a primary teacher develops with their pupils. Again her immigrant status has meant she stays within a working-class frame. Cloe failed her 11 plus and went to a Secondary Modern School. Her school changed to a Comprehensive the year she was supposed to leave at 15 to be a shorthand typist, so she stayed on and did an extra year to get her A levels. From there she went to training college. Vincent, the head teacher, began his working life as a hospital porter and consequently gained his qualifications late but has since then committed himself to teaching and working in one London borough.

The rise from working-class backgrounds to respected professionals in an inner city school is to be celebrated and not denigrated by government rhetoric about ill qualified teachers. Secondly, they have all committed themselves to the working-class pupils of this particular area with some of them specifically rejecting the chance of more middle-class teaching. I'm aware that these classifications are problematic but their use is initially limited to this memo.

It was a chance comment that prompted me to delve into their backgrounds and I was urged on by my similar experiences. The data enabled me to identify teacher commitment as a defining characteristic of the sample and to describe commitment in more depth. However, the characteristic was also subjected to negative comparisons (Strauss and Corbin 1990). Both emotional and experiential identification led to appreciation.

Appreciative Identification

My identification with the teachers developed into an appreciation of teachers' work and was written up in *Appreciation* which contrasted a Royal Ballet review (Parry 1995) of Twyla Tharp's new ballet *Mr. Worldly Wise* with a school's Ofsted inspection report.

The review interprets scenes—"the image is a metaphor"—whereas the report appears to present scientific truth. Performances in the ballet are danced "with heartbreaking grace" whereas the "quality of teaching is sound or better in most lessons'; "the cutting edge choreography is both goofy and rhapsodic" whereas "where teaching is good it is characterized by effective organisation and management, good subject expertise and clear planning." There is an air of appreciation in the review as one of the principal dancers "while dancing with crystal clarity was concentrating too hard on the opening night to enjoy herself." There is no attempt in the report to acknowledge the humanity of an inspection situation, only a criticism that, "some teachers fail to use an appropriate range of teaching approaches."

The differences between the functions of a review and a report were acknowledged in the memo but teaching is also an appreciation of qualities (Eisner 1979) and an artistic activity (Woods 1996). Surrender to the object is essential to activate the creative process (Bruner 1962). It is the sustained intensification with the data and analysis, the reciprocity that brings creativity (Ely et al. 1997). The self is acknowledged as a daily part of analytical practice through the importance of the concept of appreciation and at the same time distance is attained through considering the teacher's practice in wider contexts.

Humane Identification

My feelings were also responsible for direct intervention in the research field described in a memo called *Confession Time*, a follow up to the *Swans* memo, which was sent to my team.

> I didn't mention in the memo how far I had become involved. There were three occasions when I offered some advice or help to people who were somewhat distressed or worried. I've been worrying myself about how to explain these incidents to you and now it seems to be the right time.

I described how I had intervened in an inspection process through the cases of "the marginalized part-timer," "the dodgy inspector," and "the worried postholder." At the end of the memo to Professor Woods I was contrite, "I trust my actions don't compromise you or the research and perhaps we ought to discuss my actions in the light of future inspections." At the time I felt guilty about my actions for I believed I was in breach of my job description which said I was not to overtly influence the process I was researching. However, Peter Woods's reply emphasized the human element in the research process.

> We are interested, like the inspectors, in educational improvement though our conception of what that constitutes differs in some key respects as does the teachers'. There are other issues related to those differences, to do with aiding people in their struggle against domination, revealing practices, particularly hidden practices, that operate against commonly held views of fairness and justice, portraying the needless misery that is caused by such practices, and providing practices that might alleviate the situation (Woods 1996, p. 113).

(For further discussion of these particular memos and the correspondence between Peter Woods and myself see Woods 1996, pp. 96-117.)

Involving oneself with people at the research site is productive in terms of data but also means that one must act humanely for it is a human practice within which researcher and respondent engage. The engagement involves feelings and judgement together and there may be times when one decides to act humanely in the greater interest of the person at the expense of the research. In an extension of these connections I made friends with some of the teachers. I became involved in their lives as indicated in a memo on *Research Methodology* written in 1994.

> My examples include: offering Theresa some of my positive observations to support her appraisal and agreeing to act as a reference; discussing the organization of Laura's MA work; acting as therapist and pedagogic friend to Grace and continuing a friendship with Marilyn and her family whom I knew prior to the research, e.g. we discussed the pros and cons of headship prior to her going to look at a deputy headship....

"Going native" arises out of anthropology and ethnography (Hammersley 1992; Wolcott 1995) and is concerned with researchers limiting themselves to following the perspective of the respondents. However, friendship does not simply imply total agreement over the interpretation of a context. In employing "key informants" (Woods 1986) often the relationship becomes a close one (Burgess 1991), but these are the very people with whom the researcher can debate some of the more controversial interpretations from the analysis. I found some difficulty in gaining respondent validation for some of my case study writing, since the teachers did not wish to be identified by other teachers in the same school, yet contextual clues often made anonymity impossible. The key informants who became my friends were the people with whom I found I could share some of the analysis. Our mutual respect enabled me to show them controversial early drafts and to encourage them to feel able to be critical of the analysis. I trusted them not to take advantage of information provided by colleagues and they trusted me to strive for authenticity (Wolcott 1995). In this way human involvement led to more rigor through a form of familial critique and therefore a distancing of the object. The identification with the research context was enacted alongside playful writing that engaged my imagination.

PLAYFUL WRITING

There is a narrative element in both life and writing (Richardson 1990) and the process and presentation of qualitative research relies heavily on both. The relationship between ethnographic description and the development of valid explanation and theory are central to the dilemma of the qualitative method. "On the one hand social phenomena cannot be understood without taking account of subjective as well as objective factors; yet, at present we have no way of capturing subjective factors that meet the requirements of science" (Blumer 1979 in Hammersley 1989, p. 4). Description is part of the qualitative method, it checks analysis (Wolcott 1994) and narrative is a method of inquiry and a way of knowing as well as a virtual experience of literary constructs, bridges to interpretation (Ely et al. 1997). The literary form may not be the one that dominates most social science writing but in the process of qualitative research it adds insight as the researcher explores the various perspectives through which the research site can be viewed. A form of playful writing is employed to construct memos and vignettes that are categorized as light narratives, evocations, stories and metaphoric analogies.

Light Narratives

The headteacher of one of my research schools had asked me to hang around so I could introduce myself to the RgI (lead inspector). She had shown the RgI a letter I had sent her outlining the project and assuring her that I would not interfere with the inspection.

> As the RgI left the parents meeting at 5:10 p.m., followed by two other inspectors, both women, they proceeded along the corridor, where I was lurking, followed by the headteacher who said as they approached me, "this is the researcher who wrote the letter I showed you." The RgI smiled, held out her hand whilst continuing her march towards the governors' meeting in the other building. I shook hands, and without interrupting her step, she passed by without an acknowledgement, a spoken word or a receding glance. The entourage followed with the HT muttering "I've got tea and cakes ready for you," as they passed into the playground. I, meanwhile, didn't quite know whether to be grateful that I had been privileged to touch the hand of this busy august personage or whether I should feel appreciative of her busy schedule. I felt as though I was in a Tudor film, lining the streets as the Royal entourage passed by, feeling gratified at the opportunity to be recognized for a brief second. Or was I in a fantasy wonderland with Alice (*The Sweep*).

There was bias in this memo. However, it is argued that some biases are good ones (Ely et al. 1997). Early writing should also "help ferret out biases and prejudices in such a way as to deal with them explicitly, from the outset of an inquiry, rather than to have to fight them off as we go along" (Wolcott 1995, p. 201). In the rest of the memo I raised an analytical issue of patriarchy.

> The women were dressed very elegantly in an official manner. They wore jackets and had a square cuboid look to their bodily outline. Bourdieu (1992) claims that *habitus* is cloaked in manners and gestures and I wondered whether I had just witnessed an example of the acting out of patriarchal manners and gestures by females. This is the first of the five inspections I have researched to be run by women and I hope to look for gender differences, but maybe Ofsted is one example where gender differences have been eradicated, by the patriarchal world of inspections.

The memo also stimulated a second insight, of which I was not initially aware. The change in power relations in an inspection was exemplified by my observation of the headteacher's behavior and further explored later in *The Inspection Week*. The playful description of obsequiousness by the headteacher challenged me to ascertain the extent to which this situation was replicated in other circumstances and in other schools. We (Woods and Jeffrey 1996) have found that tone and atmosphere offer insights into the nature of research sites and playing with these observations provides an ethnographic perception while at the same time providing new categories that can be tested in other research sites or against triangulated material.

Evocations

Ethnographic description was used to describe the atmosphere in a school during the weekend before an inspection (*The Calm*).

It's ten past ten on Saturday morning. I'm sitting in the infant hall with my back to the windows facing the display boards. It is very quiet and a contrast to the normal buzz and chatter of a school. I can hear a blackbird singing in the garden. The light, albeit filtered through tall pot plants climbing up the large window frames, shows up the highly polished floor. Every display board has uniform three centimetre borders made from black sugar paper—one was removed because it didn't conform. The contents of the displays are all mounted and uniform computer printed labels explain the contents or challenge the reader to respond mutely. There are very few written labels written by teachers. All is nearly ready for the inspection event....As I contemplate the school's quiet confidence the calm is punctuated by the moving of furniture, the playing of some music, the hammering of a staple gun or the sudden whistling of a teacher leaping briskly down the stairs. Or more unusually the burst of laughter from two or three teachers gathered in a corridor or in someone's classroom. The silence is again disturbed by the low hum of two petrol lawn mowers as they circle the lone willow tree cutting the grass of the main green play area. This is Saturday morning and one wonders if the workers are being paid overtime rates. The Premises Officer is playing his full part in the preparation. The teaching staff have already commented on the surprise of having new locks on the loo doors. All is nearly ready for the inspection event....The main hall in the upper school is totally covered with a school journey display that spills out onto the corridor. Every piece of wall is covered with over 400 treble mounted pieces of work and photographs representing this year's journey to Kent. The windowsills are used to display artefacts and folders of children's work. All is nearly ready for the inspection event.

   The hall is set up for assembly on Monday. There is a newish lectern bought by the head after she first heard about the Ofsted visit and in keeping with the school's developing emphasis on religious assemblies. (She hoped that the lectern would bring "a sense of awe." Some teachers would have preferred the money spent on books.) There is a matching chair and another one on the other side of the lectern. There are two tall pot plants behind the chairs flanking the lectern and the chairs. A music stand is to one side waiting for a child to play some music. Large printed numbers have appeared on the walls in recent days to indicate where each class should sit. I thought, at first, they were hymn numbers. All is nearly ready for the inspection event.

This form of writing brings me closer to the research site because I have invested my "self" in the site and I literally "feel" my interpretation. Seamus Heaney (1995) talks of poetry being the crossing from the matter of fact to the domain of imagination, the frontier of writing. Via a poem by Robert Frost, Heaney describes the frontier for the child as that between the farmhouse and the imaginative play area elsewhere on the site that a child creates to understand his or her home and life. He sees the same situation applying to adults.

> He (Frost) convinces us that the playhouse has the measure of the other house, that the entranced focus of the activity that took place as make believe on one side of the yard (by the child) was fit to match the meaning of what happened in earnest on the other side (in the main home) and in doing so Frost further suggests that the imaginative transformation of human life is the means by which we can most truly grasp and comprehend it. What Virgil called *lacrimae rerum*, the tears of things, can be absorbed and re-experienced in the playthings in the playhouse—or in other words in the poem (Heaney 1995, p. xv).

In the same way, a social science writer needs a play area—the literary memo perhaps—to interpret and understand his or her research engagement. Heaney goes on to suggest that writing is "the movement from delight to wisdom and not vice versa" (p. 5). The early days of analysis are not all to do with coding and categorizing. The memos, which connect personal interests and analysis, are not poems but they are expressions of engagement as I attempt to understand the "other" world I am encountering. However, although I avail myself of poetry's techniques my task is not poetry, it is understanding, analysis and conceptualization. Playful writing assists this process but I also have to be conscious of the danger of being captured by the data (Ely et al. 1997). In doing so I distance that world.

Stories

Stories illuminate a reality (Rowland 1996) as does this description of the school staff room on the Monday morning of the inspection, before teaching began.

> I have been restricted to the staff room during the day and as I make my way there I don't come across anybody. They are already in their classrooms. The staff room is deserted, only the occasional sound of the water heater is heard. Ava, the job share nursery is the first to come in the staff room. She has come in to see what the inspectors look like and to wish the staff good luck....She describes how the Chair of Governors appeared in the school at ten past eight and visited every classroom to wish all the teachers good luck. "It was like inspecting the troops before the battle, like Monty did, to show how the general cared about them." At 8:44 the rest of the staff arrive. There is much talk and occasional jocularity....There are three boxes of sweet things, milk chocolate marshmallows, a packet of dark and white chocolate biscuits and a tin of butterscotch shortbread, on the main central table around which people sit. The marshmallows are opened and Angelina and Aileen declare they are "eating for Ofsted." Most of the teachers have put on their smarter clothes.
>
> At 8:47 the inspection team led by the Registered Inspector enters the room....The RgI then explains the procedure for grading teachers and the atmosphere changes as people quieten down and serious expressions are maintained....She asks if there are any questions. There is a silence of about ten seconds and at this point the inspectors take their leave....The head then breaks the quietness with a call for Amy to read her Ofsted poem. There are some cries of agreement and some laughter, as some teachers have already heard it, and Amy stands on a chair to declaim it.
>
> During this rendition, focused on by all the teachers round the table...the teachers laugh at the appropriate points and at the end they clap loudly. The poem is ceremoniously pinned to the centre of the notice board and Amy declares, in answer to a question, that it took her only five minutes or so, for "if there's the feeling it comes easily." There is loud chatting and amongst this hubbub Laura notices me scribbling quickly and with a glint of humour tempered by the euphoria and tension of the moment she says "you're just a vulture" and Esther gives me a short diary of her last week. The head then raises her voice above the chatter, and says "once more into the breach, dear friends" and all the teachers begin to leave the staff room for their station, some of them trying to break into singing "we shall overcome." With loud laughs and chatter the event has begun.

My impressionistic playing with the scene, using phrases such as "quietness punctured," "circling the lone willow tree," "ceremoniously pinned" is an evocation that excites my imagination even though I know it may well not have a final place in any academic paper. However, it appealed to some of the teachers who elaborated on their experiences and they re-interpreted those experiences after reading it. This is not to be seen as unduly influencing the respondents but opening another window on their world, part of the ethnographic process (Woods 1996, Wolcott 1995). It also gives me a memorable picture of the research site with its contrasts explicitly portrayed and these contrasts play a central part in the distancing process. The playing with the empirical data encourages one to experiment with metaphors.

Metaphoric Analogies

According to some, all writing—even scientific writing—is metaphorically based (Harrison and Gordon 1983; Jeffrey 1997; Richardson 1990; Rose 1990; Tanesini 1995):

> Metaphor is the backbone of social science writing, and like a true spine it bears weight, permits movement, links parts together into a functional coherent whole—and is not immediately visible (Richardson 1990, p. 18).

To be conscious is to discern relations between things and to begin to construct metaphors (Harrison and Gordon, 1983). Although aware of Becker's (1986) advice to search for fresh metaphors the playing with the data initially uses old metaphors. In one memo, *The Examination*, I not only pushed the context to the limit but mixed my metaphors.

> The similarities of a Ministry of Transport Test (MoT) for a motor car and an Ofsted inspection are that the mechanic has a set of components to investigate and he is looking for those component parts that are failing. Ofsted inspectors have a framework that identifies parts of a school or classroom activity and they, like the mechanic, attempt to identify the failing parts. The mechanic marks certain components as failing and then leaves it up to the car's owner to go and get the components fixed, as does the Ofsted inspector. It also has to be noticed that a mechanic in pursuance of his investigation climbs into the body of the car to check various components, into its bowels. They shake components, tap various parts of the bodywork and swivel moving parts to test their functionality. In a similar fashion the inspector creeps into the body of a teacher's classroom, observes and evaluates working activities, questions and examines the children, and investigates activities for functionality but, unlike the mechanic, with no indication of what kind of evaluation they are making.

The analogy exercise heightened the contrast between the teachers experiencing inspection and the inspector's examination process and this was further developed in *Inspection Week* where a First World War metaphor was employed.

> At 10:20 the head popped in to say that the RgI had already made some complimentary comments to her about some of the lesson plans. She seemed pleased and relieved and I was glad for her but being somewhat distant from the action I wondered how far the

compliments not only reassured the head, but also at the same time legitimated the RgI's power position in relation to the school and the staff. There was clearly more than one interpretation to any incident that occurred. There were many more such reports to me from the head and to anyone else who happened to be in the staff room. She buzzed around tweaking a bit of organisation here and there, reporting all positive comments and events and rushing off in mid sentence to do something else. This was not the General evaluating the battle plan and devising new strategies, this was the adjutant ensuring that everything went smoothly, clearing away newly emerged obstacles, making sure papers and people were in the right place for the inspectors, reporting positive events and generally boosting morale....

The war metaphor pervaded the rest of the *Inspection Week* memo and in discussion with colleagues the relative merits of it were assessed. Other metaphors were proposed and we discussed whether any overt metaphor was necessary at all. The discussion was another part of the process of analysis and distancing, stimulated firstly by my playfulness and imagination. The *Undressing* memo followed a similar theme:

> However, there is something fundamentally different. The school and the teachers have been re-dressed by Ofsted. The clothes may look the same but they have been re-dressed with Ofsted's hands of approval or disdain. There is a new inner lining to their clothes. One which reminds them constantly that Ofsted's priorities and pedagogy are paramount and that Ofsted has the power to undress you, gaze at you and, in the spotlight of their supporters, re-dress one with care or brutality as they see fit. They have effectively colonized (Hargreaves 1994) the primary teacher's domain, their classroom and their identity.

Metaphoric analogies are used for emphasis and are often "over the top" and are later examined for appropriateness. Are the inspectors merely technicians or do they invoke human and professional values? Does the body metaphor make victims of mainly women teachers? Does a war situation reflect accurately the contact between teachers and inspectors? In this process, the research site is seen in many different ways which ensures a rigorous effort to discern an appropriate reality, albeit a partial one. It is more than a triangulation, which is a limited technical approach (Massey 1997), it is a crystallization of reality (Richardson 1990). However, metaphoric analogies also act as a cautionary warning concerning the analytical process, for they have to be examined for appropriateness and often rejected. In this process a critical climate is developed. Nevertheless, they are used as recognition points, as signs on the path to a more distanced representation.

ENGAGING LIFE INTERESTS

The influence of self upon the research process and the delight of writing are complemented by the way my personal life impinges on the analysis. Music has been used extensively as a means to encapsulate my reflections and analysis; for example, I used some musical terms to describe the tone of some creative teachers' classrooms (Woods and Jeffrey 1996). I have also used my interests in opera and ballet to "play" (Rowland 1996) with the research although other personal interests, such as gardening or football, might well be used by others. The use of life interests is slightly more distanced than playful writing and again a little more distanced than subjective identification. The life interests are used more conceptually to stimulate analytical insights, provide comparative contexts and to engage with methodological issues, and although these often overlap within specific memos they have been differentiated here more for emphasis than the portrayal of distinct analytical writing.

Analytical Insights

An account of sitting with a silent but intense audience at a performance of *La Traviata* was used to reflect upon the idea of social learning in a research project concerned with creative teaching (Woods and Jeffrey 1996).

In the opera, Violetta, a courtesan slowly dying of consumption, who lives in nineteenth-century Paris, has found love with Alfredo and she has moved to his country home leaving her past life behind her. Germont, Alfredo's father, secretly begs Violetta to give him up, for the gossip is affecting his family's interests and Alfredo's sister's planned engagement. Caught between her personal love for Alfredo and sacrificing herself for his family she chooses the latter and returns to her life in Paris.

> This stillness dominated the theatre. So, what was happening in this stillness? Was it just three thousand individuals soaking up the emotion of the moment alone? Were they all just appreciating the pure sound produced by the singers? They could have done that at home under the headphones alone with their imagination. No, there was something else happening to these three thousand people sat closely together enfolded by the horse-shoe shape of the theatre. As I engaged with the emotional musical scenes and watched the audience I suddenly felt close to these strangers. I had watched many of them arrive in their expensive evening dress, listened to many middle-class accents and reflected on the differences between us. But at this moment I felt close. Perhaps it was the darkness and the stillness that dispersed our differences. No, it wasn't just that. We were having a shared experience. We were sharing an emotion—many emotions. I was able to share my humanity with them through the emotions being wrought on the stage. I knew they had felt some of these emotions in their time and I could empathize with them.
>
> Teachers who are engaged with creative teaching understand the fundamental pedagogic principle of *shared learning*. By sharing experiences through the emotions they not only wish to develop considerate people, but they appreciate that emotional connections with other people are the same connections that pupils make with knowledge; i.e., imaginative and empathetic ones. To this end they encourage and develop many close connections amongst the pupils and between the pupils and themselves.

Analytical insights are made in other memos too but this form of memo is specifically written to highlight an analysis that was constructed or at least reformed through my life in other contexts. It is less about identification with my subjectivity and the research site and more about conceptualizing the research site. It enlarges the conceptualization through the use of analogy and enables me to bring more depth to the analysis. As indicated in the introduction, a specific feature of distancing is the extent to which the analysis is supported by the empirical evidence. The decision as to whether to write up a life interest memo is first of all dependent on the amount of evidence in the data to support the analysis. This type of memo is therefore not only less subjective and playful but more substantial in content.

Comparative Contexts

A feature of this form of memo is the comparative element. A Janácek opera *Kát'a Kabanava* and a television play were used to show the influence of power in teachers' working lives in a memo entitled *Constrained.* The opera, through its powerful music, showed the stifling constraint of an authoritative regime located in Tsarist Russia in the nineteenth century. The situation was portrayed through the story of a love affair in a small community living on the banks of the River Volga, a metaphor for the deterministic oppressive power that led to feelings of guilt and cowardice if resisted.

> Janácek's powerful music describes how Kát'a, within a repressive context, is propelled by forces of liberation and humanity. The opera describes how she struggles to resist both these strong forces. Firstly, she gives in to liberation forces as she follows her feelings, unprotected by her family, and then she takes on feelings of guilt perpetrated by the repressive context and central to the maintenance of that particular order. She "cannot endure the lie" and so she takes her own life, as is expected of anyone breaking those social codes.

This opera plot was compared with a television play, in a modern setting, entitled *Stone, Scissors and Paper* and written by a teacher. It portrayed the story of how a married man, consumed by the loss of his young daughter some years before, acted as a support, for a short time, to a married woman suffering domestic violence and it showed how the relationship helped both of them for a short time. However, their constraints were not easily overcome. Kát'a committed suicide after the affair by throwing herself into the River Volga and the woman in the play was forced to leave the town as the only way to avoid further violence and her "support" reverted to sitting alone with his daughter's keepsakes.

The two dramas were contrasted with primary teachers' constrained working conditions, particularly under an Ofsted inspection, and how they coped with them.

> Their lives, like all four characters in the two plays, are ones which engender great emotions, for they are morally and emotionally committed to their work and they are also constrained within the circumstances of their environments. The powerful Volga was a metaphor for the condemnatory potential of the community of politicians, parents and media, and for teachers a new form of social conscience called accountability engenders the guilt. Are there similarities

to life in a small town in Russia in the mid-1850s, with its patriarchal establishment, and if so are these directed towards to women in particular?

In the *Swans* memo another comparison is made:

> The swan maidens in *Swan Lake* are forced to play the role of swans during the day as a result of becoming victims of an evil spirit. The spell can only be broken if one who has never loved before swears to love Odette, the swan maiden's leader, forever. Odile, an evil spirit, tricks her lover Siegfreid into swearing love to her but when he realizes his mistake he is reunited with Odette. They have only two options: he can marry the "other" Odile and the evil spirit will release Odette from her role as a swan, or they can both die together by drowning themselves in the lake of her mother's tears and destroying the evil spirit in the process. It's not difficult to guess which option the lovers take. Let's hope there is another solution for the teachers affected by Ofsted inspections. For marriage to the Ofsted values of managerialism and constant examination is generally not acceptable to most primary teachers, and the unity in death of the spirit and the self, however harmonious, will cause a loss of commitment to their work.

These comparative writings are playful but they are also more serious attempts to analyze the research site through my other life interests. They provide insights and maintain an abiding involvement with the research site even in my leisure moments.

Methodological Issues

Methodological problems of representation and the debate between ideographic and nomothetic writing have resulted in a series of memos concerning my duty, as I see it, to the people who have been so open with me and the requirements of the social science exercise. A *Don Giovanni* memo, *Representation*, is used to show how the librettist constructs flat characters (Atkinson 1990) to suit the plot and how we often do the same, in order to service a typology.

> The opera *Don Giovanni* may appear at first sight to contain a number of rounded characters, but in fact, I argue, all of them are flattened characters who show particular characteristics to enhance the plot and help define the central character Don Giovanni—an amoral philanderer and murderer. Leporello, his servant, is a coward and a "moneygrubber" with no feelings of sympathy at all. Donna Elvira, the rejected wife, represents sexual frailty and pomposity, and Donna Anna, the abused young noblewoman whose father was killed by Giovanni, represents revenge and purity and has no real feelings for her suitor Don Ottavio, who represents a wimpish gentleman with only beauty but no anger. The peasant character Masetto, the wronged man, is typically bullish and cowardly at heart. Zerlina, his fiancée, an accommodating seducee, is probably the only rounded character in the whole opera in that she doesn't resist Giovanni too much and yet she really loves Masetto and eventually embraces him....An Ofsted inspection is not a theatre or a play but research based on real people who we are re-constructing as characters to gain some insight into their problematic lives and so typologies or flat characters may not reflect the complexity of these reconstructions.

As a consequence of these concerns, I wrote some individual profiles as part of the Ofsted research entitled: *The Restructuring of an Ofsteded Teacher, The Disinclined Engager, The Pedagogic Adjuster, The Jaded Self, The Reluctant Leaver, The Reflective Realist.* I passed these on to the particular teachers for comment and received some mixed reactions. Their main criticism was that these more specific profiles still did not represent the "whole" of them and that being defined by someone else induced feelings of loss of control similar to the feelings engendered for many of them by an Ofsted inspection. Even teachers I have become quite friendly with through the research are somewhat reluctant to give whole-hearted support to what they see as a partial representation even though they appreciate our aim of theorizing contexts. So, attempts to resolve an issue of representation only confirmed earlier theoretical assumptions that all representation is partial. This particular issue was encapsulated for me via the *Don Giovanni* opera experience and supported a critique of our work in representation. The distancing of the issue was achieved through further critique brought about by critical respondent validation, which worked to assist the articulation of our methodological limitations.

CONCLUSION

The memos, in large part, have not appeared in the main social science books we have produced (Jeffrey and Woods 1998; Woods and Jeffrey 1996; Woods et al. 1997), nor have the personal experiences and literary styles appeared in full as ethnographies. However, we did include a chapter on three "rounded characters" (Atkinson 1990) in our first book (Woods and Jeffrey 1996) and we have included *The Event* and *The Inspection Week* as a piece of ethnographic writing interwoven between the social science chapters in our Ofsted book. Ironically, the "individual profiles" found themselves used as parts of a typology (Woods et al. 1997), though we clearly expressed our concerns about the limitations of the methodology.

The war metaphor was abandoned, as was the invasion of the classroom body, and most of the MoT image. The "undressing" metaphor was used in the main text of the Ofsted book and the colonization metaphor became a main theme of the research analysis (Jeffrey and Woods 1998). The actual inspection context was eventually considered to be more complex than most of the metaphors used in the memos. Discourse theory was used to show how differences between teachers and inspectors emerged and how each acted to affect the context. *The Swans, Confession Time* and *The Art of Appreciation*, together with e-mail replies from Peter Woods were used as a chapter to highlight the art of research (Woods 1996) and the rest of the memos, including many not mentioned in this chapter, lie expended in various files.

Woods (1986) urges involvement, a measure of distance and a constant debate with oneself achieved through immersion and empathy, a "warm hearted approach" but triangulated by merging the self and other, art and science in the memo, in other words research as praxis (Woods 1996). The constant writing of varied memos is a form of personal discipline to illuminate stance, to keep in mind how we are kidnapped by the data and how we must try to maintain the data's integrity (Ely et al. 1997). This discipline inspires self-reflection and is an answer to the charge of self-indulgence for it acknowledges the influence of culture upon my observations and constructions (Ellis and Bochner 1996). I cannot ignore my history or my "self" but I can employ a variety of perspectives and varied forms of representation—narratives, anecdotes, stories, poems, layered accounts, pastiche, vignettes, written dramas (Ely et al. 1997).

The memos perform a range of functions. They:

- develop and generate insights and understandings,
- create a series of dialectics as they are contrasted with each other,
- bring a critical edge to the process of analysis,
- are a form of intellectual inquiry and debate,
- bring more concentrated activity to the construction of reality,
- widen the field of vision,
- bring bias into the open,
- engage the researcher's general life interests and enthusiasms,
- develop self-understanding and consciousness.

However, there are some more questions to be answered. Could much of this analysis have been conceptualized without the written expression of the involvement of the self? Certainly some of the analysis might well have been recorded in a social science form as categories without the experiential identification memo, for example, teacher commitment. The engagement of the self is a very productive aspect of ethnography (Atkinson 1990) and is often achieved through the development of empathy. This entails placing oneself, as far as is possible, into the research context. The use of empathy results not only in a more authentic account of the research site but the possibility of being able to use one's imagination as one empathizes. This enables the researcher, like the research site inhabitants, to create "a reality" of that site, for their perspective of reality is also a construction of their own based on experience, imagination and reflection. In this way the researcher's creative constructions are put alongside the site member's constructions and compared and contrasted.

Not only does the writing of memos and vignettes bring about the possibility of creative insights and bring the researcher's bias to the foreground, it also places the craft of writing (Wolcott 1995) at the centre of the research process. It is mainly through writing that the researcher represents the research site and communicates with an audience. The development of that craft is as important to the research process as is analysis (Becker 1986; Ely et al. 1997; Wolcott 1995; Woods 1996).

There is still, moreover, the question of the extent of distance achieved. As each memo and vignette is critiqued, developed or discarded, as each prejudice and interest is illuminated and as each analytical process is rigorously triangulated and negatively compared so the researcher distances himself or herself from the object. However, distance is not detachment from the object. It is a construction of the research site from many perspectives, an acknowledgement that the self's involvement has been integral to the process but that it has been taken into account, and that the final outcome of any research is still an interpretation of the researcher. In this way the memos and vignettes are treated as data to be considered, coded, compared, negated and problematized alongside other triangulated perspectives. As each construction is compared and contrasted, a gradual distancing through comparison and reflection is achieved until the researcher is confident that his or her methodology has been as open as is possible and examined rigorously for authenticity of construction. The researcher is on that high point overlooking the course, reflecting on his or her experiences of its intricate features, comparing it to other courses they know and considering how to represent it to a related community. Distance is relative and continually connected to the research site through the researcher's self.

There are strategic activities that can assist in research writing gaining credibility and plausibility within this model of research through the self. Firstly, there is publication of details of the research process (e.g. Richardson 1990; Wolcott 1990, 1995; Woods 1996). Secondly, there is the inclusion of alternative forms of research writing in standard social science texts (e.g. Jeffrey and Woods 1998; Woods and Jeffrey 1996) and thirdly, there is research writing for different audiences (Richardson 1990).

Memo and vignette writing opens the writer to opportunities for analysis and appreciation (Eisner 1979) by using the full force of his or her experience and self. As writers we can use typologies and develop categories providing we are explicit about our wide-ranging methodology and the involvement of our subjectivity. As social scientists we may be able to satisfy the more generous of our colleagues that subjective involvement is positive providing we continually look for negative comparisons (Glaser and Strauss 1967) and continually filter our texts through increasingly fine strainers (Ely et al. 1997). If we inhabit a continuum (Ely et al. 1997) with Hammersley's stress on explanation and prediction at one end and Ball's (1991) understanding and insight at the other the implication is that we can influence one another and shift, depending on audience (Richardson 1990), backwards and forwards along the continuum.

REFERENCES

Atkinson, P. 1990. *The Ethnographic Imagination.* London: Routledge.
Ball, S. J. 1991. "Power, Conflict, Micropolitics and All That!" In *Doing Educational Research,* edited by G. Walford. London: Routledge.

Becker, H. S. 1986. *Writing for Social Sciences*. Chicago: University of Chicago Press.

Bourdieu, P., and L. J. D.Wacquant. 1992. *An Invitation to Reflexive Sociology*. Cambridge: Polity Press.

Burgess, R. G. 1991. "Sponsors, Gatekeepers, Members and Friends: Access in Educational Settings." In *Experiencing Fieldwork*, edited by W.B. Shaffir and R.A. Stebbings. London: Sage.

Bruner, J. 1962. *On Knowing: Essays for the Left Hand*. New York: Atheneum.

Eisner, E. 1979. *The Educational Imagination*. London: Collier Macmillan.

Ellis, C., and A. P. Bochner. 1996. *Composing Ethnography: Alternative Forms of Qualitative Writing*. London: Sage.

Ely, M., R. Vinz, M. Downing, and M. Anzul. 1997. *On Writing Qualitative Research: Living by Words*. London: Falmer

Glaser, B., and A. Strauss. 1967. *The Discovery of Grounded Theory*. Chicago: Aldine.

Guba, E.C., and Y.S. Lincoln. 1994. "Competing Paradigms in Qualitative Research." In *Handbook of Qualitative Research*, edited by N. K. Denzin and Y. Lincoln. Newbury Park, CA: Sage.

Hammersley, M. 1989. *The Dilemma of Qualitative Method: Herbert Blumer and the Chicago Tradition*. London: Routledge.

_____. 1992. "Some Reflections on Ethnography and Validity." *Qualitative Studies in Education* 5 (3): 195-203.

Hargreaves, A. 1994. *Changing Teachers, Changing Times: Teachers' Work and Culture in the Postmodern Age*. London: Cassell.

Harrison, B., and H. Gordon. 1983. "Metaphor as Thought: Does Northtown Need Poetry?" *Educational Review* 35 (3): 265-278.

Heaney, S. 1995. *The Redress of Poetry: Oxford Lectures*. London: Faber and Faber.

Jeffrey, B. 1995. "Problematising Conversations." Presented at St Hilda's at Warwick Ethnography Conference. September, unpublished.

_____. 1997. "Metaphors and Representation: Problems and Heuristic Possibilities in Ethnography and Social Science Writing." *International Education* 27 (1): 22-50.

Jeffrey, B. and P. Woods. 1998. *Testing Teachers: The Effects of School Inspections on Primary Teachers*. London: Falmer.

Massey, A. 1997. "Why the Concept of Triangulation Should be Banished from Qualitative Work (a Memo)." September. Department of Educational Studies. Oxford, unpublished.

Parry, J. 1995. "Two Wise Men." *Observer*, December 17. Observer Publications, London, Guardian Newspapers.

Richardson, L. 1990. *Writing Strategies: Reaching Diverse Audiences*. London: Sage.

Rose, J. 1990. *Living the Ethnographic Life*. London: Sage.

Rowland, S. 1996. "A Lovers' Guide to University Teaching?" Presented to BERA at Lancaster. September, unpublished.

Stake, R.E. 1981. "A Needed Subjectivity in Educational Research." *Discourse* 1 (2): 1-8.

Strauss, A. and J. Corbin. 1990. *Basics of Qualitative Research—Grounded Theory Procedures and Techniques*. London: Sage.

Tanesini, A. 1995. "'The Spiders Web' and 'The Tool': Nietzsche vis-à-vis Rorty on Metaphor." In *Nietzsche: A Critical Reader*, edited by P.R. Sedgewick. Oxford: Blackwell.

Thrasher, F. 1927. *The Gang*. Chicago: University of Chicago Press.

Wolcott, H. 1990. *Writing Up Qualitative Research*. Newbury Park, CA: Sage.

_____. 1994. *Transforming Qualitative Data: Description, Analysis, and Interpretation*. London: Sage.

_____. 1995. *The Art of Fieldwork*. London: Sage.

Woods, P. 1986. *Inside Schools: Ethnography in Educational Research*. London: Routledge.

_____. 1996. *Researching the Art of Teaching*. London: Routledge.

Woods, P., and B. Jeffrey. 1996. *Teachable Moments: The Art of Creative Teaching in Primary Schools*. Buckingham: Open University Press.

Woods, P., B. Jeffrey, G. Troman, and M. Boyle. 1997. *Restructuring Schools: Reconstructing Teachers*. Buckingham: Open University Press.

METHODOLOGICAL TRIANGULATION, OR HOW TO GET LOST WITHOUT BEING FOUND OUT

Alexander Massey

The English language is an arsenal of weapons. If you are going to brandish them without checking to see whether or not they are loaded, you must expect to have them explode in your face from time to time (Stephen Fry, The Liar).

STARTING THE JOURNEY

Looking Ahead: Aims of the Chapter

In his book *Images of Organisation*, Morgan (1986) shows how metaphor can illuminate and challenge our everyday thinking, but also constrain it, leading sometimes to the uncritical adoption of certain views and the ill-advised neglect of others. He argues that "the use of metaphor implies a way of thinking and a way of seeing that pervade how we understand our world generally" (p. 12). In particular, he suggests that "metaphor exerts a formative influence on science" (p. 13).

Studies in Educational Ethnography, Volume 2, pages 183-197.
Copyright © 1999 by JAI Press Inc.
All rights of reproduction in any form reserved.
ISBN: 0-7623-0563-0

Table 1.   Common Error Types in Methodological Triangulation

Type A	Using a second method to "prove" the truth of a first method, rather than simply define it as true.
Type B	Claiming that agreement between the results of two methods "proves" the validity of the second method as well as the first (the principle of mutual confirmation, also known as "arguing in a circle").
Type C	Taking answers that look the same to mean the same thing.
Type D	Assuming that the researcher can accurately convert a qualitative statement by a respondent in such a way as to plot it on the same place in a scale as a respondent would if asked (a development from Error Type C).
Type E	Assuming that propositions and answers derived from different methods can converge or diverge (i.e. "agree" or "disagree').
Type F	Believing that the "strengths" of one method can offset the "weaknesses" of another, leading for some researchers to the illusion of a problem of how to prioritize the findings resulting from different data sources (the "weighting problem").
Type G	Comparing the results of two samples as though they belong to the same population when there is no methodological or statistical demonstration that they do.

The purpose of this chapter is to examine the metaphor of triangulation—in particular methodological triangulation—in the social sciences, to demonstrate the power it still holds over some researchers, and to argue that trust in this form of triangulation is misplaced. Blaikie (1991, p. 131), in a very clear and convincing article, argues that "triangulation means many things to many people and...none of the uses in sociology bears any resemblance to its use in surveying." However, this chapter will show that some researchers have mistakenly assumed that the ontological and epistemological bases of certain sociological activities are the same as those underpinning the triangulation methods used in surveying.

The result of this philosophical and methodological confusion is that in studies that use multiple methods, many misleading and invalid claims are made in the name of triangulation. This has profound implications for ethnography, since one of its defining characteristics is that it uses multiple methods (Massey and Walford 1998, p. 6).

In order to head off some of the confusion which can arise from doing multiple method research such as ethnography this chapter has two parallel objectives. The first is to highlight an area of philosophical dispute, and the second is to identify a number of common logical errors underpinning the practice of so-called methodological triangulation (Table 1).

Where the Journey Started: The Origin of Triangulation

Blaikie (1991), a land surveyor for 16 years before turning sociologist, gives a clear and detailed description of the original concept of triangulation in surveying, navigation and military strategy. Essentially, the aim is to establish the position of a point, which can be achieved in several ways:

(1) A point can be located "from two others of known distance apart, given the angles of the triangle formed by the three points" (Clark 1951, p. 145). The absolute position of the point can be established only if the absolute positions of the two reference points are known. Otherwise, the most one can establish are the positions of the three points *relative* to each other.

(2) A topographical feature can be plotted by observing it "from a number of known positions, thus forming a triangle in which one side and the adjacent angles are known" (Blaikie 1991, p. 118). In this method (intersection), the absolute as well as the relative position of the feature can be calculated.

(3) An unknown position can be fixed by measuring, *from it*, the angles to at least two other known positions (resection).

The ontological foundation of each of these three forms of triangulation is that there is a reality separate from the observer. The epistemological assumption is that the set positions are not open to interpretation, but can be established through a direct correspondence between the positions and sensory experience of them.

"This Path Looks Promising!"
The Appropriation of Triangulation
by the Social Sciences

Knafl and Breitmayer (1989, p. 227) suggest that the appropriation of the concepts of triangulation preceded the adoption of the term itself in social science research:

> It was first used metaphorically in the social sciences to characterise the use of multiple methods to measure a single construct (Campbell 1956; Campbell and Fiske 1959; Garner 1954; Garner, Hake and Eriksen 1956), a practice also referred to as multiple operationism, convergent operationism, operational delineation, and convergent validation (Campbell and Fiske 1959).

In the literature on triangulation in the social sciences, it is usually Webb and colleagues (1966) who are attributed with the first use of the term itself. This early thinking and writing was soon to be taken up enthusiastically in research methods textbooks (Denzin 1970; Smith 1975), thus reinforcing the use of triangulation as a legitimate technique within the social sciences research which has continued to this day (e.g., Hammersley and Atkinson 1995). It is not difficult to find numerous references to triangulation throughout methodological writing in social research. For example, Mathison (1988, p. 15) states: "Extending this metaphor to social phenomena, the researcher (navigator or military strategist) can use several kinds of information to determine the truth (location) about some social phenomenon (an island or the enemy)." Moreover, triangulation is a standard topic on methodology courses where, while seen as sometimes problematic, it is nevertheless regarded as appropriate in social scientific thought.

Typologies of triangulation have proliferated: data, investigator, theoretical, methodological, multiple, between-methods and within-methods triangulation (Denzin 1970; Jick 1983); simultaneous and sequential triangulation (Morse 1991); planned and unplanned triangulation (Deacon et al. 1998). Knafl and Breit- mayer (1989) have managed to organize these many types into two strands based on what they see as the two principal aims of triangulation in the social sciences: convergence and completeness.

> In the measurement of discrete variables, triangulation contributes to the investigator's efforts to achieve confirmation or convergent validity. In studies that address more encompassing domains of interest, multiple triangulation contributes to the investigator's ability to achieve a complete understanding of that domain (Knafl and Breitmayer 1989, p. 237).

Both of these aims of triangulation will now be examined in detail in order to show that their conceptual basis is fundamentally flawed to such an extent that generations of researchers and readers have lost their way through their very attempts to improve sociological "navigation" techniques.

LOOKING INTO A MIRAGE: DO THE PATHS CONVERGE?

A Fixed Social Reality? The Spectre of Positivism

One of the principal aims of triangulation in the social sciences seems to be to corroborate one set of findings with another; the hope is that two or more sets of findings will "converge" on a single proposition. This view holds much weight in literature on triangulation:

> Once a proposition has been confirmed by two or more independent measurement processes, the uncertainty of its interpretation is greatly reduced. The most persuasive evidence comes through a triangulation of measurement processes. If a proposition can survive the onslaught of a series of imperfect measures...confidence should be placed in it (Webb et al. 1981, p. 35).

> Investigators engaged in qualitative research will have increased confidence in the credibility of their results when multiple data collection methods yield consistent findings (Knafl and Breitmayer 1989, p. 238).

> Multiple and independent measures, if they reach the same conclusions, provide a more certain portrayal of the...phenomenon (Jick 1983, p. 136).

As Blaikie (1991) points out, such views can make sense only if the researcher works within a "positivistic frame of reference which assumes a single (unde- fined) reality and treats accounts as multiple mappings of that reality" (Silverman 1985, p. 105). Of course, triangulation in surveying is based on such a premise.

The question is whether it makes sense to conceive of social reality in this way. According to Blaikie (1991, p. 120), for the strict interpretivist, "social reality is not some "thing" that may be interpreted in different ways; it is those interpretations." Guba and Lincoln (1989) are anxious about a simplistic notion of a fixed social reality that remains basically unchanged regardless of one's investigative stance: "...triangulation itself carries too positivist an implication, to wit, that there exist unchanging phenomena so that triangulation can logically be a check" (p. 240). And if one takes the position that there is a reality "out there" separate from ourselves which, however, cannot be known but only hinted at through our constructions, then it is difficult to see how any amount of triangulation (as conceived in the social sciences) can get us any "closer" to knowledge of that reality.

Arguments about the nature of social reality are well documented, and do not need to be rehearsed here. However, it is clear that if a researcher were to reject the notion of a fixed "social reality" (knowable or not), then the idea of there being a method that could help a researcher home in on a social reality would make no sense; "the image of data converging on a single proposition about a social phenomenon" would have to be regarded as a "phantom image" (Mathison 1988, p. 17), and the researcher would have to give up all thoughts of using triangulation as a methodological resource.

Let us assume, however, for the moment, that there is a social reality that can be mapped, in order to investigate the ways in which methodological triangulation is conceived and widely employed. The rest of this chapter is a discussion of some significant errors which are often committed by those who attempt to conduct methodological triangulation. Regardless of one's ontological or epistemological position, the discussion raises serious questions about what kind of claims could be generated through such a strategy, or what could count as good practice.

Pulling Yourself Up by Your Own Bootstraps: The Logical Fallacy of Mutual Confirmation

Commonly "triangulation" is used as a means of establishing the truth of propositions while simultaneously establishing the validity of the methods which are used to reach those propositions:

> In several instances in the present study, there has been achieved what might be called methodological triangulation, in that several different methodological approaches have been employed to get at the same variable, psychologically conceived....The process is one of mutual confirmation among the various approaches (Campbell 1956, pp. 73-74).

> [Between-methods triangulation] is largely a vehicle for cross-validation when two or more distinct methods are found to be congruent and yield comparable data (Jick 1983, p. 136).

Underlying both the above quotations is the belief that the results generated from one method can somehow confirm those of another. There are two logical fallacies bound up in such a belief.

First, there is a confusion between the "truth" function of a technique, and its operational function. Operationally, one can define a priori that one measure can serve in place of another. In such circumstances, the proposition developed through one strategy could then be said to be the same as one that would have emerged had the strategy's "operational twin" been employed (concurrent validation). A logical error in the confirmatory type of social scientific triangulation is that a second strategy is commonly used to *prove* the truth of a first, rather than simply *define* it as true; this I call Error Type A. For a second strategy to be able to prove that propositions generated from the first were "true"—or to establish the degree of validity, reliability of bias—it would first have to be defined as a strategy which itself produced "true" propositions.

The equivalent in land surveying would be to claim that one bearing alone could locate the true position of a point, which is clearly impossible; for this reason alone, the term triangulation would be misleading in social research. In practice, social scientists rarely claim that any one method can by itself produce "true" propositions because if a particular strategy was deemed to be able to produce "true" propositions, then no "triangulation" by using a second data source would be necessary.

The second logical fallacy is that agreement between the results of two methods is taken to prove the validity of the second method *as well as* the first (the principle of "mutual confirmation")—the logical equivalent of arguing in a circle: "Proposition/method A is valid/true. Why? Because it agrees with proposition/method B. How do we know proposition/method B is valid/true? Because it agrees with proposition/method A." In layman's terms it is like trying to pull yourself up by your own bootstraps. This I call Error Type B.

The difference with triangulation in land surveying is that, barring very minor error margins, the instruments are assumed to be reliable and able to provide valid measurements from the outset. The process of triangulation is to locate a point or true position of an object, not to find out whether the instruments actually work (or how they work): for the final answer to be useful at all, the readings must be assumed to be true. In addition, in the form of (land surveying) triangulation known as intersection, the locations from which the readings are taken are also known. However, in the confirmatory function of triangulation in the social sciences, the researcher is simultaneously trying to establish the validity of a proposition and the validity of the method used to produce it, moreover without knowing all the relevant social dimensions (the "location") of each investigator. The equivalent in land surveying would be to claim to be able to establish the exact geographical position of an object without knowing beforehand which instruments worked, how to interpret the measurements, or what were the locations of the points from which the bearings were taken. Triangulation in land surveying is logically consistent internally; confirmatory triangulation in social research is not remotely logical and the appropriation of the term triangulation gives such activity a veneer of logic and respectability which it does not deserve.

One option is to adopt an operational definition of truth as the agreement between propositions arrived at through two or more different procedures, a form of consensual truth (e.g. intersubjective agreement). Stated as boldly as this, it is hard to say how many social researchers would want to subscribe to this definition of truth. That does not stop many, however, from implying it in their methods when they adopt a "mutual confirmation" approach. There is a dilemma whether to adopt a positivist position on truth, or to define truth in Humpty Dumpty fashion as whatever one wants it to mean. Neither position is satisfactory, but advocates of the "mutual confirmation" theory seem to try to adopt both positions simultaneously.

Methodology textbooks do not always clear up this confusion. For example, Hammersley and Atkinson (1995) seem to reject "confirmatory" triangulation, for fear that "confirmation" could simply reinforce prejudice or bias, while "disconfirmation" might lead one to replace one "mistaken" proposition by an equally misguided one:

> In triangulation, then, links between concepts and indicators are checked by recourse to other indicators. However, triangulation is not a simple test. Even if the results tally, this provides no guarantee that the inferences involved are correct. It may be that all the inferences are invalid, that as a result of systematic or even random error they lead to the same, incorrect, conclusion (Hammersley and Atkinson 1995, pp. 231-232).

That a conclusion could be "incorrect," "a result of error," or "invalid" or that "links between concepts and indicators" could be "checked" presupposes that there is a correct conclusion at which one could arrive. Either this hides a positivist stance, which the authors reject, or a view that there is a reality but we just cannot know what it is. If the latter is true, then it is hard to see how Hammersley and Atkinson's comments could be useful, since one would not be able to know if one was getting any closer to the "truth" of this reality. This point will be explored further in the next section.

False Signposts:
The Myths of Convergence, Divergence, and Bias

The key mistaken assumption in much triangulation work in the social sciences is that answers that look the same mean the same thing (e.g. Campbell 1956; Webb et al. 1966; Denzin 1970; Jick 1983; Mitchell 1986; Mathison 1988; Morse 1991; Deacon et al. 1998); this I call Error Type C.

Let us examine a hypothetical example of answers in a survey that appear to conflict in some way, despite the fact that they are apparently about the same phenomenon (e.g., happiness). One question may require responses on a defined scale, while another may ask a qualitative question. The scaled answers may appear to express a generally lower degree of happiness than the qualitative answers suggest. However, this would be a very sloppy way of thinking. The general statements one could derive from the scaled answers would demonstrate where the members of the sample fitted themselves on the scale. In contrast, the general statements derived from the qualitative answers represent where the *researcher* placed (through personal interpretation) the members of the sample on the scale. This would still be so even if the researcher were to compare the two answers of just one individual from the sample.

As has been argued earlier, if the answers apparently "disagree" this can in no way disconfirm the validity of one of the answers (Error Type A); ideally, it would simply alert the researcher to the fact that two different phenomena are present (or being socially constructed). Unfortunately, if the answers apparently "agree," this is taken as confirmation of some truth (Error Type A), or a form of mutual confirmation (Error Type B)—both of which have already been shown to be flawed procedures—and the researcher is then likely to overlook the fact that the questions represent enquiry into (or construction of) two different (albeit perhaps related) phenomena.

To summarize this hypothetical example, there are two mistaken beliefs:

(1) that the two different types of question will uncover the same phenomenon, in this case, the same aspect of a respondent, and
(2) that the researcher can accurately convert a qualitative statement by a respondent in such a way as to plot it on the same place in a scale as a respondent would if asked (Error Type D).

Unfortunately, such errors committed in the name of triangulation are not merely hypothetical; even a cursory glance at literature across the social sciences shows them to be all too real. In fact, even in the triangulation literature the same sorts of mistake occur. For example, in a piece of methodological triangulation, Mathison (1988, p. 16) was concerned about inconsistent findings when "teachers reported using the activity cards extensively but in over 200 classroom observations only 14 such activities occurred." It was perhaps a little naïve to assume that the number generated for frequency of card use would be the same whether the researcher elicited teachers' perceptions or observed behaviors. The point was that effectively different questions were being asked, although they appeared to be questions of the same type ("How many times were activity cards used?") with answers of the same type (numbers).

One should seriously question Jick's (1983, p. 136) claim that multiple methods can be used "to examine the same dimension of a research problem." After all, the meaning of an answer can only really be fully understood by reference to the meaning of its corresponding question, which, in turn, is embedded in a particular research method and ontological/epistemological perspective. Consistencies or inconsistencies therefore only appear to be so because the propositions derived from two sources have been removed from their fuller context of meaning.

Given that propositions derived from two separate methods must mean different things it does not make sense to say that they can conflict or agree: the claims made are not of the same type, and as Blaikie (1991) takes pains to point out, the methods used to produce the claims are usually not even based on the same philosophical premises. The assumption that propositions derived from different methods can converge or diverge, I call Error Type E.

The whole issue of convergence becomes even more of a mystery when one compares methodological triangulation with the original concept of triangulation. Land surveying depends on the knowledge that each new piece of information (bearing/reading) is based on the same framework of measurement (i.e., the same kind of question), so that each answer can be understood in the same way. This is a single method approach—and necessarily so—unlike the multi-method approach of triangulation as conceived in the social sciences. Moreover, in land surveying triangulation, the issue is not *whether* the two bearings will converge, but where. Convergence always happens eventually; this is a fundamental geometrical truth.

One kind of misleading rhetoric in social scientific literature is that two or more "bearings" may not converge. This is not necessarily seen by social scientists as a problem, but as a strength of triangulation (e.g., see Mitchell 1986), the belief being that "the effectiveness of triangulation rests on the premise that the weaknesses in each single method will be compensated by the counter-balancing strengths of another (Jick 1983, p. 138)." Denzin (1970), one of the early authors of this view, wrote:

> Triangulation, or the use of multiple methods, is a plan of action that will raise sociologists above the personalistic biases that stem from single methodologies. By combining methods and investigators in the same study, observers can partially overcome the deficiencies that flow from one investigator and/or one method (p. 300).

This view, which I call Error Type F, is countered by Morse (1991, p. 122):

> Methodological triangulation is not a matter of maximising the strengths and minimising the weakness of each. If not approached cautiously, the end result may be to enhance the weaknesses of each method and invalidate the entire research project.

Clearly, if one does not know a priori which method is closest to the "truth," or how close it is, then it is not possible to use any method as a yardstick to assess degrees of bias or validity in other methods. As Knafl and Breitmayer (1989) point out:

> To use triangulation for the purpose of confirmation necessitates the identification of data collection instruments or techniques whose strengths and weaknesses are both known and

counterbalancing with regard to threats to validity....Any claim to triangulation based on
such an approach would have to be supported by a discussion of the complementary nature
of the...approaches and evidence that the weaknesses of one were offset by another
(p. 228).

However, it is hard to imagine what would count as a satisfactory outcome of such
a discussion. Deacon and colleagues (1998, p. 57) set out the problem:

Where there are no grounds to query the internal robustness of particular strands of
evidence, the only way to privilege certain findings over others is to resort to
epistemic prioritization, e.g., that large-scale random samples inevitably have a
greater validity than smaller, purposively selected samples, or that quantitative
methods always obscure rather than reveal the complexities and contradictions of
social life. In our view, deploying such preferences is a particularly unsatisfactory
way of resolving the impasse, not least because to do so would demonstrate a basic
intellectual inconsistency. There is no point developing a multi-method approach if
the researcher resorts to methodological purism at the first sign of trouble.

Silverman's (1985, p. 105) view that "the sociologist's role is not to adjudicate
between...accounts" does not help, and Jick (1983) and Mitchell (1986), while
recognizing the problem of how to weight different data sources, provide no
answers either. Blaikie (1991, p. 123) believes that "regardless of the methodological perspective adopted, decisions about the relative merits of different
sources of data can only be settled in the context of some theory; and the choice
and application of the theory is a matter of judgement."

What is one to do, though, if such "methodological purism" (Deacon et al.
1998, p. 57) is rejected? Mathison (1988) suggests that "all the outcomes of triangulation, convergent, inconsistent and contradictory...need to be explained." If
divergence is no more informative than convergence, then why bother to make the
distinction, and do such terms mean anything at all in this context?

In fact, what I have argued is that the weighting problem (Error Type F) and the
problem of how to interpret divergence/convergence (Error Type E) do not even
exist, since propositions derived from different methods or data sources are not of
the same type and therefore not open to comparison. The widespread belief that
answers from different methods or data sources can converge, diverge or deviate
from a social "truth," and Mitchell's (1986, p. 24) question of "how to interpret
divergent results between numerical data and linguistic data" (Error Type F), turn
out to be more unwitting pieces of misdirection and illusion which nevertheless
capture many social researchers in their spell.

How to Be Lost Without Even Knowing It: A Recent Example

Deacon and colleagues (1998, p. 49ff.) ask how one is "to handle instances
in which there is a clear inconsistency between data deriving from quantitative
and qualitative research," describing this as a "failure to triangulate" and insist

that one should find a way to "deal with the clash." Morse (1991, p. 122) is unequivocal:

> If contradictory results occur from triangulating qualitative and quantitative methods, then one set of findings is invalid and/or the end result of the total study inadequate, incomplete, or inaccurate.

The following discussion illustrates just how lost researchers can get when attempting to conduct triangulation in social science research. Deacon and colleagues (1998) conducted a large-scale investigation into social scientists and their media relations in Britain. Six methods (out of a total of eight used) are discussed in the article:

(1) Quantitative content analysis of written and broadcast journalistic items (random sample: 592 items over 10 months).
(2) Mail questionnaire survey of those social scientists covered in (1) (81% usable response to 151 questionnaires).
(3) Mail questionnaire survey of social scientists (stratified random sample: 62% usable response to 1139 questionnaires).
(4) Semi-structured interviews of social scientists (small purposive sample: 20).
(5) Semi-structured interviews of journalists (quota sample of 34 from those covered in 1).
(6) Participant observation of journalists at conferences (opportunity sample).

By their own admission there was "only one instance in which similar or the same respondents were being researched," and that was where some social scientists were in the samples for both (2) and (4). The declared objective of this was not triangulation but elaboration of quantitative findings through qualitative means (p. 51).

Deacon and colleagues compared the findings from (4) and (5), interviewing social scientists and journalists respectively. They claim that social scientists' answers about the existence of conflict and tension corroborated those of journalists. In doing so, they commit several errors. First, there is an assumption that the perceptions as expressed by one group were the same as those of another group (interaction of Error Types D and F). Second, they are committing Error Type A if they believe that one set of answers can confirm the truth of another. Third, it seems that where in their eyes the two sets of answers agree, a truth has been established, an interaction of Error Types C and A in which the implicit claim is "this is The Truth, because these two data sets agree."

Such problems abound throughout the article; careful reading will show that all the comparisons of findings from the different methods are illegitimate according to one or more of the Error Types I have identified. For example, method (3), the second survey, was used to "appraise the validity of the first survey's [2's] findings" (p. 56) (Error Type A). Deacon and colleagues use the "clear consistency between the two surveys"

(p. 56) simultaneously to establish the validity of method (3) (Error Type B). All the concerns about results from the different methods apparently diverging, and the uncritical acceptance of results that apparently converge, are a commission of Error Type E.

Finally, in following up their declared need to investigate various "clashes" (p. 50) between the different studies, Deacon and colleagues add one more type of error to those already identified. The claims on p. 52 made about what social scientists and journalists feel and think are based on the interviews in method (4) and (5). Such generalizations to the wider populations of social scientists and journalists are wholly unreliable and illegitimate since these were not randomized but purposive, quota and opportunity samples—an elementary methodological mistake.

But this is not a triangulation error, and therefore is not included in my Error Types. Even if all the samples *had* been randomized, so that they were all generalizable to wider populations, this would still not have validated the comparison of the studies. The point is that, since each sample was constructed on a different basis, one has to assume, unless it is proved otherwise, that the social scientists in samples 1, 2, 3 and 4 represent different populations, as do the journalists in samples 1, 5 and 6. Therefore, even if each of the six studies had used the same method and questions, any apparent "inconsistency" could be attributed to nothing more remarkable than the fact that the samples did not belong to the same population— indeed the same wider populations of "all social scientists" or "all journalists." The studies were conducted on different methodological grounds, and dissimilar samples. It is therefore a mystery how the researchers—without even recourse to statistical or probability statements—were able to decide whether or not the apparent differences in results were significant. Comparing the results of two samples as though they belong to the same population when there is no methodological or statistical demonstration that they do belong to the same population is a commission of Error Type G.

Such a catalogue of muddle-headed errors would not be so worrying if only neophyte researchers had committed them; perhaps then these researchers could be put back on the straight and narrow path by vigilant supervisors and teachers before too much harm was done. However, the seriousness of the problem becomes apparent when one finds studies such as the above published by such highly respected and influential researchers.

A SECOND MIRAGE:
IS THIS THE END OF THE PATH?

The Goal of Completeness

As well as identifying the "confirmatory" function of triangulation in the social sciences, which has been seriously questioned in this chapter, Knafl and

Breitmayer (1989) suggest that "multiple data collection techniques contribute to the completeness function of triangulation by providing explanatory insights about data from varying sources" (pp. 234-235). This seems similar to Jick's (1983, p. 138) holistic type of triangulation which enables the researcher to elicit data and suggest conclusions "to which other methods would be blind." The general idea behind the "completeness" idea is that triangulation, in this form equated simply with multiple methods, leads to a "holistic" account where all the "gaps" are plugged by each successive method/data source. However, the "completeness" application of the term triangulation in sociology falls so far outside the definition or use of it in land surveying, it is difficult to see why it is applied at all in this context (Knafl and Breitmayer 1989).

JOURNEY' S END:
CONCLUSION

In this chapter, I have argued that a number of philosophical assumptions within the original conception of triangulation (as practiced in land surveying and so on) simply do not translate into the field of multiple methods research in the social sciences. At least seven types of logical error have been identified in the practices which can be generally grouped under the designation of methodological triangulation. In addition, the goal of completeness bears little or no relation to the original concept of triangulation. Several conclusions follow from this.

First, the adoption of the term triangulation by the social sciences is often inappropriate. None of the practices carried out in multiple method research such as ethnography under the name of methodological triangulation is in fact triangulation at all. Each is simply a unique technique to construct a unique kind of data or information.

Second, this misappropriation of the term would not be a problem but for the fact that the resonances and associations of the word are just too powerful and misleading. Morgan (1986, p. 382) stresses that we must "recognise that our seeing and understanding of the world is always 'seeing as,' rather than a 'seeing as is'." The mistake of those social researchers who have retained the term triangulation is that they have stretched the metaphor too far, taking it too literally, and believing that they can reach the same kind of certainty about social reality as land surveyors can about physical reality. Insistence on using the term may be the result of a need to establish authority for one's claims beyond one's own subjectivity. Whatever the reason, for the unsuspecting, it leads to claims of convergence, truth, validity, control of bias, completeness and so on looking far more solid than they really are.

Third, it is hard to see how completeness could be achieved without the existence of a fixed social reality. Even if there were such a thing, how could one know it had been achieved? What could count as a workable definition of complete-ness? Jick (1983, p. 144) claims:

> Overall, the triangulating investigator is left to search for a logical pattern in mixed-method results. His or her claim to validity rests on a judgment, or as Weiss (1968, p. 349) calls it, "a capacity to organise materials within a plausible framework."

Implicit in this seems to be a post-modern idea that the world is coherent and that any commentary on it must reflect this. However, it has been argued in this chapter that the capacity for methods to complement each other in the drive towards "completeness" should not be assumed; nor should "corroboration" between methods (whatever that might mean) automatically be considered unproblematic, and therefore precluding the need for further investigation.

Fourth, I agree with Blaikie (1991, p. 131) that there is a need to "identify appropriate and inappropriate combinations of methods." Ideally, those methods or combinations which are governed by one or more of the errors identified in this chapter should be seen for what they are—seriously flawed—so that researchers can properly evaluate under what circumstances such methods should still be used, if at all.

Finally, the current confusion which characterizes the use of methodological triangulation leads to weak research and plays unnecessarily into the hands of those who are already keen to discredit mixed or multiple method research. If this chapter has encouraged in social researchers—ethnographers especially—a healthy distrust of the term triangulation and those techniques it is used to signify in social science research, then perhaps it will help provide more tools for evaluating work which uses so-called methodological triangulation, and strengthen future multiple method research such as ethnography.

ACKNOWLEDGMENTS

I would like to thank Geoffrey Walford for his close reading of and helpful comments on an earlier draft of this chapter. Thanks also go to Thomas Spielhofer for his feedback on earlier drafts.

REFERENCES

Blaikie, N. 1991. "A Critique of the Use of Triangulation in Social Research." *Quality and Quantity* 25: 115-136.

Campbell, D.T. 1956. *Leadership and Its Effects upon the Group*. Columbus: Ohio State University Press.

Campbell, D.T., and D. Fiske. 1959. "Convergent and Discriminant Validation by the Multitrait-Multimethod Matrix." *Psychological Bulletin* 56: 81-104.

Clark, D. 1951. *Plane and Geodetic Surveying for Engineers, Vol. 2* (4th ed., revised and enlarged by J. Glendenning). London: Constable.

Deacon, D., A. Bryman, and N. Fenton. 1998. "Collision or Collusion? A Discussion and Case Study of the Unplanned Triangulation of Quantitative and Qualitative Research Methods." *International Journal of Social Research Methodology* 1 (1): 47-63.

Denzin, N. 1970. "Strategies of Multiple Triangulation." In *The Research Act in Sociology: A Theoretical Introduction to Sociological Method*, edited by N. Denzin. New York: McGraw-Hill: 297-313.

Garner, W.R. 1954. "Context Effects and the Validity of Loudness Scales." *Journal of Experimental Psychology* 48: 218-224.

Garner, W.R., H.W. Hake, and C.W. Eriksen. 1956. "Operationism and the Concept of Perception." *Psychological Review* 63: 149-159.

Guba, E.C., and Y.S. Lincoln. 1989. *Fourth Generation Evaluation*. London: Sage.

Hammersley, M., and P. Atkinson. 1995. *Ethnography: Principles in Practice* (2nd ed.). London: Routledge.

Jick, T.D. 1983. "Mixing Qualitative and Quantitative Research Methods: Triangulation in Action." Pp. 135-148 in *Qualitative Methodology*, edited by J. van Maanen. Beverley Hills, CA: Sage.

Knafl, K.A., and B.J. Breitmayer. 1989. "Triangulation in Qualitative Research: Issues of Conceptual Clarity and Purpose." Pp. 226-239 in *Qualitative Nursing Research: As Contemporary Dialogue*, edited by J.M. Morse. Rockville, MD: Aspen.

Massey, A.S., and G. Walford. 1998. "Children Learning: Ethnographers Learning." Pp. 1-18 in *Children Learning in Context,* edited by G. Walford and A.S. Massey. London: JAI Press.

Mathison, S. 1988. "Why Triangulate?" *Educational Researcher* 17 (2): 13-17.

Mitchell, E.S. 1986. "Multiple Triangulation: A Methodology for Nursing Science." *Advances in Nursing Science* 8 (3): 18-26.

Morgan, G. 1986. *Images of Organisation*. London: Sage.

Morse, J. 1991. "Approaches to Qualitative-Quantitative Methodological Triangulation." *Nursing Research* 40 (1): 120-123.

Silverman, D. 1985. *Qualitative Methodology and Sociology: Describing the Social World.* Aldershot: Gower.

Smith, H.W. 1975. "Triangulation: The Necessity for Multi-Method Approaches." Pp. 271-292 in *Strategies of Social Research: The Methodological Imagination*, edited by H.W. Smith. Englewood Cliffs, NJ: Prentice-Hall.

Webb, E.J., D.T. Campbell, R.D. Schwartz, L. Sechrest, and J.B. Grove. 1966. *Nonreactive Measures in the Social Sciences*. Chicago: Rand McNally.

Webb, E.J., D.T. Campbell, R.D. Schwartz, L. Sechrest, and J.B. Grove. 1981. *Nonreactive Measures in the Social Sciences* (2nd ed.). Boston: Houghton Mifflin.

Weiss, R. S. 1968. "Issues in Holistic Research." Pp. 342-350 in *Institutions and the Person*, edited by H.S. Becker, B. Geer, D. Riessman, and R. Weiss. Chicago: Aldine.

NOTES ON CONTRIBUTORS

Maria Birbili is a doctoral student at the Department of Educational Studies, University of Oxford. Her thesis is on the workplace experiences of academics from different types of higher education institution. She has an MA in early childhood education from Boston College, USA, and an MSc in educational research methodology from the University of Oxford, UK. She taught early childhood issues for four years at the Technological Education Institution of Athens while at the same time working as a coordinator for a European Union funded program for childminders.

Mari Boyle is a former primary teacher. She was until recently Research Fellow at the School of Education, The Open University, Milton Keynes, UK, researching child-meaningful learning with particular reference to young bilingual children during the first two years of their school careers. She is currently preparing a book on this topic, and working toward a PhD. Her publications include *Restructuring Schools: Reconstructing Teachers* (Open University Press, 1997, with Peter Woods, Bob Jeffrey and Geoff Troman).

Phil Francis Carspecken is an associate professor of educational sociology at the Department of Cultural Studies, College of Education, University of Houston. His academic interests include social theory, critical theory, and cultural studies. He is author of *Community Schooling and the Nature of Power: The Battle for Croxteth Comprehensive* (Routledge, 1991), *Critical Ethnography in Educational Research: A Theoretical and Practical Guide* (Routledge, 1996) and *Four Scenes for Posing the Question of Meaning, and Other Explorations in Critical Philosophy and Critical Methodology* (Peter Lang, 1999).

Sam Hillyard is a final year doctoral student at the University of Warwick. She has a BA in sociology, also from Warwick, where she lectures in qualitative field research and the sociology of education. Her main research interests are the relationship between theory and method in ethnography, the sociology of childhood and interpretative social theory.

Bob Jeffrey is research fellow at the Open University and has published research, together with Peter Woods, on teacher creativity, primary teacher discourses on work, pupils' perspectives of creative learning and the restructuring of primary teachers' work. His books include: *Teachable Moments* (Open University Press, 1996, with Peter Woods), *Restructuring Schools: Reconstructing Teachers* (Open University Press, 1997, with Peter Woods, Geoff Troman and Mari Boyle), and *Testing Teachers: The Effects of School Inspections on Primary Teachers* (Open University Press, 1998, with Peter Woods).

Alexander Massey taught in state and private schools for ten years, heading both music and drama departments, and has done LEA consultancy work and run workshops on supply teaching issues. He completed an MSc in educational research methodology in 1995, and continued with DPhil research within the Department of Educational Studies, University of Oxford. He has published several papers on research methodology and was co-editor of *Children Learning in Context* (JAI Press, 1998). He runs "Free Your Voice," a voice consultancy for theatres, businesses and therapy centers, and is a professional solo singer, performing opera, oratorio, cabaret and folksong.

Jim Mienczakowski is a former Deputy Dean (Research) of the Faculty of Education and the Arts, Griffith University and is currently the Director of the Ethnographic Performance Research Unit at the Gold Coast Campus, Queensland, Australia. Trained in theatre in the UK, with a background in theatre, television and radio performance, Jim has many years of experience teaching in Inner London, Dorset and the Caribbean as well as in Australia. Since 1990 he has been developing ethnographic performance research as a way of explaining and debating health consumers' experiences of illness and institutional treatment. His research unit is now developing, among other things, ethnographic methodologies to help explore family and individual experiences of cosmetic surgery and the efficacy of anti-youth suicide campaigns.

Marlene Morrison is a lecturer in education at the School of Education, University of Leicester. Until recently, she held a joint lectureship at the Center for Educational Development Appraisal and Research (CEDAR)/Sociology at the University of Warwick. Research and evaluation studies have focused upon emerging developments in the University for Industry and library-focused research for citizenship and lifelong learning. Other research interests include: supply teaching and the growth of private teaching agencies, professional and school development, and the sociology of food and eating in schools. Articles, books and reports reflect her research interests.

John Schostak is professor of education at the Center for Applied Research in Education at the University of East Anglia. His interests focus on applied research methodologies appropriate to understanding educational processes in all spheres of social life: private and public sector organizations in health, business, media, politics, law and order and educational institutions, as well as the more informal institutions of the family, street and Internet.

Ana Vasquez is a former professor in the psychology of education at the University of Chile who has lived and worked in Paris since 1974. She received a PhD in psychology from the University René Descartes-Paris V in 1977, and is now a senior researcher at the French CNRS (National Centre for Scientific Research) within the CERLIS (Research Centre for Social Relations) team at University René Descartes. Ethnography of education is one of her principal research interests, and she is now developing a conceptual analysis of culture, transculture and cultural identity on the basis of ethnographic research. Her academic publications include: *La malédiction d'Ulysse: exils latino-américains* (with A.M. Araujo) and *La socialisation à l'école: approche ethnographique* (with I. Martinez). She is also a published novelist, and is particularly interested in the field of narrative and the links between fictional and ethnographic writing.

Geoffrey Walford is reader in education policy and a fellow of Green College at the University of Oxford. He was previously senior lecturer in sociology and education policy at Aston Business School, Aston University, Birmingham. His recent books include: *Choice and Equity in Education* (Cassell, 1994), *Educational Politics: Pressure Groups and Faith-Based Schools* (Avebury, 1995), *Affirming the Comprehensive Ideal* (Falmer, 1997, edited with Richard Pring), *Doing Research about Education* (Falmer, 1998, editor) and *Durkheim and Modern Education* (Routledge, 1998, edited with W.S.F. Pickering). His research foci are the relationships between central government policy and local processes of implementation, choice of schools, religiously based schools and ethnographic research methodology. He is currently directing a Spencer Foundation funded comparative project on faith-based schools in England and The Netherlands, and is Joint Editor of the *British Journal of Educational Studies*.

Angela Xavier de Brito received a PhD in sociology from the University René Descartes-Paris V in 1991, and is now a senior researcher at the French CNRS (National Centre for Scientific Research) within CERLIS (Research Centre for Social Relations) associated with the University René Descartes. Her research work in Brazil and Chile guided her interests towards qualitative research, and she is now involved in developing theories about photographic ethnographic approaches that draw on symbolic interactionism, history and epistemological reflection about the research process. Her main research themes are the socialization process, the foreigner in various social situations (exile, migration, academic training), gift theory (as developed by Mauss), and academic cooperation between France and Latin America. She has published many academic articles and produced ethnographic films.